I WAS SENT TO ATHENS

Books by
HENRY MORGENTHAU

AMBASSADOR MORGENTHAU'S STORY

ALL IN A LIFE-TIME

I WAS SENT TO ATHENS
(*In collaboration with French Strother*)

P. 39 also
"Secrets of
the Bosphorus"

I WAS SENT
TO ATHENS

BY HENRY MORGENTHAU

In Collaboration with
FRENCH STROTHER

ILLUSTRATIONS FROM PHOTOGRAPHS

DOUBLEDAY, DORAN & COMPANY, INC.
GARDEN CITY, NEW YORK
MCMXXIX

TO

THE CREATORS OF THE LEAGUE OF NATIONS
WHO ORIGINATED THE FIRST SERIOUS
EFFORTS TOWARD A BETTER UNDER-
STANDING AMONGST NATIONS

CONTENTS

LIST OF ILLUSTRATIONS

CHAPTER I

The Epic of the Modern Greeks

I PROPOSE in this book to tell the story of an epic enterprise. Heroic figures crowd the busy scene: Venizelos, a modern Pericles in his nation-building genius; Karamanos, just such a flashing figure as Achilles, born leader of men; Delta, benevolent, energetic, wise; Charilaos, bold as Hector and more successful in a better cause; Diomede, man of money, man of courage, man of heart; and many another, whose names and deeds will appear as the story unfolds.

The scenes of this drama are as old as history, and as new as the newest suburb of Los Angeles: romantic Smyrna, which six years ago was a great commercial seaport, and which to-day is again decaying under Turkish rule; immortal Athens, now more populous than ever before in history, as teeming and alive as in her Golden Age; cosmopolitan Salonica, that has known the armies of every great soldier from Philip of Macedon to Haig and Foch; picturesque Cavalla, old when St. Paul landed there from Asia Minor on his way to answer "the Macedonian cry," and thriving to-day upon a huge tobacco industry, whose principal managers are Americans and whose principal market is the United States; and those "isles of Greece" that so thrilled Lord Byron, and still so thrill all visitors from distant lands.

I

These present-day Greeks, in this illustrious arena, have just performed one of the most epochal and inspiring achievements of modern times—a veritable modern labor of Hercules, in which any race or nation might take a glorious pride. Just how great is this achievement can perhaps best be pictured by drawing an analogy:

Suppose that something like this had recently occurred: that twenty-six million men, women, and children had suddenly and unexpectedly arrived by steamer at the ports of Boston, New York, Philadelphia, and Baltimore. Suppose, further, that this mighty host was well-nigh starved, was penniless, was without any worldly possessions beyond the clothes they stood in, their bodies covered with vermin and filth and ravaged by typhoid and smallpox. Imagine these twenty-six million human beings (chiefly women, children, and old men) to be absolutely dependent upon American charity for immediate food, for shelter, and for medical attention. Imagine that they must depend entirely upon America for an opportunity to make their homes and their livelihoods for the rest of their days.

Now imagine that America had magnificently met this challenge to its humanity and resourcefulness, had fed these starving, sheltered these homeless, healed these sick, found work for the less capable among them, financed a new start in life for them, built modern group houses for most, found land for the farmers, sold them seed and implements and animals at cost—in brief, had rehabilitated twenty-six million wrecked human lives, and had done all this within six years from the date

2

they landed on her shores. Would not the world resound with praise of American humanitarianism, American bounty, American energy and resourcefulness?

Exactly such an achievement, not in absolute numbers but in percentages, has been accomplished by Greece in the last six years—and yet the world at large has heard almost nothing about it!

Nothing in Homer is more exciting than this modern epic of the Greek people, which I have made my theme. These present-day Greeks have exhibited the qualities that made their ancestors illustrious: the courage of Achilles, the wisdom of Agamemnon, the ingenuity of Ulysses, the pity of the High Gods themselves. The frightful catastrophe at Smyrna in 1922, when the victorious Turks killed Greeks by the uncounted tens of thousands, and forced the surviving hundreds of thousands to proceed at once to Old Greece, created in that tiny nation of five million people just such an emergency as we have imagined for America—the sudden influx of a 25 per cent. addition to its native population, requiring instant relief and eventual permanent rehabilitation.

This challenge to Greece's "humanity and resourcefulness" it met most magnificently. It fed and sheltered this great army of brothers from Asia Minor, granted them immediate citizenship, and promptly evolved a plan to absorb them into the life of the nation. Six years ago I was sent to Athens to become the first chairman of the Refugee Settlement Commission, the international agency set up by the League of Nations to plan and supervise the staggering work of repatriating the million-odd destitute refugees from Asia Minor. What I saw six years ago, when the first chaos of a great calamity seemed to have caused a hopeless disorganization of a nation's life, and what I saw last year, when I again visited Greece accompanied by my collaborator, French Strother, and found the Greeks of their Great Exodus established in orderly urban and rural settlements, busy at the normal tasks of daily life, affords such a striking contrast, and is so wonderful a demonstration of the force of human character, that I feel the story will be read with eager interest wherever men take pride in glorious achievement.

CHAPTER II

Ten Paragraphs of Recent Greek History

EVER since Moses led the children of Israel out of bondage in Egypt the story of the Exodus has thrilled the human heart. It was the birth of freedom to a race, the beginning of the history of a nation.

Only six years ago there occurred another exodus, not far from the scene of the first. This time the fleeing multitude were Greeks and the pursuers were Turks. The sea to be crossed was the Ægean. No Providence intervened to protect the innocent and destroy the guilty. The righteous were slaughtered by the tens of thousands, whilst the guilty remained unharmed at the scene of their crimes. Yet much the same final result has issued from the second exodus as issued from the first. The flight of the Greeks from Asia Minor was the birth pangs of the Greek Republic. Out of their bitter tribulations has arisen a new nation, welded by suffering into a closer bond of union, and destined, I believe, to revive in great measure the ancient glories of that rocky land where Western civilization was born.

I would not presume to write upon so great a theme were it not that I was an eye witness of some of its most significant events, and was, moreover, privileged to have a guiding hand in several of them. This book is written

5

in part to add to the data available to those later historians who will describe this crucial epoch in the life of a great people. I shall hope it will find present acceptance with the general public by reason of the intrinsic interest of the subject.

First, let me crowd eleven years of recent Greek history into ten short paragraphs.

In 1913 the Turks, having determined to drive the Greeks out of Asia Minor, began a systematic deportation of whole Greek settlements there. Resistance at Phocæa, northwest of Smyrna, led to the massacre of fifty Greeks. To facilitate these deportations, the Turkish Government bought a warship from Brazil for the purpose of destroying the Greek Navy, so as to have a free hand in the Ægean Sea. The Greeks then bought from the United States the battleships *Idaho* and *Mississippi*, thus checkmating the Turkish scheme.

In 1915 King Constantine of Greece, who was the Kaiser's brother-in-law, dismissed the Prime Minister, Venizelos, who was pro-Ally.

In 1916 Venizelos set up a secessionist government at Salonica, and soon had a considerable Greek army fighting with the Allies against Bulgaria and Turkey.

In 1917 Constantine abdicated, under Allied pressure, and his son Alexander became King, with Venizelos as Prime Minister.

In 1918 Greece had 250,000 soldiers in the Allied offensive in Macedonia that led to the capitulation of Bulgaria and Turkey.

In 1919 the Treaty of Versailles was signed, leaving the question of Turkey to be settled by a separate treaty. Greek troops were landed at Smyrna, at the request of the Supreme Allied Council, to patrol western Asia Minor while the Allies were deciding what should be the ultimate fate of Turkey.

In 1920, by the Treaty of Sèvres, the Allies announced their decision regarding Turkish territory. By this treaty Smyrna and the Ionian hinterland were placed under Greek administration for nine years. Thereupon the Turkish Nationalists revolted as a protest against the treaty. They set up a government at Angora under Mustapha Kemal and organized an army to defend Asia Minor. In Greece, King Alexander died of a monkey bite, Venizelos was defeated in the general elections, and Constantine returned to Athens as King.

In 1921 the Allied powers agreed to reconsider the Treaty of Sèvres, and held a conference at London for this purpose. The Greek representatives rejected the alternative treaty proposed by the conference, and the Greek Army started a military offensive against the Turkish Nationalist positions in Asia Minor. Constantine proceeded to Smyrna to direct this offensive in person, and the Greek Army penetrated Asia Minor to a point within sixty miles of Angora, where it was disastrously defeated by the Turks.

In 1922, after frightful mismanagement of the situation by Constantine and his government, the Turks entered Smyrna. They massacred a large proportion of the Greek population, burned the Greek quarter, and deported hundreds of thousands of Greek civilians in the most barbarous manner. The Greek Army revolted and forced Constantine to abdicate again; whereupon

7

his son, George II, became King. The League of Nations sent Dr. Fridtjof Nansen to study the problem of the Greek refugees from Smyrna and other parts of Asia Minor, who had been landed penniless in Greece, where they were now in danger of starvation. Dr. Nansen reported that they could be effectually aided only by helping the Greek Government to raise a foreign loan for this purpose.

In 1923 the League of Nations created the Refugee Settlement Commission, to handle this whole problem on the scene in Greece. This Commission was to have four members—one American, one Britisher, and two Greeks, the American to be the chairman. I was offered the post, accepted it, and hence this book.

CHAPTER III

Rumblings of the Approaching Storm

THE Commission's task was to deal with the Greek refugees from Asia Minor, a people totally unlike their conquerors, the nomadic Turks. These Greeks had a brilliant heritage of their own as direct descendants of the Ionian Greeks who settled the Ægean coast of Asia Minor. It was in their land that Homer, perhaps the greatest poet of all ages, sang their early history. The scene of the Iliad is the plains of Troy, on the Asia Minor coast, south of the Dardanelles. In Homeric times not only the Ionian coast, but also the southern shore of the Black Sea, were populated by Greeks, who engaged in agriculture and carried on a lively commerce by sea.

Soon after Athens had reached the height of its glory under Pericles in the Fifth Century, B. C., and had started on its decline, the rise of Macedon under Philip carried Greek influence into new regions. The glory of Athens had been based upon sea power, but the conquests of Macedon were the work of land armies— Philip invented the invincible phalanx. Upon Philip's death his son, Alexander the Great, set forth to conquer the whole of the then known world, and as that world in his day lay to the east, his marches were in that direction. In a few years he had overrun the fertile plains

9

and opulent cities of Asia Minor, Syria, Mesopotamia, and Persia, and had carried his conquests to the gates of Delhi. In all the cities in the intervening countries he left large garrisons of Greek soldiers. In many of these countries he founded flourishing new cities. In every place his soldiers were followed by large colonies of Greek civilians. The result was that the whole of western Asia, and of what we call the Near East, including Asia Minor, Egypt, Palestine, Syria, Babylonia, Mesopotamia, Persia, and northwestern India, was saturated with the Greek influence and with Greek colonies.

The imagination of these conquered peoples was dazzled by the introduction of Greek art, literature, philosophy, and public works. Though the successors of Alexander were unable to maintain the political control of the lands he conquered, and though successive waves of Roman, Arabian, and Tartar conquests swept over these lands in succeeding centuries, none of the later conquerors has been able wholly to eradicate the influence of Greek culture, nor to exterminate that element of population which was of Greek blood.

Thus it becomes clear that when, nearly seven hundred years ago, the night of Turkish oppression began to settle down upon the Near East, the Greeks who were caught beneath the Turkish darkness were not merely the inhabitants of Greece itself, but were also those several million Greeks who had been settled for more than a thousand years in Asia Minor. This fact has played a decisive part in the recent history of both Turkey and Greece.

To understand the modern history of the Greeks,

Western readers will have to get one idea clearly in mind—an idea that will probably astonish most of them. This is, that the modern Greek thinks no more about the Greece of the Classical Age than we do. The modern Greek shares our veneration of that golden epoch of the human intellect, but it is just as remote to him, and just as unrelated to the immediate interests of his life, as it is to us. Until six years ago no modern Greek ever dreamed of reconstituting Athens as the permanent capital of the Greek world. On the contrary, every Greek in the world shared a passionate devotion to the ideal of reërecting the ancient Byzantine Empire in its prime of glory as of, let us say, the Ninth Century, with Byzantium (Constantinople) as its capital. Not to the Parthenon at Athens, but to the Santa Sofia at Constantinople, did his mingled emotions of religion and political greatness yearn with a burning zeal. If this animating principle be kept firmly in mind the whole course of Greek political aspirations in the Nineteenth and Twentieth Centuries becomes clear.

The Greek War of Independence, which came to a successful conclusion in 1832, affected less than one half of the Greeks in the Turkish Empire. It did not bring freedom to the Greeks of Macedonia and Thrace, of Crete and the Ægean Islands, nor to the more than two million Greeks in Asia Minor and Constantinople. For ninety-five years following the War of Independence, down to the destruction of Smyrna in 1922, the consuming ambition of the Kingdom of Greece, shared by the "unredeemed Greeks" of Asia Minor and the islands, was the liberation of this majority of the Greek race. Along with this ambition went the desire to control the territory over which all these Greeks were scattered.

When I arrived in Constantinople as American Ambassador in 1913 the second Balkan War had just come to a close. My two and one half years at the Embassy there not only gave me an intimate knowledge of Turkey and the Turks, but of the Greeks in Turkey as well. To my astonishment I then learned that the Greeks comprised a considerable percentage of the population of the Turkish Empire. In Constantinople alone there were between three hundred and four hundred thousand permanent Greek residents. They were one of the strongest elements of the population. I learned that, not only in Constantinople, but also throughout Asia Minor, the Greeks largely controlled the banking, the shipping, and the general mercantile business. Some of the Greeks in Constantinople were among the most brilliant and cultivated people I have ever met anywhere in the world. Highly educated, fluent linguists, and very prosperous, they would have adorned any society. Some of them were the only non-diplomatic residents of Constantinople who were admitted into the diplomatic social circles.

I found that the Greeks, like various other non-Mohammedans, occupied a peculiar legal status in Turkey, for which there is no parallel in any European country. They constituted a separate legal community, and exercised all community rights for themselves. They organized and supported their own schools.

This peculiar status arose from the theocratic nature of the Turkish Government. To the Turkish mind, civil government and religious government are inseparably intertwined, the civil government deriving its sanctions and its authority from the Mohammedan religion. Consequently, the Turk has always regarded the non-Mohammedan minorities as being simply other religious communities. The Turkish Government has dealt with them as such. Therefore, the Metropolitan, or chief bishop of the Orthodox Greek Church, was officially recognized by the Turkish Government as the head of the Greek community. He was held responsible for the orderly behavior of his co-religionists, and for their obedience to Turkish laws.

When I came to Constantinople the revolutionary Committee of Union and Progress—better known to the world as the Young Turks—was in control of the government. They had deposed the former Sultan, Abdul Hamid, and had placed upon his throne Abdul's brother, Mohammed. Utterly incompetent and hopelessly weak, Mohammed was ruler merely in name. The real power was exercised by the Young Turks, whose outstanding conspirators were Enver, Talaat, and Djemal. Their men had set up the machinery of a sham constitutional government, including a parliament of two houses, a senate, and an assembly. The Greek community had representatives in this body. It was of no advantage to them, however, as the parliament had no real authority.

As a result of the two Balkan Wars the relations between the Turks and the Greeks were considerably strained in 1913. The first Balkan War (in which an alliance of Greece, Serbia, and Bulgaria had decisively defeated Turkey) had resulted in the lopping off from the Turkish Empire of Albania, Macedonia, and Thrace, leaving Turkey only a few miles of European territory just north of Constantinople. This disaster had followed close upon the almost equally disastrous war between Italy and Turkey in 1911, wherein Italy wrested Tripolitania from Turkey. I could readily understand the bitter feelings harbored by the Turks. They were being pushed out of one after another of their possessions, and were beginning to be fearful of being crowded to complete extinction as a nation. The instinct of self-preservation was aroused within them. They hated with a deadly hatred all Italians, Bulgarians, Serbs, and Greeks. They yearned for an opportunity to strike back and take vengeance for their losses and humiliations.

The Greeks were the only one of these hated races within striking distance of Turkish vengeance. The Greeks alone had a considerable body of their population living within the Turkish borders. It was deplorable, but by no means unnatural, that they should speedily become objects of petty persecution wherever they happened to be living in Turkey.

They became also objects of official suspicion on the part of the Turkish Government. That government was concerned with more than mere revenge. It was fighting for the life of Turkey as an independent nation. Recently deprived of many of its richest territories, Turkey was menaced with other losses at the hands of ambitious neighbors. Its capital, Constantinople (now within sight of enemy guns), had been coveted by Russia since the time of Peter the Great, and by Greece for many centuries before that.

Thus, the Young Turk government had reason enough to be fearful of the future. But the Young Turks had friends who took pains to increase their fears. These friends were the German Ambassador at Constantinople and the German army officers who had been brought in to organize and train the Turkish Army. It developed later that the German Ambassador and the German officers were already feverishly engaged in paving the way for the World War that broke out in the following year. They were scheming for Turkish coöperation in that conflict.

I have explained the German plan at length elsewhere. Briefly, it was to use Turkey and Bulgaria during the impending war for the purpose of wholly segregating Russia from her Western allies. After the war Bulgaria and Turkey were to be made into tributary states, forming the opened corridor of German expansion through to Mesopotamia and India. In working out the details of this scheme Germany had foreseen that the presence of large bodies of recalcitrant Greeks and Armenians within the Turkish Empire would constitute a serious military difficulty. In the excitement and confusion of war, these minorities would be strongly tempted to organize into hostile armies threatening the German-Turkish lines of communication. Even if they did not carry their hostilities so far as this, they would almost certainly use their knowledge of the country

15

to act as spies for the benefit of Turkey's enemies. Especially could they be dangerous along the coasts of Asia Minor, both to the north on the Black Sea, and to the west on the Ægean, where the Germans had planned to establish submarine bases. The majority of the inhabitants in the cities and towns on these coasts were Greeks. For the foregoing reasons, the German agents in Constantinople did everything in their power to heighten the fears of the Turkish Government and to incite it to violence against the Greeks and Armenians.

Already in the early spring of 1914 the Young Turks were scheming and preparing to go to war with Greece. They were not going to submit calmly to the dissection of their nation. To defend themselves, they were determined to take the offensive. It soon became evident that they had been advised that, in anticipation of their entering the Great War, it was essential to remove the Greeks from the seashores. Consequently, they began a systematic petty persecution of the Greeks in the coast towns, with the purpose of so frightening and discommoding them as to induce them to move out. The results of their reign of terror were apparent to those of us who lived in Constantinople. Whenever we passed the Greek Consulate we could see a throng of excited Greeks besieging its doors in an effort to get passports to leave the country. Our friends among the wealthy Greeks told me they were removing their valuables from the country; and they repeated to me endless stories of the persecutions and hardships of their less fortunate brethren. The Greek

Metropolitan told us something of his difficulties. The poor man was in a truly tragic position. Appeals to him, as the head of the Greek community, poured in by the thousands from every part of Turkey. He had attempted to obtain redress from the Turkish Government, but had been met with rebuffs and insults. Only too plainly he perceived that the sufferings of his followers were more than the result of sporadic outbursts of local patriotism: they were the result of a systematic policy emanating from the government at Constantinople itself.

Intolerable as the government was making it for the Greeks in the coast towns, the Greeks were not leaving their homes fast enough to suit the Turks. More strenuous measures were therefore adopted, and the atrocious murder of fifty Greeks at Phocæa followed.

The Phocæa incident brought the designs of the Turks out into the open, and made it evident to all that a war between Turkey and Greece was practically inevitable. The Young Turks realized that in such a war they could not attack Greece by way of the traditional route through Thrace and Macedonia. Both Bulgaria and Serbia might join Greece to bar the way. To succeed, the attack would have to be launched by sea. The Turkish Navy and the Greek Navy were so evenly matched that the Turks had no assurance of victory on the water.

My office at the American Embassy now became the local scene of a strange and subterranean battle for the control of the Ægean Sea. I have once before told this incident in print, and I cannot do better than quote it here from my *Ambassador Morgenthau's Story*:

. . . early in June, I received a most agitated visitor. This was Djemal Pasha, the Turkish Minister of Marine and one of the three men who then dominated the Turkish Empire. I have hardly ever seen a man who appeared more utterly worried than was Djemal on this occasion. As he began talking excitedly to my interpreter in French, his whiskers trembling with his emotions and his hands wildly gesticulating, he seemed to be almost beside himself. I knew enough French to understand what he was saying, and the news which he brought—this was the first I had heard of it—sufficiently explained his agitation. The American Government, he said, was negotiating with Greece for the sale of two battleships, the *Idaho* and the *Mississippi*. He urged that I should immediately move to prevent any such sale. His attitude was that of a suppliant; he begged, he implored that I should intervene. All along, he said, the Turks regarded the United States as their best friend; I had frequently expressed my desire to help them; well, here was the chance to show our good feeling. The fact that Greece and Turkey were practically on the verge of war, said Djemal, really made the sale of the ships an unneutral act. Still, if the transaction were purely a commercial one, Turkey would like a chance to bid. "We will pay more than Greece," he added. He ended with a powerful plea that I should at once cable my government about the matter, and this I promised to do.

Evidently the clever Greeks had turned the tables on their enemy. Turkey had rather too baldly advertised her intention of attacking Greece as soon as she had received her dreadnaughts. Both the ships for which Greece was now negotiating were immediately available for battle! The *Idaho* and *Mississippi* were not indispensable ships for the American Navy; they could not take their place in the first line of battle; they were powerful enough, however, to drive the whole Turkish Navy from the Ægean. Evidently the Greeks did not intend politely to postpone the impending war until the Turkish dreadnaughts had been finished. Djemal's point, of course, had no legal validity. However great the threat of war might be, Turkey and Greece were still actually at peace. Clearly Greece had just as much right to purchase warships in the United States as Turkey had to purchase them in Brazil or England. . . .

To Djemal and the other Turkish officials who kept pressing me I suggested that their ambassador in Washington should take up the matter directly with the President. They acted on this advice, but the Greeks again got ahead of them. At two o'clock, June 22d, the Greek *chargé d'affaires* at Washington and Commander Tsouklas, of the Greek Navy, called upon the President and arranged the sale. As they left the President's office, the Turkish Ambassador entered— just fifteen minutes too late!

Djemal treated his failure in the negotiations for the American battleships as a personal defeat and humiliation. His anger could not, of course, find any outlet upon me. It could, however, be turned upon the Greeks who lived in Turkey. Djemal was the most relentless of the group of desperate leaders of the Young Turks. Realizing that the Turkish Navy was now outmatched, and that Turkey would have to give up the idea of open war with the Greeks to recover the Ægean Islands, Djemal's implacable hatred took a new direction. At his insistence the Turkish Government began the deliberate effort to remove all Greeks from the seashores of Asia Minor—that I have mentioned above—and to molest them in other ways.

These Greeks were completely at the mercy of the

19

Turks. The Greek Government was impotent to help
them. Whole settlements of Greeks in Asia Minor were
rounded up by the Turkish troops, were loaded like
cattle on to ships and deported from the country.
On shipboard these Greeks were treated with the greatest brutality. They were given neither food nor water
—in some cases for such long periods of time that their
tongues clove to the roofs of their mouths. En route
to Greece the ships called at the Island of Prinkipo, in
the Sea of Marmora. Notwithstanding the terrible sufferings of the refugees on board, the Greek residents
of Prinkipo were not permitted to do anything to help
their brethren on these ships, which were anchored
within sight and sound of the shore.

I came into intimate contact with this whole problem
through the Greek Metropolitan at Constantinople.
Powerless to be of any assistance to his fellow countrymen, he appealed to me for help for them. I sent a boat
to Prinkipo with barrels of water and boxes of crackers,
with instructions to distribute them to the distressed
refugees.

The Prinkipo incident was so flagrant and was so
obviously approved by the Turkish authorities that
it dispelled any lingering doubts I might have had
that an organized effort was being made to frighten
the Greeks out of Turkey. This incident had the same
effect upon the minds of the Greeks themselves, and
many of the leading Greek bankers and merchants
of Constantinople left Turkey with their families, many
of them removing to Athens and Paris.

The World War broke out shortly after the Prinkipo

incident. The Greeks in Turkey were now more alarmed than ever. The Greek Government was a traditional friend of Great Britain's, and Great Britain was now at war with Turkey's military advisers, the Germans. The Greek inhabitants of the Turkish Empire were therefore more than ever under the suspicion of the Turkish rulers. The stream of Greeks besieging the consulate with applications for passports to leave the country now became a veritable deluge.

The Greek inhabitants of Turkey were, of course, citizens of the empire, and, as such, were liable to military duty. Not unnaturally, they were regarded by the Turks as unreliable soldiers in the Turkish Army. Consequently, they were not permitted to bear arms. Those who had the means to do so were coerced into buying exemption from military service at the rate of about forty English pounds per capita. The less affluent Greeks—who, of course, comprised the great majority—being unable to purchase exemption, were enrolled in so-called "labor battalions," and were put to work at menial tasks under the direction of Turkish officers. They built military roads, erected barracks, and performed other tasks of manual labor behind the lines. They were subjected to iron discipline, as the Turks regarded every Greek as a potential traitor, insurrectionist, and spy.

I would be the last person to condone the Turkish brutality toward the Greek labor battalions—for the Turks, undoubtedly with deliberate intention, so overworked and underfed these men as to cause the death of several hundred thousand of them. Nevertheless,

21

it is only fair to the Turks to say that they were largely justified in their fears that the Greeks would have availed themselves of any opportunity to hamper Turkish military efficiency.

After the World War had been in progress for two years Venizelos took Greece into the war on the side of the Allies. From that moment onward the Turks no longer treated their Greek citizens as merely potential traitors, but began to treat them as avowed enemies, and to make their lives miserable in every possible way. I was besought upon scores of occasions to use my influence with the Turkish Government to help Greek individuals and Greek communities out of critical difficulties with the Turks. Happily, I was able on a good many occasions to be of real service to these distressed people.

The ending of the World War, with the incidental complete defeat of the Turks, by no means ended the troubles of the Greeks. The Kingdom of Greece, to be sure, would inevitably gain great advantages when the terms of the peace settlement were finally written. The Greek inhabitants of Turkey, however, were left in little better state than they had been before. Indeed, as will appear shortly, the extraordinary success of Venizelos at the Paris Peace Conference, in securing for Greece exceptional advantages in the peace terms there, eventually operated indirectly to bring overwhelming disaster upon the Greeks in Turkey.

The conference at Paris did not include the Turkish problem in the peace settlement. The Allies, themselves, had too many conflicting interests involved in the Near

East to permit an immediate agreement. Consequently, that whole subject was laid aside for separate treatment after the Versailles Treaty should be out of the way.

Even during the peace conference, however, the Turkish problem could not be kept submerged. The Italians were determined to gain special advantage from the dismemberment of the Turkish Empire, and Greece was only little less anxious to do so. Italy announced her claims and proceeded to overt acts. Italian troops seized the port of Adalia, the key to southwestern Asia Minor, which Italy coveted. The Greeks protested that this move was intended solely to anticipate their own claim in Asia Minor. President Wilson attacked the Italian move so vigorously that Premier Orlando for a time withdrew from the conference. President Wilson now announced his support of the long-debated claim of Greece to the possession of Smyrna, Aidin, and the Ionian coast. Partly to block further the Italian aggression, and partly to protect the Greek inhabitants of Asia Minor from the fury of the vanquished Turks, President Wilson now consented that the Greeks be invited to send an army of occupation to police this region until the Powers could finally agree on its ultimate disposition.

Apparently, President Wilson's theory in proposing this move was that the nearest friendly troops were the Greek divisions in Macedonia, and that prompt action was necessary to protect the Christians of the Smyrna district. Winston Churchill has only recently asserted that the American missionaries in Smyrna added their

23

warnings against this move to the warnings of the British Foreign Office and British General Staff, declaring that it was fraught with the gravest dangers, not only to the Greek Army itself, but to the Christian population of Ionia as well. In any event, Lloyd George cordially approved President Wilson's proposal, Clemenceau offered no objections, and the occupation was ordered and quickly accomplished. Greek troops landed at Smyrna under the protecting fire of Greek battleships, killed a number of Turkish soldiers retreating from the city, and quickly occupied advanced positions in the hinterland.

Churchill has described vividly the bewilderment and alarm with which he heard the news of this action. He had made a special study of the Turkish problem in both its military and political aspects. He was convinced that the Greek Army would eventually meet with disaster in the exceedingly difficult mountainous interior of Asia Minor. But he was even more alarmed, he declares, at the political complications that would be engendered. The defeated Turks were growing restive. Constantinople was strongly held by the Allies with their fleets in the Bosphorus, but the dwindling Allied armies retained only a few precarious footholds in Asia Minor, where most of the Turks lived. This half-savage warrior race was already angry enough at its military defeat, but to have a part of its very homeland occupied by Greeks, whom it regarded with age-long hatred and contempt, fanned resentment to active fury.

The results that Churchill foresaw actually came to

24

pass. The Turks felt that their very existence was now threatened, and they resorted to desperate measures. Mustapha Kemal, the ablest officer the Turks had had during the war, now emerged as the political and military leader of an organized movement to defy the whole world, if necessary, to preserve a Turkish nation in Asia Minor. Withdrawing from Constantinople, and setting up headquarters in the mountain fastnesses at Angora, a group of determined Turkish leaders issued a manifesto to the world, in which they declared that Turkey would fight to the death of her last man to preserve Turkish nationality.

This was the beginning of the Turkish Nationalist State, which has persisted to the present day. Kemal rapidly organized an efficient army and proceeded to recapture the ammunition "dumps" of arms laid down when Turkey had capitulated the year before. The Greek Army in Ionia was soon confronted with the menace of a well-equipped Turkish army waiting only for a favorable opportunity to join battle.

Meanwhile, in 1920, the Allies gathered at the Conference of Sèvres to thresh out the peace settlement for Turkey.

Before discussing the Sèvres Conference, however, I should go back a moment to the decision at the Paris Conference to have the Greek Army occupy Ionia. Quite independently of Churchill, I came to the same conclusion he had reached, for I, too, was intimately familiar with the Turkish problem from my residence in Constantinople in the first years of the war. I told Henry White, one of the American peace commissioners, my views on the subject. I once before described this incident and I quote what I then printed:

When discussing with Henry White the Greek invasion of Smyrna, I told him that the Greeks were making a mistake and that they would be drawn into a tedious struggle with the Turks. They would have to draw heavily on their resources and on their people's patience, which would be severely strained if, as I feared, the war lasted for years. White was deeply impressed.

"I want you to tell that to Venizelos," he said.

He knew everybody, and his bringing people together was not the least of his services to our Commission. He invited the Greek Premier to his rooms in the Crillon, and there I repeated my opinion.

I told him in great detail the changes that had taken place in Turkey since the beginning of the war, and described to him the characters of the men that were now in power. I also explained to him the great importance they put on retaining possession of the Port of Smyrna, now that they had lost most of their other ports on the Mediterranean. I felt certain that they would draw the Grecian Army back into their hinterland, and away from their base of supplies, and then would continue to fight them by legitimate, or even guerrilla, methods, until they exhausted them. I reminded him how the Turks not only forbade their own people to employ Greeks, but even insisted that the American firms could not use Grecian workmen to collect the licorice root, or the Singer Manufacturing Company continue to have Greeks in charge of their Turkish agencies. I also alluded to the difficulties of governing Smyrna from Athens, as Constantinople would divide their country, and the cost of administration would be beyond the present and prospective resources of Greece, and, finally, I reminded him that they would antagonize Italy and said: "You know better than I do what that means for Greece."

Venizelos listened patiently to my elaboration of this theme.

"Perhaps we have acted too hastily," he said, "and if all you say is true, it may have been unwise for us to send an army into Smyrna, but now that the army is there, it would be more unwise to withdraw it—to do so would admit military and court political defeat. The Monarchists are plotting constantly against me in Athens, and they are backed by the merchants and shipping men who are over-ambitious and want new territory for their operations."

The conference at Sèvres finally worked out a treaty of peace which everybody signed. It satisfied nobody. Turkey was to be dismembered and left with no territory to call her own except the interior of Asia Minor and the city of Constantinople. The independent Republic of Armenia was erected to the east; Mesopotamia and Palestine were put under British mandate, Syria and Cilicia under French mandate, and to Italy was assigned Adalia and its hinterland. Smyrna and Ionia were held by the Greeks, pending further discussion of their eventual disposition.

The relations between Turkey and Greece now moved rapidly toward a tragic conclusion. The Turkish Nationalists announced they would never accept the Treaty of Sèvres, and bent all their energies toward getting their army into condition to defend their country. They were also determined to seize the first opportunity to drive the Greeks out of Ionia.

At this juncture, when Greece had the greatest need of the genius of Venizelos, that far-sighted statesman was overwhelmingly defeated in the Greek general election in the fall of 1920. His Royalist enemies in Greece

27

were almost as much astonished at the result of this election as Venizelos himself. Immediately, however, they hastened to take vengeance on his adherents. Their first act upon organizing their government was to repeal the decree of exile against Constantine, and to recall him to Athens to resume his throne.

Reinstated in power, Constantine pursued his advantage by removing from command all the officers of the Greek Army who owed their positions to Venizelos. It so happened that these officers were by far the most experienced commanders amongst the Greeks. They were replaced by favorites of Constantine. The most grotesque example of this favoritism was his appointment of General Hadjanestes to the supreme command of the army of occupation in Ionia. This was the most important command in the army at the moment. The Greek troops in Ionia were operating in a most difficult country in the presence of a skilful and implacable enemy. General Hadjanestes, upon whom was placed the terrific responsibility of guiding this army in its precarious situation, was notoriously a nervous wreck at the time Constantine appointed him.

Early in 1921 representatives of the British, Frencn, and Italian governments met in London to reconsider and revise the impossible Treaty of Sèvres. The London Conference worked out a set of tentative proposals for a revision of that treaty. These proposals were indignantly rejected by the Greeks. Constantine now thought he saw an opportunity to eclipse the glory that Venizelos had gained by his acquisition of Ionia. He thought he saw an opportunity to drive the Turks out of Asia Minor and to assert Greek sovereignty over the whole of that country. He accordingly committed the supreme folly of ordering a general offensive against the Turkish Nationalist position. The Greeks were defeated in this attack, and Constantine left Athens and took personal command of the army in Asia Minor on June 11th. He left Greece hailed by the government-inspired press as Emperor-Designate of Constantinople, thus vaingloriously appealing to the traditional ambition of the Greek nation to reconstruct the Byzantine Empire.

The Turkish military commanders in Asia Minor now followed the strategy that I had foreseen in Paris three years before. The Turks retired before the Greek advance, permitting the Greek Army to capture difficult mountain passes with only feeble resistance. Thus the Turks lured the Greeks farther and farther into the difficult mountains just west of Angora. The Greek line of communications was thus extended until Greece's army was barely able to maintain its supplies from the coast. Then, one day in August, the Turkish Army, in accordance with its long-meditated plan of action, attacked the Greek Army on the banks of the Sakkaria River. The Greek Army was compelled to withdraw westward until it could reform its lines on a continuous front about four days' march east of Smyrna.

Then followed a year of international negotiation. The conflicting ambitions of the Allied Powers regarding the future of Asia Minor resulted in some of the most disgusting intrigues in modern history. Of these, two were especially disgraceful. The first was the so-called Franklin-Bouillon Agreement, arrived at between France and the Turkish Nationalist Government. This agreement was signed on October 20, 1921, at Angora, by Kemal for the Turks and by Franklin-Bouillon for the French. It was dictated by the greed of French capitalists seeking concessions from the Turks for railways and commercial privileges. In exchange, the French shamefully deserted their support of the Greeks, whom in 1919 they (along with Great Britain and the United States) had invited to take over the military occupation of Asia Minor. Not only did the French withdraw their moral support from the Greeks and transfer their friendship to the Turks, but they "abandoned" great quantities of French ammunition in Asia Minor—practically making a present to the Turks of munitions of war with which to destroy their former allies, the Greeks.

Italy, like France, deserted her Greek ally. During the Paris Conference the Italians had entered the southern coast of Asia Minor at Adalia, and were still in possession there whilst the Greeks were operating against the Turks from Smyrna as a base. While this Greek campaign was in progress it soon became notorious to military observers of all nations that the Turks were being continually supplied with ammunition "bootlegged" to them from the Italian base at Adalia. Italy's ambitions with regard to Asia Minor were stronger than her sense of duty to an ally. Italy already occupied the Dodecanese Islands off the coast of Asia Minor, and the peninsula itself has long been an object of Italy's scheme of colonial expansion. To

have remained faithful to the Greek alliance would have
been to help Greece eventually to become the owner of
Asia Minor. On the other hand, to have helped Turkey to repel the Greeks was to weaken both of Italy's
rivals. The temptation was too strong for Italy to
withstand it.

Greece was almost hopelessly weakened, not only by
the active betrayal of France and Italy, but as well by
the inactivity and indifference of Great Britain, her
third ally. The United States likewise shared in this
disgrace. The request that Greece should occupy
Smyrna and police the Ionian shore was initiated by
President Wilson. It implied the assistance of all four
of the Great Powers, including the United States. But
in 1920, following the victory of the Republican Party
in our national election, the United States rejected
practically all the commitments of the Wilson Administration. They gave not the slightest regard to the ful-
fillment of our arrangement with Greece, which was
part of the general scheme of ending the war. We
precipitately retired from the scene, and so far as
we were concerned left Greece to her fate.

This fate speedily descended upon the Greeks in
the most terrible form. Following the year of futile
negotiations among the European Powers, the Turks
attacked the Greek Army in Asia Minor, defeated it
decisively, and put it to ignominious rout. Two weeks
later, on September 9, 1922, the Turks entered Smyrna.
Then followed the orgy of looting, outrage, massacre,
and burning which desolated the city. The Turks
segregated all the able-bodied Greek men of mature

age and drove them into the interior of Asia Minor, where practically every one of them died of starvation, forced labor, or assassination. The old men, the women, and the children were herded upon any kind of craft that was available and without more ado were shipped (to the number of several hundred thousand) to the mainland of Greece and to the Ægean Islands under Greek sovereignty. The sudden inforced exodus of this vast number of people, all unexpectedly uprooted from their ties of home and occupation, all of them completely impoverished, and all of them thrown chaotically upon Greek soil without any regard to their future welfare, marks the beginning of the refugee problem in its most acute stage.

CHAPTER IV

Britain Saves Us From Another World War

IN 1922, just as the Greek tragedy was drawing to its catastrophe and during the fateful two weeks preceding the destruction of Smyrna, I happened to be in London, on my way home from a tour of Europe. There I ran across my old friend, the father of the House of Commons, T. P. O'Connor, with whom I had often exchanged hospitality, both in England and America. He invited me to have luncheon with him on September 2d. He turned the conversation to the situation in the Near East. This was natural, as the newspapers were filled with big headlines on the overwhelming defeat just suffered by the Greek Army, now in headlong flight back to the west coast of Asia Minor, closely pursued by the Turkish conquerors. "Tay Pay" was of course familiar with my experiences with the Turks while American Ambassador at Constantinople, and he was anxious to have my views regarding the effect of this unexpected Nationalist victory upon the situation in the Near East.

When I explained to him that I did not limit its possibilities to the Near East, but regarded it as a menace to the safety of the Balkans and quite possibly to the peace of all Europe, he was so impressed that he asked me for an interview for the London *Daily Telegraph*, with which he was associated. He felt that the country at large had no idea of the possible effect of this Turkish victory upon Europe, and that the British public should at once be informed of my views.

Consequently, on the Monday following, Mr. O'Connor called on me again, bringing with him Mr. Gerothwohl, a writer on the *Daily Telegraph*. I repeated my opinion of the situation, in detail, and the interview was published in the paper next morning as follows:

"I wonder," stated the Ambassador, "if 400,000,000 Christians in full control of all the governments of Europe and America are again going to condone these offences by the Turkish Government! Or will definite steps be promptly taken to rescue permanently the remnants of these fine old civilized Christian peoples from the fangs of the Turk?"

Mr. Morgenthau agreed that there were only two methods by which the present emergency could be met. "We should help," he said, "to remove these refugees from Anatolia to Thrace, in view of our pledges to them. The Powers should also be absolutely adamant in refusing to allow the Kemalists to cross the Straits.

"If the European countries have control of Constantinople, they can eventually influence the Turks and keep them in check, because the possession or non-possession of Constantinople determines the status of Turkey. If she obtains Constantinople she becomes a world power again. If she does not, she becomes a succession state. There is the point. Now what sensible person wants Turkey to be a world power again, with increased powers for the making of international mischief? No matter how other countries may differ on other matters, they must unite and agree on this: To keep Constantinople out of the hands of the Turks.

"Constantinople is the sixth largest and sixth most important city in the world, after London, Paris, Berlin, New

York, and, possibly, Vienna. To put it again into the hands of these people, who can neither govern themselves nor anyone else, would be the most terrible blunder of the age, because it would simply give them a chance to reëstablish themselves in a place where for the last one hundred years we have heard of 'the dying Turk,' and where they could tyrannize again. There is no need to recapitulate the doings of the Turks—their incapacities, how they have been the parasites of those countries they have attempted to govern. They have never assimilated the people nor assimilated with them, and have always been merely the collectors of revenue, the farmers and the butchers. The Chauvinism of the Turks is so well known and so extreme that, unless restrained, they will not permit the minorities to exist. They will find some new device or resort to some of the old devices for exterminating the non-Moslem populations. The waterway through the Dardanelles and the Bosphorus should be internationalized."

This interview in the *Daily Telegraph* created something of a sensation. An immediate result of it was that the *Sunday Times* (not to be confused with *The Times*, the daily of world-wide fame) promptly sent Captain Townroe to interview me for that paper, and this article appeared on the following Sunday—the morning after the Turkish Army, pursuing the Greeks, entered the doomed city of Smyrna. This interview was as follows:

The events of the past week in Asia Minor have increased the magnitude of the task which lies before Great Britain. Turkey is again trying to establish herself as a world power. This new fact is spreading unrest throughout the Moslem world, and in the chancelleries of Europe the new situation is being considered in all its bearings. Still more significant to a war-wearied world is the rustle of the operation maps which naval and military officers are studying.

The immediate outcome of the Turkish threat will be further massacres of the Armenian, Greek, and Syrian Christians if Turkish power is allowed to pursue its course as a conqueror unchecked. The Christian governments of Europe and America must help to rescue the survivors of these unhappy races.

But the issues involved in the new crisis reach further than Smyrna or Athens. The prestige of the British Empire is far more seriously threatened by the success of the Turkish arms than is, I find, generally recognized in London, except in official circles. The conditions that have arisen are too tangled to be analyzed in one article. I can only hope here to touch briefly on certain points, and to give some reasons for my conviction that Great Britain, France, and Italy must suspend all personal jealousies and prejudices, and in mutual agreement refuse to allow the Turk under any pretext again to control Constantinople and the Dardanelles.

Mistakes occurred when in the peace negotiations the Allies favored Greece and allotted to her Smyrna and part of the hinterland. The negotiators apparently were ignorant of the fact that the Greeks of Athens are entirely different from the unredeemed Hellenes of Asia Minor. Further, the Allies seemingly failed to appreciate the threat to Turkey if the Greeks were allowed to be in occupation both in Thrace and in Asia Minor. When M. Venizelos was displaced by the brother-in-law of the late Kaiser, the Turkish leaders inevitably supposed that before long the Greeks would try to connect their two possessions in Europe and Asia by occupying Constantinople, a city which contains a Greek population of nearly three hundred and fifty thousand.

Faced with this supposed menace, Turkey tried again her old game—a game as old as Æsop's fables. She tried to divide her enemies and so to benefit herself as a result of their quarrels. She found all the Allies foolishly cherishing

36

old mutual jealousies, ambitions, and suspicions. The hard lessons taught by disaster in war, and the value of unity in command, had all too quickly been forgotten in peace. Turkey received help from Italy, and now with French ammunition, guns, tanks, and possibly aided by the directing ideas of French officers—the most capable strategists in the world—Turkey has delivered a knock-down blow to Greece.

Many English people probably have not followed the kaleidoscope of Turkish affairs. Certain main facts must be recognized in order to appreciate the present crisis. The Turks have refused to sign the treaty of peace with Great Britain and so, technically, there is still a state of war between Turkey and this country. Italy has made a secret peace. France, after her troops were in danger of annihilation, signed the Treaty of Angora, which, when fully known, may be called the surrender of Angora. Thus have the Allies been divided by the wily Turk, and, owing to Entente mistakes, the Turks again hold the upper hand in Asia Minor, and will mercilessly use the same.

If only Great Britain and France will even now come to an agreement on the questions over which they have differed, there is time to prevent further mischief. The peace of the Balkans depends largely to-day on the Allies retaining command of the Dardanelles. The door must be kept open in the Mediterranean for the trade of all nations with Russia. Otherwise Russia will continue to be largely dependent on Germany for its supplies and its trade. A false step now, and the Allies may to-morrow find the German military party and the Russian Bolsheviks have again allied to threaten the world's peace. If Turkey, defeated primarily in 1918 by Lord Allenby's army coming through Palestine, and so compelling them to lay down their arms, has so revived in 1922 as to demand a place again as a world power, what may not Berlin and Moscow together accomplish?

I speak without reserve, as the exigencies of the case demand it. If there had been harmony between the Allies, and if the United States had agreed to take part in the League of Nations, I believe the peace of the Near East would have now been secured. During the week thousands of men have lost their lives, and thousands of women have suffered unprintable horrors, because there has been discord among the Entente Powers.

Those Americans who believe in, and have fought for, the League of Nations are convinced that American influence ought to have been at work to prevent this wrong. Instead of pursuing selfish aims, it would have been a wiser policy if the Turks had been definitely relegated to Asia Minor, and the Dardanelles permanently converted into a great international waterway. Constantinople should be under the protection of the League of Nations. The Turks cannot govern an empire, nor have they the revenue to maintain even Constantinople, the sixth most important city in the world. This city should be a storehouse and distributing centre between East and West, and governed, policed, and civilized under the combined control of Great Britain, France, and Italy, and possibly in due time the United States would join.

Those who have heard from French and British lips what a salutary and sane influence has been exercised by Major General H. T. Allen in the Rhineland believe that the time has come when other Americans might take their share in the international task of keeping the Turk in Asia, where he belongs, and assisting in making Constantinople a free city, and the Dardanelles a free waterway for the world. The majority of the residents of Constantinople are non-Turks, and it requires no plebiscite to establish the fact that they are determined not to come again under Turkish rule.

For the present, the chief burden of ensuring the freedom of the Dardanelles rests upon Great Britain. If all Americans understood the terrific task that the British race have on their hands to-day in order to preserve Western civilization in Europe, they would not long withhold their hearty co-operation.

On the day after the *Sunday Times* printed the fore-going interview I had luncheon with Winston Churchill and his wife at their home. Churchill was full of the Near Eastern question. We discussed not only the news of the day, but he carried the subject back to the World War. He had been chiefly responsible for the British expedition to force the Dardanelles in 1915, the expedition that had failed so miserably; and he had been savagely criticized for it by members of Parliament and the press. In my book about my experiences at Constantinople (published in England under the title of *Secrets of the Bosphorus*) I had told of the nervousness of the Turks at that time. It was common knowledge to them that if the British had pressed on instead of retiring they would have been able easily to force the Straits and capture Constantinople. Churchill recalled this part of the book, and expressed his gratitude that I had recorded these facts, which vindicated his plan.

Churchill talked with the utmost freedom about the Near Eastern situation. Like myself, he believed the Turkish victory the prelude to a great débâcle in the international situation, fearing that the world was in grave danger of a fresh outburst of war.

When I was leaving the Churchills I told them that Mrs. Morgenthau would be deeply disappointed at having missed the interesting discussion we had just been having, and said that they must repair this loss by dining with us on Tuesday of the following week. Mrs. Churchill could not come, so he came alone.

Before Tuesday came, however, I had a long talk with Lloyd George, at breakfast at No. 10 Downing Street. Lloyd George had read my interviews in the *Daily Telegraph* and the *Sunday Times*, and he wished to get my ideas at first hand. I arrived at No. 10 Downing Street a few minutes after nine in the morning, and we sat down at once to breakfast. But what a repast, to bear such an humble name! For me, it was the equivalent of a five-course luncheon.

I remarked to Lloyd George on the fact that he spoke to the servant at the table in a foreign language.

"There's a method in that madness," he rejoined with a chuckle. "Every servant in the place is Welsh, and not one of them speaks a word of English. There'll be no leaks of news about important political conversations in this place while I am here, on account of some servant's indiscretion!"

Lloyd George was a delightful host. He did not rush at once into the subject he wished most to discuss with me, but talked of many things, and with a most engaging frankness: about German reparations, his own continuance in office (he thought it would be a good idea to get out and let some of his critics see what they could do with the impossible situation they damned him for not settling), about his forthcoming book and his intention to show in it the mistakes made at the Dardanelles, about his solicitude concerning American politics and our attitude toward international affairs after our impending Congressional election, and even

about the Underwood typewriter he used in his office.
He evidently knew that I was a director of the company
—I believe he had pursued the usual method of having
me looked up in *Who's Who* before I called.

In discussing America's international policy, he frequently mentioned his contact with Woodrow Wilson,
and several times he characterized one or another of
Wilson's traits as "weaknesses." The last time he said
this he realized that he had been rather critical of the
President and that I was unsympathetic with his attitude, and so he added, with a twinkle in his eye, "But
doubtless I have a lot of weaknesses of my own that I
overlook—they're much more obvious to us in the
other fellow than they are in ourselves."

At length Lloyd George turned the conversation to
the Turkish issue. At once there became evident one
of the reasons for his phenomenal success as a politician.
Here was a subject upon which he could not be intimately informed, but he speedily emptied my knowledge of it into his own head. I have often been on the
witness stand, but no skilful lawyer ever subjected me
to a more searching cross-examination than did Lloyd
George on the Turkish problem. Question after question was fired at me, and when they were all answered
he had secured a picture of the situation that was
pretty complete, covering all its essentials. And he was
thoroughly stirred by what I had told him. I said to
him that the triumph of the Turks was fraught with the
gravest possibilities of danger to the peace of the world.

Kemal's government and army, I continued, were a
Turkish Nationalist protest against the terms of the

41

peace settlement, which had been dictated by the Allied Powers and which had imposed upon the conquered Turks the most drastic limitations of territory, armament, and power. Kemal and his Nationalist government had rejected these terms and had defiantly retired inland into Asia Minor, to pursue their own aims in their own way. Now they had suddenly achieved a dramatic military success over the Greeks, to whom the Allies had allotted the Ionian coast and the city of Smyrna. Intoxicated by this success, the Turks would doubtless take Smyrna, in defiance of the Allies, and would doubtless massacre the defenseless Greeks in that city.

But, I continued, even that would not be the most serious result, viewed from a world perspective. The Turk would not stop there. He would also cross the Dardanelles, invade Thrace and seek an alliance with the Bulgarians, who likewise were smarting under the sting of defeat and who would be only too glad of a chance to recapture ports like Cavalla and Dedeagatch, which the peace settlement had allotted to the Greeks. Worse yet, both Turks and Bulgarians would be glad of a chance to even old scores with the Greeks by an invasion of Greece itself, which would be a perfectly feasible enterprise, once the Turks got into Thrace. In other words, I concluded, I foresaw a violent reopening of the whole Balkan question, with the possibility behind that of a renewal of the whole European war—unless the Turks were at once forcibly prevented from crossing the Dardanelles back into Europe.

At this point I became quite emphatic. "You must," I exclaimed, "prove to the Turk that you mean business! Words are not enough. The only language he understands is force. He must be told that if he attempts to pass the Dardanelles he will be met with the armed might of the British Empire and hurled back into Asia!"

"Mr. Morgenthau," rejoined Lloyd George, "I simply can't do it. The Labor crowd and the pacifists right now are trying to make me demobilize the entire army—even trying to make me withdraw the troops in Palestine. They wouldn't stand for a government's spending a shilling on anything that involved a military expedition for any purpose."

"But you don't need to spend much money," I retorted. "All that is needed is a threat. That threat will be no good if the Turk knows it is a bluff. But if he thinks you mean it nothing more than the threat will be needed. And if he is not stopped he will produce a situation in Europe that even the Laborites will have to admit will compel Britain to intervene. The real interest of Labor is to back you up in an effective threat, so that no expensive, forcible action may become necessary. Why not call in Ramsay Macdonald and explain the situation to him, and get his support in a stiff warning to the Turks?"

"That's a good suggestion," Lloyd George replied, "and I'll follow it up."

Later, I learned that he did so. He sent for Ramsay Macdonald and explained to him my view of the possibilities of the Turks invading Europe again. Macdonald was deeply impressed. "But," he said, "this is too serious a question for me to undertake to commit the Labor Party on it. I will bring a group of Labor leaders here and have you explain the situation to them."

So seriously did his followers regard the matter that when Macdonald brought his delegation to Lloyd George they were so numerous that they filled to overflowing the big reception room at No. 10 Downing Street. Lloyd George laid the situation fully before them and satisfied them that no force need be sent from England, as the local British troops quartered at the Dardanelles would be able to handle the Turks if prompt action were taken. The Laborites agreed to support the government, with the result that not a word of criticism of its subsequent action was later heard in Parliament. The British at once fortified Chanak, on the Straits, and notified the Turks that if they attempted to pass the Dardanelles or come within fifteen miles of Chanak the British guns would shell them. The Turks disregarded this warning to this extent: they approached to within *twelve* miles of Chanak—they had learned that this was the effective range of the British guns! But they did not approach nearer. And they did not pursue their intention to invade Greece. Thus, thanks to Great Britain's prompt action, another Balkan outburst was prevented.

That I had a good deal to do with this result was indicated to me that very evening. When Lloyd George and I had finished our breakfast and our conversation he accompanied me to the entrance hall. There, as I was leaving, I encountered Winston Churchill, who was just arriving, and we stopped long enough to exchange greetings.

That evening Churchill came and talked with delightful freedom for hours, and I enjoyed his conversation thoroughly. Soon after we got under way in our tête-à-tête, he said abruptly: "By the way, I want you to know that I agree perfectly with everything you said to Lloyd George about the present Turkish situation."

I was astonished and asked him, "How do you know what I said to Lloyd George?"

He laughed and said: "When I ran into you in Downing Street this morning I was on my way to a Cabinet meeting, and Lloyd George took quite a bit of time at the meeting in giving us a synopsis of what you had just said to him. I wouldn't say that it determined our position as to what the British Government intends to do in that quarter, but it certainly had a strong influence upon it."

I soon received additional confirmation of what Churchill had said about my having influenced the British decision. A few days after our dinner Lord Lee of Fareham invited me to have luncheon with him at the Admiralty. Other guests were Sir James Grigg and two admirals, one of whom, Admiral Webb, had recently returned from Constantinople. They devoted a large share of the luncheon hour to quizzing me about the Turkish situation, and it was clear that Lord Lee, following the discussion of my views in the Cabinet, had arranged the luncheon in order to get these views at first hand for the information of the Admiralty.

Thus it came about that a social call from my old

friend T. P. O'Connor led to newspaper interviews, that led to conversations with the Prime Minister and Cabinet officers, that somewhat influenced a decision of the British Government, that undoubtedly prevented a fresh Balkan outburst and a possible rekindling of the war in Europe.

CHAPTER V

The Storm Breaks at Smyrna

THE Smyrna disaster of 1922 needs be only briefly mentioned here. It was the cause of the great exodus of all the Greeks of Asia Minor, but it happened so recently that many of the details are still fresh in the public memory. Let me itemize a few of these details:

The systematic burning of the Greek quarter of Smyrna by the Turkish troops under the very eye of Kemal;

The systematic slaughter of Greek men, women, and children;

The organized looting of houses and churches;

The unchecked, wholesale raping of women and young girls;

The segregation of all able-bodied Greek males from sixteen years of age to fifty, who were then driven inland, where practically all perished of forced labor, their destruction being hastened by starvation and assassination;

The deportation of the remaining women, children, and old men to Greece.

All these atrocities were clear evidence of the deliberate intention of the Turks to remove utterly all Greek population from Asia Minor, in pursuance of the program of the Turkish Nationalists under Kemal, by which Asia Minor was to be completely "Turkeyfied."

This plan to deport or exterminate the Greek population, thus made plain by the horrors of Smyrna, caused the immediate flight of thousands of Greek families from the other ports of Asia Minor. In many cases they were pursued out of their houses by their Turkish neighbors, who seemed spontaneously to attack them, in imitation of the Smyrna example. These thousands likewise poured in upon the seaports of Greece proper, swelling the flood of destitute refugees that was overwhelming the ancestral land. Within a few weeks seven hundred and fifty thousand people were dumped like cattle at the ports of Salonica and Athens, and upon the larger Greek islands of the Ægean Sea, such as Crete, Mytilene, Chios, and Eubœa.

The condition of these people upon their arrival in Greece was pitiable beyond description. They had been herded upon every kind of craft that could float, crowded so densely on board that in many cases they had only room to stand on deck. There they were exposed alternately to the blistering sun and cold rain of variable September and October. In one case, which I myself beheld, seven thousand people were packed into a vessel that would have been crowded with a load of two thousand. In this and many other cases there was neither food to eat nor water to drink, and in numerous instances the ships were buffeted about for several days at sea before their wretched human cargoes could be brought to land. Typhoid and smallpox swept through the ships. Lice infested everyone. Babes were born on board. Men and women went insane. Some leaped overboard to end their miseries in the sea. Those who survived were landed without shelter upon the open beach, loaded with filth, racked by fever, without blankets or even warm clothing, without food and without money.

Besides these horrors the refugees endured every form of sorrow—the loss of husbands by wives, loss of wives by husbands, loss of children through death or straying, all manner of illnesses.

If ever the Four Horsemen of the Apocalypse rode down upon a nation it was when this appalling host appeared upon the shores of Greece, that was trampled by the flying hoofs of their chargers and scourged by the spectral riders of War, Famine, Pestilence, and Death. But the little Greek nation, of only five million souls, met their brothers in distress with unshaken courage and with open arms. Every home in Greece threw wide its doors and took in some of the refugees. In Athens more than five thousand rooms in private houses were opened to them. Public schools were turned into hospitals, town halls were used as barracks, even the beautiful National Opera House in Athens was filled with refugees, each of its velvet-lined boxes becoming the home of a whole family, while scores more slept upon the floor of the auditorium and on the stairways.

Relief work was organized on every side. In Athens the famous Old Palace on Constitution Square was turned into a headquarters where bread was distributed daily to thousands of refugees, where lists of names were posted for the purpose of reuniting families that had been separated in the chaos at Smyrna, and where the general direction of all relief measures was centered.

The streets of Athens were transformed by the surging multitude that now invaded them. The city had been almost somnolent before this irruption. It had been living the staid life of an orderly small capital, where business had grown into established channels and where life had settled into an easy and familiar routine. Overnight all this was changed. Now the streets were thronged with new faces. Strange dialects of Greek assailed the ear. The eye was caught by outlandish peasant costumes from interior Asia Minor. Sidewalks were crowded. Avenues that had been pleasantly ample were now filled with peddlers' carts of refugees who were trying to make a living by selling a few strings of beads or bits of finery. Cobblers set up their stools and trays along the most fashionable thoroughfares. The great rock of the Acropolis, that rises with almost sheer sides in the very heart of Athens, looked down upon as strange a sight as it had seen since the days when Phidias was adorning the Parthenon at its summit. At its base sprung up a new Angora, a new marketplace, packed with tiny shops displaying all the varieties of small merchandise that refugees could scrape together for sale.

These petty merchants, however, were the fortunate aristocracy of the refugee horde. Upon the bare hills about Athens, now bleak and cold with approaching winter, were camped the less fortunate tens of thousands, huddled in tents pieced out of burlap bags, or in huts extemporized out of the ubiquitous five-gallon

Standard Oil cans. Some, who could find not even these crude materials, dug desperately into the earth and found a damp refuge from the elements in caves. At the Piræus, the port of Athens, eleven miles away, the beach was lined with the tatterdemalion encampment of other thousands of refugees.

Misery is always picturesque, the one sorry virtue of human sorrow. Shoes made of pieces of discarded automobile tires became almost the standard footwear of the refugees. Clothing made of flour sacks was a fashion born of necessity, and was hard-pressed for first place by garments improvised out of burlap or pieced together from mere rags. The simplest implements were hard to come by. Tin cans served for cooking utensils, rusty nails were substituted for pins, and a real needle was as valuable a curiosity as it is to an Esquimau.

Tennyson said that "sorrow's crown of sorrow is remembering happier things." These wretched myriads knew that heavy truth. Even the humblest had been happy peasants, in a familiar land, accustomed to the pleasures yielded by a few vines and fig trees, eating their pilaff at ease after the day's labor, comfortably clad and sheltered. Many had been used to every luxury. Women who now stood in line for hours to receive a half loaf of bread had once been able, only a few weeks before, to command every delicacy that the palate could crave. Many shivered in rags, who had lately been dressed in Paris fashions; and cowered in mud huts, who had been mistresses of palatial mansions. Now they shared the great democracy of misery, mourning the loss of the men of their families, and shuddering at horrible memories of frightful scenes along the quay at Smyrna.

Everywhere in camps, markets, barracks, and streets you might see thousands of forlorn, grief-stricken, bedraggled people, many of them with histories as sad and appealing as Longfellow's "Evangeline," except that they told no stories of love.

They were no longer wandering about. Their journeys had ended, and now they were divisible into various groups. Thousands and thousands of them were most heroically facing this almost irremediable situation. They girded on their armor and entered this new fight for existence with a grim determination that foretold their eventual success. Many of them had acquired in their past independent positions amongst their people, and those were gathering their neighbors around them. They planned to recreate their old surroundings and make a joint effort to reproduce their past conditions. The spirit shown by these leaders was admirable. They seldom presented to us their individual claims. They always said "our people" should be placed here or there, and "our people" are especially fitted for such and such work. It showed what long usage had done. These leaders treated all their villagers as their families. Of the unattached, few asked for charity, but nearly all implored for work. They spurned permanent doles. They begged for opportunities which would make them self-supporting. The big camps that were thrown up in the vicinity of Athens soon became villages and early showed signs of being citified. It just required a little guidance and the temporary support of the Greek Government, the Refugee Settlement Commission, and the other help-rendering activities to bring order out of chaos and render first aid to those injured people. Their injuries were not merely physical, affecting single individuals. Their injuries were the total disruption of a fine civilized people, the destruction of family life, the uprooting of villages and towns and casting the survivors pell mell into new surroundings. They were deprived of their accumulations of wealth, their government, their traditions, their families, and those fine interrelations which make up society.

The worst predicament that confronted them was that their breadwinners and their youths had nearly all been killed or imprisoned. Here was an unusual condition. A rearrangement had to be made for these people in spite of all these shortcomings. It required the acceptance by the survivors of additional burdens. Fortunately they were ready and almost anxious to assume them. The very extreme depression they were facing seemed to restore to them the energies of their youth. They did not sit down and mourn for their sons and their sons-in-law, but apparently threw off ten or twenty of their years and successfully replaced the lost members of their families.

Great credit should be given to the young women. Their heroism and devotion were simply amazing. It showed what stuff these people were made of. They did not succumb to the temptations of those miserable miscreants of society, the cadets, who hovered at the

53

entrance of these camps and tried to beguile these fine
girls into the pleasure haunts of Athens. Fortunately,
with the assistance of the police we were able to make
short work of these rascals. Many of these girls single-
handed supported families of three and upward. They
worked at anything they could find, in the shops of
Athens, in rug and other factories, as domestic servants,
and some of them on their sewing or knitting machines
in their own homes.

Of course there were tremendous numbers of completely forsaken people and shiftless ones. Their dilemma
was indescribable, and so was that of a number of victims
of tuberculosis and malaria. In this big broad readjustment these latter people had to meet their fate.
It could be softened a little, but there were no means
at hand to remedy it completely. They were doomed.

Immediately after my arrival in Athens I was visited
by a number of refugees whom I had known in Constantinople. They implored me to use their services in any
capacity at all. One of them, Alexandra Joanides, reminded me how when we first met at the Constantinople
College for Women she had been dressed as an American
Indian, and how I had walked with her in the college
grounds. She was now anxious for a position that would
give her a living. She is a brilliant woman, full of life
and mental resources. She had become a very active
feminist and republican. As an adherent of Papanastasiou she was in constant touch with the activities of these
progressives. She was sprightly, irrepressible, and full
of hope for "her people," as she called the refugees.
As secretary of the commission she reported to me all

the activities of the various political factions, and her reports were very intelligent and instructive. Eventually she married a man who became Governor of Mytilene, and she helped him most gracefully and effectively to fill this post.

Another old acquaintance who called was our former steward at the Embassy in Constantinople, a man who had owned two houses and a vineyard in Therapia. He took the post of steward at the Embassy because it was the height of the ambition of all men in his profession to end their career in that way. He had a wife and four children, and was out at his elbows. His property had been confiscated, and he was walking the streets of Athens looking for work. He was a sad contrast to the gentleman who so meticulously functioned in our American Embassy. I appointed him custodian of the Refugee Settlement building and manager of the messengers. Now, in 1928, he is fully reëstablished, owns a nice refugee home in one of the settlements, and two of his daughters are working and helping to support the family.

Rose Sartinsky, another graduate of the Constantinople College for Women, applied for work and became my private secretary. She did not possess the exuberance of spirit of Alexandra Joanides. She felt the grief of her people as though it were partly her responsibility to bear it. She was a most amiable and tireless worker, and used her evenings to teach stenography and typewriting to the girls at the Y. W. C. A. Little pleasure did she seek or have. Her greatest joy was to supervise a summer camp for these waifs of the Y. W. C. A. I took her with me on my tours of inspection, showing her how to make them, and then having her go by herself. I felt that only a Greek refugee could secure from these sufferers their real stories. Anyone who really wants to secure an exact picture of these poor sufferers can do no better than to read her unedited account of these various visits. Miss Sartinsky's little personal comments add a charm to her statements, and rob them of some of their gruesomeness. I am going to give you her reports exactly as written by her:

Report on Koundouriotis Camps. (Dated Athens, May 9, 1924.)

These camps are at Polygene, near the military school, one of the best situations in Athens. There are in all 463 houses giving shelter to more than 5,000 people, but in view of the fact that newcomers have arrived and there was no room for them, tents have been added and the refugees themselves have built some wooden barracks, which are more private than the other dwellings, where two, and in some cases three, families live together.

This is one of the first camps erected, and its inhabitants, some of them camped there over a year, have had sufficient time to make a sort of living and become more or less self-supporting.

They are not beggars, they do not ask for charity but for work. Work! Work! this is their cry, but alas! little or no work is to be found. They do not mind what work they have to do, or how hard they have to work, so long as they get a few drachmas a day. Women who in their country did nothing else than take care of their children and house are now working in factories, 8, 10 and even 12 hours a day. They go as washerwomen, char-women, use all their efforts, never grumbling, but pleased when they earn enough to bring some food to their hungry children, and even, whenever they can manage it, they help those who being old or sick cannot go out to work.

The streets of this Liliputian town are very clean and in some of them there are trees planted. In front of almost every house there is a tiny garden with two or three flowers in it, as there is no room for more. In the evening, after the day's work, the women and young girls take their chairs and sit in the open air, chatting, while their fingers are busily engaged in some needle work, the mothers mending the family's clothes while the girls make lace or some embroidery work, which they afterward sell at rather low prices. When they have a little piece of stuff and some minutes to spare, they make little curtains for their windows, and covers for the tables, which are made out of cases.

Nothing is missing in this place. They have two large laundries with plenty of water, well ventilated and lighted, where twenty women can wash at a time.

They have their school, which unfortunately I could not visit, as it was too late, and the teacher who had the key was away, but I saw several little girls sitting on their doorstep with their books on their knees absorbed in study.

Farther off there is the market place. Some of the men who were fortunate enough to find people enough interested in them to lend them some money, built small barracks which they are using as shops. A few sacks of sugar, potatoes, beans, some boxes of cigarettes, not of the best quality of course, etc., represent the stock of the grocer, who, when I asked him if business was getting along well, said that he was doing fine work. He hoped he would soon be able to pay off his debt and afterward try and enlarge his enterprise. Next to him is the butcher and green-grocer. You can also see a coffee house and a pastry shop which, except on Sundays or some holidays, are not very active. The shoemaker and the carpenter also have their quarters. They seem less fortunate than the others, however, as shoes are rather a luxury and are worn only on great occasions; and as for furniture, the refugees make themselves their stools and tables out of cases. They cannot find any work outside of the camp, as there are many more shoemakers and carpenters in Athens than are needed.

There is not that look of despair which you see on the faces of the refugees in the National Theatre. These seem ready for a new life. Perhaps this is due partly to the fact that the place is bright and sunny and not dark as the former.

I went to one of the tents which is large enough and inhabited by Erano Housetian, his wife, three daughters and two sons. The place is spotless and the ground is covered by mats. All round the tent there are crude *divans* made of mattresses and covered with blankets. They also have some stools, a table and a set of shelves on which you can see a few cups, glasses and plates neatly placed and very clean. Some knits and knots give to the place a homelike atmosphere and there is an air, if not of cheerfulness at least of satisfaction. The father, the two sons and one of the daughters are working, so that they are well fed and properly dressed. One of the daughters, a beautiful young girl of about 18, was making a dress for her younger sister. I asked her if she was pleased with her present life.

"Yes," she said, "compared to others we are rather fortunate, as none of our family has been killed or kept prisoner, and we are also able to earn our living, but I can never forget our house with its big garden all around. It was so well furnished and we had plenty of dresses to wear. I had my trousseau ready; I have been working on it for years and years, and now everything is burnt."

Tears filled her eyes at these last words. They lived in the interior of Asia Minor, and some time before the catastrophe they took as many of their belongings as they could and went to Smyrna. As soon as they arrived the Turks came and they had to fly, leaving everything behind. In their country they also owned many shops which they used to lease. The father was working for the railway company and getting a substantial salary, which shows that they were amongst the wealthiest people of their country. The girl asked me if I thought there was any hope that they would be allowed to go back to Asia Minor. "We love Greece"—they say—"but we cannot forget our birthplace, our homes, our lands, where we have been happy for so many years. The people here have done so much for us, but we are dependent more or less on others, while there we were our own masters."

Close to that tent there is another one where conditions are not so good. Indeed it is bare of all furniture and in it lives an old woman of about 65, Ekaterian Aslanoglou, with a little blind boy. You can at once see the hopeless look on the woman's face and understand the struggle for life. She also has a daughter of 30, who, far from being a help to her, is a burden as she is sick and most of the time is at the hospital. She was away and I could not understand from the mother what was the trouble with her. When I went there the woman was busy making bricks out of mud which she dried in the sun. She is doing this work when she has some spare time and hopes that before winter she will succeed in building a hut where she and her children shall find a better shelter against the rain and cold than under the tent. She is the only support of the family. She is doing some washing and gets about Drs. 20 a day, but the misfortune is that she cannot find work every day, and sometimes a whole week passes without her being able to earn a cent. You can see from her manners and talk that she was used to quite a different life. They are from Neni-Hissar (near Kessaria), where they owned a large house, besides another house in Constantinople which they leased. And now this woman, who had two houses of her own, is trying to build a hut out of dried mud and is looking forward to it just as if it were the nicest dwelling.

At some distance from the tent I saw a sort of hole in the rocks and to my great surprise a woman was standing at the opening. She greeted me with a smile and asked whether I would not like to go and have a little rest in her home. She seemed to be proud of being its owner, and indeed when I went in I saw that her pride was justified. When she and her husband first arrived at the camp it was late in the year, all the houses were occupied, the few tents were crowded and there was no room for them anywhere. At last they found a grot under which they went to get shelter. Some time after they understood that there was no way of getting another house or anything better, so they decided to make the best of it and give to their grot a more comfortable look. The task was far from being an easy one but they did not lose hope. They started digging the rock and after much effort and many days' work that former hole was transformed into a rather large and suitable dwelling. Now the room was ready but bare, so they had to get to work and furnish it. No sooner said than done. They found some packing cases, from which they made a bed, some stools, and a table, as also the indispensable set of shelves for their cups, glasses, etc. The husband did his best to find some work. The only thing he was offered was to break stones. He would have to work eight and sometimes ten hours a day under the scorching sun or in the sharp cold, but, although he is more than 60, and of course not very strong, he did not hesitate one minute to accept it, for he had to choose between this and starvation. His wife told me that this job is very trying for him. In the evening he comes back dead tired and she is afraid he will not be able to stand it much longer. All he gets for this is Drs. 3 a day [Note: the drachma was then worth about $1\frac{2}{3}$ cents; later it was stablized at $1\frac{1}{3}$ cents] and they manage with them to feed and dress themselves, and now and then buy something for their little home. They bought some blankets with which they covered the walls and floor. There is a nice cover on their bed, as also on the table and shelves. The woman wished she could work and help her husband, but she is rheumatic and therefore unable to do so. I do not think the dampness of the grot will do her much good although she is

The Fire in Smyrna

pleased and says that she does not fear winter this year as she is safe from the rain and cold. The place does not seem to be very comfortable for winter, however, as it is impossible to have a window made and there is only a hole for a door.

One of her brothers, a nice young boy, has been killed by the Turks. They are from Vourla, where they were the owners of a house and many vineyards. The husband was supervising the works and they were exporting wines and currants. They had to flee from their house in the middle of the night. She cannot forget the terrible scenes she saw in the streets. Amongst others she says that the place was full of heads of young girls whom the soldiers after maltreating had killed. They were placed in rows just as a sort of decoration of the roads. I wanted to get some more information about what she had seen but it was impossible because the remembrance of these sights made her weep and one of the neighbors told me I had better not make her speak any more as she is subject to fits of hysteria whenever she remembers those dreadful scenes.

Another woman confirmed the statement about the heads of the young girls. Some of them, those who could escape, fell into the sea, preferring to be drowned rather than fall in the hands of the Turks. None of them from 10 to 30 and even 40 escaped. Vourla was the place where the most beautiful girls of Asia Minor were found. The inhabitants were proud of this, but the time came when this pride had to be paid by death. The Turks fell upon them as flies on the honey, and killed, killed, killed, finding a fierce pleasure in exterminating those unbelievers, who, despite all the efforts of the Mohammedans, continued to rebel against them, and even those who could escape went so far as to prefer to be drowned than deny their faith, be taken in the harems and become the wives of the murderers of their fathers and brothers. Well so much the worse for them. Those who were caught had to pay for the whole lot.

After this I went to one of the big houses, composed of two

rooms in which two families (6 people, relatives) live. One of the rooms serves for bedroom and sitting room, the other as bedroom and kitchen. These people are amongst the most fortunate of refugees. The men were working at the railway company in Smyrna, as engineers, when the city was captured by the Turks. For five months after the catastrophe the Turks kept them without doing them any harm, because they needed engineers to mend the railway machines, etc., which had gone to pieces. As soon as the railways were in a good shape again these men were discharged, and after paying tremendous sums of money they got permission to leave Smyrna, bringing with them one or two trunks, their clothes, mattresses and blankets. They were also able to save part of their money. Their rooms are furnished with luxury compared to others. They have real beds, chairs, a table and also a petrol machine. They have one or two Turkish rugs on the walls too. Three days ago the husband of one and the brother of the other family found a good job and they are grateful and hopeful. Up to now the women were selling their jewels, one after the other, so as to live, and considering from the few rings and brooches that remained, they must have been rather valuable things. Two of their houses in the suburbs of Smyrna have not been burnt and they continue to hope that some day they will be allowed to go back and start their former life again. In one of the corners a watch light is burning before some ikons. It is burning there day and night. "We have to pray God for the return of our eldest son, who is still with the Turks," they said.

In fact, every family, even the poorest, has its ikon; those who can afford it have more, and the watch light is always burning. Those who are safe thank God for it and place some hope in the future; others, who have some members of their family still in the hands of the Turks, pray for their safe return; and those, the more numerous, whose many a beloved one has been killed, pray for their souls. Their faith never fails them, and I have seen a woman whose husband and two sons were killed, who was living in a hut by herself, with not even a chair to sit on, but she never forgets to light her watch light before the ikon and never did she utter a word of protest. "God took from me everything I possessed, husband, children, house. *Such was His will*, and my only hope now is that I may soon be called to go and meet them."

The last house I visited did not bear such an air of desolation. On the contrary, it was one of the cases where there seemed to be some hope and relief, and this is because these people have been assisted in the beginning and were able to buy some yarn and start making carpets. The mother, Ourania Armoza, is too old to work, but her son and daughter are working hard. The daughter is making carpets and her brother is selling them. She seems to be satisfied with her earnings. She showed me some nice little rugs for which she was asking 600–700 drs. each. It takes her from 15 to 20 days to finish one. They also have a little grocery shop in the same room and are selling sugar, coffee, rice, cigarettes and candy. They are from the interior of Asia Minor. Their room is clean and tidy and no effort is spared to make it look cosy.

I was then conducted to one of the barracks occupied by P. Palassakis and his wife. It has the size of a rather large room. Two of his brothers went lately to the United States and as soon as they got a job they did not forget their brother here. They sent him some money with which he was able to buy boards and build his barrack and furnish it with a bed, two chairs, a table and a small cupboard. The wife made the curtains and the covers, and the room looks very smart. In Melemeni, where they come from, they possessed several houses, one of which has not been burnt, and they too hope that some day they will go there and continue their former lives.

I picked up all this information from different points of the camp, going into the little houses and speaking with the women in their own language. I showed that I understood their sorrows and felt for them. Some of the women thought that I went there to give them some news of the prisoners. They were depressed when I told them I was not in a position to give them any information. They ask me if I could help them to find out what had become of their beloved ones. Poor souls! A month ago the last prisoners arrived and it was announced that no more were left. But these people are still hoping against hope and watching for their husbands, sons, brothers, fiancés, until some day a friend comes carrying the sad news that those who are so anxiously awaited will never come back, they have been killed or have died from starvation or ill-treatment.

Seeing those little houses and grots one is reminded of the story of Robinson Crusoe, with the difference that instead of its being displayed in the wilderness it takes place in the midst of the busy and civilized world of the Twentieth Century.

I left the camp full of admiration for these brave strugglers with life who, with but a little assistance, would accomplish wonders.

Report on the Refugees at the 7th Boys' School. (Dated Athens, May 31, 1924.)

This school, located near Athens, is composed of three large rooms, giving shelter to 22 families, or 91 individuals, amongst whom there are only 17 men, 7 of whom are too old to be of any help to their families. The others are women, quite a number of whom are above 60–70. Most of them have to support three, and even in several cases five, children. Nearly all the men who have been kept by the Turks have not and probably will not come back.

The clothes of the women and children, although worn out, are clean and tidy. They were kind and ready to answer all my questions, although many a time their words were broken by tears when they wanted to describe to me how they used to live in their own country, and when they remembered those who were left behind and whom they would never see again.

All the men and nearly all the women were away at work. They leave their children to the care of the old women or others who for some reason or another cannot go out to work and must stay there all day long.

Kallipoi Pantopoulou is the mother of six children and a two-months'-old baby. She showed me, with great pride, the three of them who were there (6–4–2 years old) and who really are beautiful little children, with fair, curly hair, and big, blue, bright eyes. They are like the mother, who probably was a nice woman before but now sorrow has broken her down. She keeps her children as clean as can be. The others are working already, although the eldest is only 14 years of age. "I wish I could send them to school," she told me—"but we can't afford it, they must work because my husband only gets Drs. 35 a day and it is not enough." They come from Aivali where they had houses of their own and the husband was a flour dealer. It appears that they were living fairly well there.

Another woman of perhaps more than 65 is taking care of her two grandchildren, while the mother is working as a servant and supporting the whole family. The little girl is not more than 12 years old, she has a sad, melancholic look and one can see in her eyes the whole drama of the family. There is none of that childish carefreeness left in her. The answers she gave me were too serious, too sorrowful for her age, and I cannot forget her eyes full of tears when to my question where her father was, she pointed to the sky with her little finger and said "There." They had been expecting him but instead someone came and said that he was killed a few days after his captivity. This little girl is now working at a shirt-factory all day long. For the present she only gets Drs. 3 a day because she is just learning and her only hope is that she will soon learn to work sufficiently well and get a raise in her pay which will enable her to help her mother. Thus at

65

the best period of life, when as a rule the children think of nothing but play, and those who are going to school consider it a hard job to study, hundreds of children like this little girl spend all their sunny days in the prison-like atmosphere of factories with the only expectation that some day they will be able to help their mammas.

Another old woman of about the same age, Eleni Lazarou, is also looking after her two grandchildren while the mother is out the whole day working at a carpet factory from eight o'clock in the morning to seven or even eight in the evening for the poor salary of Drs. 800 a month. Her husband was a prisoner, he came back four months ago but owing to the ill-treatment of the Turks he is suffering from consumption. He is at an hospital but his wife has to pay for his medicines, etc., which cost at least Drs. 100 a week. "We had no time to rejoice for his return"—said the mother-in-law—"ever since he came he has been in bed. At the beginning we thought that with proper care and solicitude we could bring him back to life, but it is too late, we soon found out that there is no hope, everything is useless and he will soon leave us." She told me she had another daughter with two children, who a week ago learned that her husband died in Smyrna. One of her sons, a former prisoner, came back in a pitiful condition it appears. He has a wife and children to support and tries to work, he is willing to do it, but he has not the power, he gets exhausted very quickly and of course the future is not at all promising for this family. "In Smyrna"— this woman told me—"I was so happy. All my children were married. They had their homes where nothing was missing. The men were working very well, all were cheerful, and now I can't send my grandchildren to school because they have no stockings and shoes to wear; every day there is some bad news, and one after the other our people are dying." She told me that sometimes she goes and does some washing so as to help her daughter, but as she is old and not at all strong she cannot do this very often.

66

THE STORM BREAKS AT SMYRNA

Socrates Illiopoulos has his wife and five children, the eldest of whom is 11 years of age. He is a shoemaker and lately he has found a job where they give him 30 drs. a day. Two of the children are sent to school, the others are too young. In Kirkayats they had two houses, lands and vineyards and now they have not even a small room of their own. "After the free country life we were living, it is difficult, specially for the children, to live in this closed atmosphere" the women told me. They had to walk four days and nights from their country to Dikeli in order to get on board a ship. They took with them as many things as they could, clothes, silver, etc., but on their way they got tired and they had to drop one by one the bags containing the few things they had saved. Nevertheless they consider themselves happy because none of their family have fallen in the hands of the Turks and this really is a great privilege.

In a small little room there remains a family of four people, Fotini Pashalopoulou, with her son, an old mother and an old aunt of hers who has been left alone in the world. It appears that her son is suffering from consumption and this is the reason why they have the room to themselves. There is some sort of furniture, some pictures hanging on the wall and it is cosy and smart. You can at once see the difference from the other rooms where several families live together. Fotini is a nice woman of not more than 28 years of age and is a widow. She was neatly and nicely dressed. As a rule she does some washing and when she is at home she does some sewing work. "We can manage to live," she told me, "but I cannot stop working even a minute." She is so delicate and seems so much unused to this hard work that one wonders if she will be able to go on with it for very long. Life was easy and cheerful for her when she was at Smyrna; now she is taught the other aspect of it too. The only thing she was able to bring is an ikon. "I could not leave it in the hands of the Turks," she told me—"it would have been a sacrilege."

Maria Pierno is living with her sister and her daughter, 25 years old. The latter has had pneumonia and was taken to the hospital. Now she is on her way to recovery and they want to send her back to the school. The hospital kept her more than four months and if now she is out of danger and on her way to recovery of course they cannot have her there any more, as there are many other people who are seriously sick, who need immediate care and who are anxiously waiting for a vacant bed in the hospital. The mother at the same time is afraid to bring her to that place lest she have a relapse again, and I think she is not wrong. How can this girl rest and regain health in that noisy and unhealthy atmosphere of the room, where all the families are cooking, and without even a bed to lie on! "The main point," said the mother, "is that I have not the means to feed her properly." She is supported by her sister who only gets about Drs. 15 a day. She herself cannot work because she is suffering from rheumatism. Their situation is really fearful.

In another room I saw the wife of Ioannis Herouvim with her baby who is only one month old. Her husband is working and gets 35 drs. a day but he has to support, apart from his wife, his old father and mother and a sister of his. He is the only man of the family left. One of his brothers was a prisoner but as no one has heard from him they believe he is dead. The grandmother had the little baby on her knees and was singing to him. "This is my only consolation now," she told me. In Smyrna they owned houses and vineyards and now their only belongings are two blankets.

Stillianos Kivopoulos was a prisoner and he just came back. I asked him to tell me how they were treated by the Turks. "I could talk for days and days and never be able to give you an idea of the horrors I saw," he said. He was a war prisoner. When they were taken from Smyrna they were 3,000. They were told that they should walk to Magnissia (near Smyrna). They were only a few miles out of the town when they met Turkish soldiers armed with clubs, guns,

knives, swords, and everything they could find. As soon as
the Greeks arrived the Turks started killing them, and as our
soldiers of course tried to escape the Turks, who were in a
hurry to finish their business and to destroy as many unbelievers as they could, found that the best method was to hit
them and then throw them into dried wells that were
around; thus even those who were not killed at once had not
the least chance to escape death; and so corpses and wounded
men were heaped up in those wells. These bodies were so
many that the wells were filled up to the top and those
who by chance were thrown in the last and were not very
seriously wounded were able to get out later. Some of them
turned mad at the time, and what was principally haunting
them was the howling of those dying men who were buried
alive in those graves. The most fortunate of course were those
who were killed at once. Some of them, very few, succeeded
in running away from the Turks while they were so busy.
Later, however, the Turks caught them again. This man
was one of them, and he told me that out of the 3,000 only
250 had not been killed. He told me that several times during
his captivity he wished he were dead and only the thought of
his young wife prevented him from committing suicide.
They were left several days without any food or water,
they had to work 14–16 hours a day, and were beaten like
dogs. When the Turks did give them some food it was 100
grammes of bread, made out of barley and some currants.
He said that later they were better treated but they had
great difficulty in getting away.

Now although he does not look strong and healthy he is
working and considers himself lucky to be back and with his
family again. "I have worked for so many years," he says,
"I had my house and some vineyards, I thought that I had
not to worry any more about the future, but the Turk
came. Everything has been destroyed and now I have to start
all over again, but in spite of all this I thank God that I am
alive and able to work."

Phili Balaban, a woman of more than 65 is supported by her granddaughter, a girl 16 years old. This child is the only member of the family left, her parents are dead as also one of her uncles. In Smyrna they had their houses, lands and vineyards. The girl was being brought up for quite a different life, which makes things more difficult for her now. When she comes home she makes the meal, tidies their little corner, etc.

Heleni Zahariou is supported by her son who is only 17 years old and he gets 30 drs. a day. One of her sons has been killed by the Turks and of course her house and all her belongings have been burnt up.

I am of the opinion that if these people are moved from that school and have their own houses their conditions will improve considerably. They will feel at home and of course this will encourage them a great deal.

In hearing their stories and thinking over the whole thing, one is bewildered at the ruin which has been caused in so short a time. Some hours have been enough to destroy the work and efforts of so many years, to make hundreds of widows and orphans, to take away from old parents their children, their only hope and joy, and to plunge these once happy and merry people of Asia Minor, into everlasting grief and mourning!

CHAPTER VI

The Tragic Flood Inundates Greece

THE Greeks themselves instantly undertook to solve the problem of their refugee brethren, unaided and alone. The Smyrna disaster began on September 9, 1922. In October the Greeks of Old Greece had perfected a non-governmental organization to deal with the rapidly arriving horde of refugees, and had raised a large sum of money for this purpose. This bold and humane enterprise was a daring thing for private individuals to undertake, but it was made necessary by the supineness—worse, by the hostility—of the King and his government, who feared that the new-comers would ascribe their sufferings (as they rightly did) to the blunders of the monarchy and were loath to strengthen the hands of the refugees even with bread and shelter.

The success of the unofficial national relief work was due primarily to Mr. Epaminondas Charilaos, a leading industrialist of Greece, who was a self-made man of great energy and courage. He had the very able coöperation of Mr. Etienne Delta, president of the Greek Red Cross, and many other patriotic citizens. At the instance of Mr. Charilaos, and under his leadership, these men organized the Refugee Treasury Fund.

71

The origin and the noteworthy achievements of the Refugee Treasury Fund, in relieving the refugees, cannot be better described than in Mr. Charilaos's own words, which he used to recount his stewardship as its president. On October 31, 1923, the fund was disbanded, to make way for the international Refugee Settlement Commission, set up by the League of Nations to carry on the whole work of relief under my chairmanship, beginning early in the following month. On that occasion Mr. Charilaos delivered a memorable address, which I have caused to be translated and which I here print in part because it gives a very striking account of a most remarkable achievement:

The Refugee Treasury Fund was formed in October, 1922. The discussions of the Great Committee for the study of all refugee matters brought out clearly that only through an independent, non-political organization could something be done. It was therefore decided to entrust the settlement of the refugees dictatorially to one person, as was done in France for the reconstruction and settlement of the devastated provinces after the Great War.

This proposal being partially accepted on behalf of Mr. Doxiades, the Minister of Providence and Security, we ended the interminable discussions of the Great Committee by the formation of the Refugee Treasury Fund.

The funds were administered by a council, in which all social parties were represented and also various government services.

The Refugee Treasury Fund was established by a decree of law, and was headed by a board of fifteen members. Some of these were higher clerks of the various ministries, whilst others were representatives of the Commercial and Industrial Chamber of Commerce of Athens and Piræus, and of the

Professionals' Confederation. Five other members were appointed by the Minister of Providence and Security.

The income of the Fund included all private contributions for the refugees, and all amounts which the government placed to its disposal for certain defined purposes.

The Fund organized over twenty sub-committees, at Piræus, Volo, Salonica, Larissa, Patras, Edessa, etc.

The General Board elected an Executive Board of three members, which, without any further formalities, could order the execution of any work, fix the method of executing the work, and determine the amount of expenditure.

In actual practice, the carrying out of the plans of the Fund, and also the executive direction of the work, was managed by the president personally and on his sole responsibility. This confidence that was invested in me by the board, and the consequent authority that I had to take any decision promptly in urgent cases, account for the greater part of the success of the Fund.

The Fund not only continued the work of helping the refugees with emergency relief, but also undertook their permanent settlement. At its first meeting, therefore, the General Board decided to use all private contributions to pay for the purchase and distribution of medicines, blankets, clothing, and other articles of first necessity; and to use all governmental allowances for the permanent civic settlement of the refugees.

In execution of the first of these intentions, the Refugee Treasury Board distributed to the refugees (through the Patriotic Establishment and Ladies' Committee at Athens, and also through their annexes and committees in the provinces) 200,000 blankets, 2,000 beds, thousands of mattresses, about 2,000 bundles of clothing (forwarded mostly from America), as well as many other things, such as medicines to be sent to the various hospitals and also to the various provincial committees. They distributed to refugee hospitals and to children, through the same committees,

73

many thousands of cases of milk, either purchased or coming as contributions from America. In relation with these contributions, we must specially mention the Pan-Ionian Corporation in America, which forwarded thousands of cases of milk, flour, and clothing.

The Fund granted to foreign relief organizations the money required to transport flour that had been supplied gratis. The Fund also paid for the fuel used in common by the refugees for cooking the common meals.

All refugees under trans-shipment were promptly supplied with the flour that was forwarded from America. On account of the Fund's excellent organization, and because no formalities stood in the way, these things were done quickly, and thus, without any exaggeration, the death of thousands of refugees was prevented.

Where no foreign organizations were installed, or where they were not sufficient, or where the government was unable to give any assistance, the Refugee Treasury Fund itself did what was needed, at any time of the day or night.

At the Lazarette of St. George the first crowded lot of refugees landed. They were cleaned, dressed, and fed until they could be transported to their settlement sites.

The Fund undertook afterward at Athens and Piræus the sanitary service of the refugee settlements, until the Ministry of Providence and Security intrusted this work in part to special government services. The Refugee Treasury Fund undertook also the evacuation of the night-soil pits of the settlements, a very needful, but also difficult, service. It distributed approximately 300,000 *okes* of soap (equal to 400 tons), thereby helping to prevent epidemic diseases. When, notwithstanding, epidemics of smallpox and typhus broke out, the Fund undertook the supply and the carrying out of all measures necessary to check these diseases.

The Fund provided the technical personnel for the formation and repair of numerous hospitals. They also supplied medicaments, clothing, tools, furniture, kitchen utensils, restaurant utensils, and very often also foodstuffs. They supplied beds, blankets, and tents for the above hospitals, and also for many provincial ones. They constructed wooden houses for over two hundred beds at various hospitals. They supplied motor transportation for the ill; the fuel for the ovens at 30 per cent. less cost than current estimates; repaired hygienic instruments; supplied disinfectants; and constructed over one thousand de-lousing machines at one third of the cost that had been indicated as necessary by a competition carried out by the Department of Health.

The success of the Fund in rendering this prompt and efficient aid was due largely to our accuracy in forecasting the necessities to be met in proportion to the funds available; and to our early analysis of the various indispensable requirements of the refugees. The utmost economy and judgment were exercised, though it must be remembered that on many occasions the urgency of the necessities did not allow time for full investigation, or for free operation and choice.

Parallel with these emergency operations of relief, the Treasury Fund had to execute also the very difficult work of *urban* settlement of the refugees. (The part of this work that concerned settlement of refugees *on the land* was undertaken by the Ministry of Agriculture.) The government decided to begin the erection of the first permanent urban settlement at Pangrati, utilizing at that site an area of approximately one hundred stremmas. [Note: A stremma is equivalent to about one fourth of an acre.]

The reason for the immediate erection of this settlement was the desire of the Ministry of Public Instruction that the refugees should evacuate at least some of the school buildings. After a long investigation of the matter by the engineers and myself, final plans were drawn up and carried into execution.

Everything necessary for the settlement, including schools, baths, workshops, parks, gardens, squares, suitable tracing

75

of roads, and even future extensions, were foreseen in the plan. An up-to-date, scientific system of sanitary dry pits was made. A water tank overlooking the settlement was built, a complete system of piping was installed, and an elevation pump with a complete machine house and independent power plant was constructed.

A machine and carpenter shop was also erected, which was utilized to do much of the wood working of the settlement.

In order quickly to finish the houses it was decided to distribute the execution of the work to numerous contractors, allowing them to utilize various systems of construction. The awarding of contracts was by competitive bids. Over two hundred well-known and honest contractors submitted sealed tenders. Thus we managed this operation of the Fund as efficiently as if it had been our own private work.

The contract for the construction of the first 800 houses was awarded to four contractors, who commenced the work during the end of December. I must emphasize the zeal and energy that were demonstrated by all of them, particularly as it must be considered that it was the first time such construction work was ever undertaken on such a scale in Greece, so that there was absolutely no previous experience to guide them. Likewise, essential materials were missing, organization was lacking, and trained help was scarce.

The unit prices of the successful bidders were judged by everybody to be satisfactory. The facilities made available to the contractors, and the prompt payment of weekly accounts due to them, were the principal reasons why the Fund got such good prices.

The execution of the work was so satisfactory that during April the first refugees were settled in the houses.

The results achieved at Pangrati demonstrated what were the most suitable methods of construction and arrangement of the dwellings. The procedure followed there having been accepted by the government, it now decided to spend

larger amounts for further urban settlements, and we therefore next studied the most suitable sites for the location of
these settlements. Sites at Podarades and also in the valley
of Kaisariani were approved at Athens, and Kokkinia at
Piræus, as being situated not far from the towns and as
having the advantages of an easy local water supply. Settlements were also projected for Volo, Patras, Eleusis, Salonica,
Edessa, etc.

We now organized a technical staff, employed engineers,
established a control office, and set up an inspection service,
with the necessary supervisors, controllers, and warehouse
keepers.

In awarding contracts for these later settlements, we tried
always to prefer those giving the most efficient guarantees,
wherever these offered equally satisfactory prices. Wherever
possible we utilized the refugees themselves as contractors
or sub-contractors, and required them to use, so far as
possible, only refugee labor.

Thus, of a total of 77 contractors, 34 were refugees, and of
a total of 5,900 laborers, 5,488 were refugees.

Supplies were generally purchased through public compe-
titions, or through requested offers from various parties, or
by an open adjudication. In special and urgent cases, they
were obtained by special agreements after carefully studying
the market. This system of course adds greatly to the responsibilities of the administrator, but as long as he does not
fear these responsibilities, and is familiar with the persons
and matters, this system is the one that gives the best
results. If the various markets should be attentively ex-
amined it will be proved that very special prices were obtained for governmental services. Taking also into consideration that in the present instance rapidity of execution
was a capital object, and that any delay, merely that certain formalities should be followed, would have brought
great losses, we shall, I hope, be justified by all that we
acted correctly.

A total of 12,000 rooms has been built or is under construction, besides 2,500 rooms at Eleusis, Volo, Salonica, Agrinion, Patras, Ægion, and Edessa.

The foregoing is a summary of work concerning which I asked to be allowed to report, and regarding which I considered that I was under obligation to do so. I received the presidency of the Fund at a time when the refugee problem was spread all over the Greek coast, and I undertook it in order to elaborate a system and draw up a service and a plan to contribute to the security and the salvation of the refugees. We all worked for over a year in order to accomplish these things. Owing to the wise and noble coöperation of all the members of the board and the employees, and owing to the vast confidence of the Minister of Public Assistance, we succeeded in all the things I have mentioned.

I do not ignore the fact that the system of concentrated authority, which I followed, approached in a way to absolutism; nor that I very likely touched other men's ambitions, weaknesses, and perhaps their interests. By all those whose ambitions I may have thwarted, I beg to ask in a friendly way to be excused. The work has been common for all of us.

In conclusion, I would emphasize that the employees and collaborators who have been engaged in this work have all shown a wonderful self-denial.

CHAPTER VII

I Was Sent to Athens

WHEN I left New York on October 23, 1923, to assume my duties as chairman of the Greek Refugee Settlement Commission, my steps naturally were turned first toward London, where the Bank of England was already pledged to advance the first million pounds to finance the work of rehabilitation.

In London I talked with the responsible men at the Foreign Office, at the Treasury, and at the Bank of England. Naturally, these three work in close coöperation; they have interests that supplement each other. The financial strength of the bank is necessarily a powerful lever in the national policy of Great Britain, and consequently no small item in its calculations of financial and foreign policy. The Foreign Office and the Treasury, on the other hand, may at any time be called upon to protect and assist any British interest abroad, and as the bank is involved in numberless important transactions all over the world, these two offices need to keep in the closest touch with the bank. In any dealings, therefore, with the center of British finance, it is necessary both that the bank shall approve the business aspects of the proposal, and that the Foreign Office and the Treasury shall approve of its political implications.

I had, therefore, the best of reasons for going to London before proceeding to Athens. The Britishers had long been purchasers of Greek Government bonds. They were familiar with Greek conditions, and the Bank of England had in its vaults a cash deposit of the Greek Government amounting to about nine million gold dollars.

I had several conferences with Mr. Montagu C. Norman and with Sir Otto Niemeyer, the Comptroller of Finance of Great Britain. They were friendly, but skeptical about a big loan. The public debt of Greece was already large in proportion to the nation's ability to pay, and many of its most valuable sources of public revenue were already pledged to the service of old debts and were being regularly handed over to an International Financial Commission for that purpose. Montagu Norman was greatly interested to ascertain whether the use of the million pounds the bank had agreed to advance was sufficient to demonstrate that the refugee problem could be solved through the placing of a much larger loan. He regarded the expenditure of the one million pounds as an experiment. Furthermore, upon one point Norman and Niemeyer were adamant, and here I agreed with them: Any fresh funds to be advanced to Greece must be used solely for permanent and productive uses, as provided in the Protocol, and none of it for charity or temporary relief. These moneys must be used to restore the refugees to self-support and economic usefulness. They must provide farmers with seed, plows, and work animals, so that Greece might become productive. They must provide artisans with tools, industrial enterprises with equipment, and working people with permanent homes. These uses of money would restore Greece to a permanent earning power that would be a blessing to the refugees and that would provide funds to repay the loan.

At the Foreign Office the political aspects naturally were stressed. Not, be it said to the credit of Sir William Tyrrell, in any but the most humane and unselfish spirit. His hopes were for an end of the internal political strife in Greece, so that the nation might be united in meeting this great crisis in its history. He assured me of official British sympathy in anything that might be done by the Greeks themselves to put their house in order.

I paid my respects also to Lord Robert Cecil, then the outstanding British leader in the League of Nations, who happened to be in London. He invited me to have luncheon with him at his home, and his delightful informality, in true British home manner, made this an occasion long to be remembered. We two were quite alone, with not even a servant in the dining room, where a buffet luncheon was spread upon the sideboard. We replenished our plates and brought them back to the table ourselves from time to time while we carried on our conversation. Lord Robert's features are familiar to all the world through his photographs, but these do not convey the complete picture of the man —his tall, lanky frame, with its rounded shoulders, surmounted by the massive head that always looks too big for the body that supports it. Lord Robert's great mind and vision, and his broad humanity, need no additional certification from me; they are known to all; and it was an inspiration to get the stimulation of his fine mind and spirit before entering upon the strenuous labors that lay before me.

Cecil explained that the reason the British had agreed to help Greece was their wish to stabilize the Balkans. That region had long been the tinder-box of Europe, and had finally set off the terrible explosion of the World War. Of that region Greece was at the moment the key position, and if her affairs could be straightened out, much would thereby be accomplished toward assuring tranquillity. A secondary reason that Lord Robert gave for Britain's interest in Greece was the desire to repay the debt to classical Greece, that great fountain head of European culture, which had made possible all that we mean by the word "civilization"—the creator of the philosophy that makes religion intelligible, the creator of the systematic thought that makes science attainable, the creator of the arts that make life beautiful.

I could not help thinking, as I talked with Cecil, of how perfectly he embodied British statecraft, in its permanency and its inheritance of steadily unfolding and expanding tradition. Cecil's forebears were counselors to Queen Elizabeth, and in every generation since, have been leaders of Britain's policy. Born to rule, breathing statecraft in the very air of the nursery and absorbing it in every contact of life from the cradle to the grave, they are representatives of a wonderful political system that has made Britain important in world affairs out of all proportion to the numbers of her inhabitants. Brains, character, and a steadfast policy transmitted by verbal tradition are at the roots of this greatness.

From London I proceeded to Paris. Here were two most important personalities whose interest I must try to attach to my undertaking. First—and here of course no effort was necessary—was Sir Arthur Salter, the financial wizard of the League of Nations. He had himself been one of the principal authors of the plan for an international Refugee Settlement Commission for Greece, and was therefore as keenly interested as I that it should be a success. I called upon Sir Arthur in Paris. He, too, is a characteristic product of British politics. Like many another high-minded British patriot, he has made the welfare of his country his sole aim in life, and has devoted his time and all his thought and energy to the intelligent advancement of her interests. He has gone about this purpose without noise or display, but quietly has made himself an expert on international affairs, and has developed his own natural gifts to make them most useful in his special field. His particular skill lies in the power of analysis of conditions in other countries, and of devising practical financial measures to relieve their necessities. His ambition has always been to play a useful part in a general plan by which Great Britain should protect and advance civilization throughout the world. In especial, he has always been most solicitous that the United States should share in this great responsibility, feeling as he does that the united efforts of the English-speaking peoples would go far toward preserving our present state of advancement and the peace of the world.

A single interview with Sir Arthur was enough to bring us into full accord as to the general plans I had in mind for dealing with the Greek problem, and to assure me that I should have his powerful backing at Geneva for whatever I should decide was necessary to do after I should actually look over the situation on the ground in Greece.

My second objective in Paris was Mr. Venizelos. I should doubtless have gone to see him of my own volition, but my intention to visit him had been fixed before I left America, for Woodrow Wilson, whom I visited at his home in Washington just before my departure, had strongly advised me to consult Venizelos, and had reminded me of the great Cretan's genius and wisdom and far-reaching influence. I was aware that to be fully successful in Greece it would be necessary—as likewise it would be a pleasure—to renew my acquaintance with that great patriot and statesman. Few men in the world are so well worth knowing. One of the greatest geniuses in the statecraft of our time, he has for years wielded an influence in European affairs out of all proportion to the leverage normally afforded by eminence in so small a country as Greece. Power of intellect, force of character, and a dazzling personality have won him international fame, and have enabled him to perform prodigies in the service of his country.

I had become well acquainted with Mr. Venizelos four years before. At that time, when President Wilson was in Paris negotiating the Treaty of Versailles, Venizelos was one of the brilliant group of leaders of the smaller democracies, that included Paderewski from Poland and Masaryk and Benes from Czecho-Slovakia. The "Big Four," Wilson, Clemenceau, Lloyd George, and Orlando, held all the trump cards in that feverish international game, but they needed all their intellectual and moral powers to outshine what might well have been called the "Lesser Four" just named. Of these Venizelos was by far the most experienced in politics, both national and international. Not even Masaryk, the Grand Old Man of Prague, wise and capable as he was, equaled in experience the Cretan patriot, whose far-sighted vision, boldness in action, and wisdom had steadily enlarged the boundaries of Greece, had taken her into the World War upon the right side before it was too late, and had enabled her to claim a favored seat in the councils of the peace conference. Nor had anyone in Paris, during those fateful months in 1919, been more astute or more persuasive in urging the claims of his country. It got to be a byword in Paris that "every time Venizelos called on Wilson the map of Europe was changed."

I had got to know Venizelos well in those days. President Wilson had honored me with several private missions to various representatives of other nations during the discussions, and I had several confidential interviews with Venizelos, among others. I, too, had learned to have an affection for this lovable man, whose personality combined all the elements that charm and impress. One of the most attractive men in the world, tall, slender, graceful in every motion and gesture, with every social gift, a mind at once subtle and profound, a lofty spirit fired with the highest ideals, not only for his country's welfare but for the whole human race, it would be a man of mean soul and little imagination who could fail to delight in contact with him.

Naturally, then, immediately after my arrival in London I had written to Venizelos in Paris, explaining that I was on my way to Greece, and that I wished very much to renew my friendship with him. I knew that he could not fail to be warmly sympathetic, and his powerful influence with at least half of the political forces inside Greece itself would inevitably affect any plans I might wish to carry through when I should arrive at Athens. His advice would be most useful, enabling me to avoid many a pitfall.

By return post from Paris I received the following cordial note from Venizelos:

> 20, Rue Beaujon,
> Paris, (VIII°),
> October 30, 1923.

MY DEAR MR. MORGENTHAU:

I now have your good letter and I hope I shall have the pleasure of meeting you either here or in London, where I shall be, at the Ritz, between November 4th and 8th.

I am very glad to see that you have accepted the chairmanship of the Refugee Commission. Your appointment, I feel, is the surest guarantee of the success of its work, which is so urgent and necessary for the welfare of Greece and for the stabilization of peace in the Balkans.

With kindest regards to Mrs. Morgenthau and your good self from my wife and myself, I remain

> Sincerely yours,
> E. K. VENIZELOS.

Accordingly, one of the first things I did upon my arrival in Paris was to get in touch with Venizelos. At his invitation Mrs. Morgenthau and I dined with him and Madame Venizelos at their apartment. M. Politis and his wife were also present—M. Politis being the permanent representative of Greece at the League of Nations headquarters in Geneva, and consequently likewise a man most useful for me to know.

I found Venizelos as cordial and inspiring as ever, full of concern for Greece's distress and full of enthusiasm at the prospect of efficient relief of it. His keen mind grasped all the financial, as well as the political, intricacies of the problem, and he assured me of his hearty benediction on my labors. I was sorry to find that he was none too well, physically. His prodigious efforts during the war and the peace conference had affected his heart, and his doctor required him to observe a strict regimen of life, with no avoidable excitements, as the path back to health. Politically, he was for the present living in retirement. The savage hatred of the Constantinist, or so-called Royalist, faction in Greece, engendered by his defiance of that brother-in-law of the Kaiser in 1916, coupled with his prolonged absence from home to further the interests of his country during the peace conference, had combined to weaken his hold upon the political machinery of Greece, with the result that he had been disastrously defeated in the election of 1920, and had wisely removed himself from the scene until events should inevitably demand his return as the one leader strong enough to steer the ship of state.

Venizelos urged me to hasten the exchange of populations under the recent treaty by which Greece had undertaken to bring all remaining Greeks out of Turkey, and by which Turkey had undertaken to take back to Turkey all the Turks now living in Greece. Venizelos's reason for urging that this movement be hastened was, that Turkish landlords occupied many thousands of acres of the most fertile lands in Macedonia and Thrace, and if these lands could be promptly vacated they would immediately provide farms and homes for thousands of refugee families now starving in Salonica and the other cities of Greece.

He urged me likewise to find means at once to provide forty thousand houses—winter was approaching, and shelter was the very first need of the refugees. The next move he advised me to make was to lay plans for the early draining of the swampy lowlands in the Vardar and Struma valleys—if this were done, great areas of highly fertile soil would be reclaimed for cultivation, and, besides, the mosquitoes would be killed off that made malaria an endemic curse in northern Greece, costing the lives of thousands of people annually and so debilitating the survivors as to reduce their productive capacity to a low level. He advised similar measures with regard to the plains of Philippi, north of Cavalla. The experience of Bailey, the English pioneer who had drained Lake Copais, near Thebes, had proved that such plans were feasible economically. Venizelos declared his belief that these three districts could thus be made to suffice for the needs of all the refugees.

In discussing the men in Greece upon whom I could

most surely depend for coöperation and counsel, Venizelos spoke with high praise of Epaminondas Charilaos, the president of the Chamber of Commerce of Athens and head of the Refugee Treasury Fund, the nation-wide private and volunteer organization that had sprung up to attempt to solve the refugee problem when the Constantinist government had shown itself averse to taking active steps for relief. Venizelos also spoke with affectionate enthusiasm of Etienne Delta, the president of the Greek Red Cross, a man of conspicuous strength of mind and benignity of character. "You can treat him with unlimited confidence," said Venizelos, a remark that my later experience bore out fully, in my many dealings with that sagacious, benevolent, and most lovable philanthropist and patriot.

Venizelos urged me to prompt but not hurried action. So vast an enterprise could not be carried through overnight, and the future must be planned for as well as the present emergency. He was pleased that the United States should be interested in the welfare of Greece, as evidenced by my appointment; and remarked that my philhellenism, as repeatedly shown in Constantinople while I was Ambassador there, proved that I would deal with the present situation in a sympathetic way. No other course could win the confidence and coöperation of the Greeks, who, though not sentimental in many things, do give their loyalty without reserve to those foreigners who sincerely love them.

Venizelos also spoke most warmly of Pericles Argyropoulos, the other Greek member of the Refugee Settlement Commission and later member of several succeeding ministries, as Minister of Foreign Affairs and, most recently, as Minister of the Interior. I too found Mr. Argyropoulos a man of steadfast courage, wide outlook upon affairs, and an intimate familiarity with Greek politicians and the intricacies of Greek politics. This knowledge he placed at my disposal, and thereby greatly facilitated my understanding of the many complications of men and parties with which I had to deal.

My meeting with Venizelos in Paris occurred on November 2d. When we parted I did not dream—and I doubt if Venizelos did either—that exactly two months later a universal demand would arise in Greece that he should again take up the reins of government, and that we should then be resuming our discusssions in Athens.

My next, and last, objective in Europe was Geneva. Here, at the League Headquarters, I familiarized myself with some of the financial details of the problem ahead, and got acquainted with that part of the League's machinery that I should have to keep in touch with later. I should have had to be much less sensible than I am to the beauties of Nature not to have drawn inspiration from the loveliness of Lake Geneva, as I strolled in the evening along the waterfront back to the hotel; and strength from the massive bulk of Mont Blanc, shining white in the distance as if it were an emblem of those more steadfast things that do remain unchanged in the midst of change. After all, the distress of the Greeks, tragic and urgent as it was, yet would be cured, and become but an incident in the great history of that great race.

A few days later, as my railroad train followed the

windings of the Vardar River southward from Belgrade, I could not help but muse upon the strange turnings of events that were again bringing me back to the Near East. Ten years before I had gone to Constantinople as American Ambassador. There I had found the Young Turks in control of the government, the so-called Committee of Union and Progress, led by Talaat, Enver and Djemal. I had seen these men take Turkey into the World War as an ally of Germany. I had come to know their savage purpose to destroy the Armenians in Turkey, and their equally obvious intention to make life intolerable for their Greek citizens.

Now, ten years later, I was going to Greece to aid the victims of this latter animosity. In Turkey new forces reigned. Talaat and Djemal had been assassinated. Enver had fled to Afghanistan, to become a nomad chieftain on the world's wildest frontier, and had been killed there. Turkey—no longer an empire, but a shrunken remnant of its former self, stripped of its control of Arabia, Palestine, Syria, and Mesopotamia— was now ruled by a single new dictator, Kemal Pasha, whose capital was not Constantinople but the ancient city of Angora, aloof from the world in the mountain fastnesses of interior Asia Minor. Under Kemal the Turks were making their last stand to preserve their national identity. Hated by their fellow Moslems, who rejoiced in their new freedom from these Tartar interlopers, execrated by the Christian world for their slaughter of the Armenians, the few remaining millions had concentrated on the plateau of Asia Minor and defied the world to interfere with them. An unwise attack upon them had been made at the instance of the Allied Powers, including the United States; and the army at hand to make it was the Greek Army. The Turks had defeated the Greek Army. Then, true to type, and more than ever determined to clear Asia Minor of all but Turks, they had killed or deported all the Greeks who had, from immemorial times, lived along the shores of the Black Sea, the Ægean, and the Mediterranean, on the northern, the western, and the southern coasts of Asia Minor.

At last the Turk was supreme—and solitary—in the land that he had first occupied in the year 1227, when his Osmanli ancestors were driven westward before the Mongolian hordes of Jenghiz-Khan.

And at last—but how tragically!—the Greeks were reunited upon the ancient soil of Greece. What migrations they, too, had made eastward, and now back! As I crossed the Jugo-Slavian border into Macedonia I realized that this was the soil from which Philip of Macedon had gone east to conquer Thrace, and from which Alexander the Great had carried Greek civilization across Asia Minor, Persia, and the Indus River to the very gates of Delhi, leaving behind him Greek settlements that had colored the life of the Near East for two thousand years. Now, that chapter of a great history was closed. Greece confronted a gigantic task of reconstructing her whole national and racial life upon a new order. Macedonia, that had slumbered under Turkish misrule for centuries, was now to be made the home of half a million Greek farmers, and the granary of the race. Athens was now to be roused from its somnolence of centuries and become the humming metropolis of a newly energized commercial and seafaring people, surpassing Constantinople in importance. Salonica, which my train was approaching, was to be made the sea portal of the Balkans, furnishing an outlet not only for that part of Greece but for the southern Serbs and Bulgarians as well. How best could I help in this great process of rebuilding an ancient nation upon new foundations?

A letter written to my children a few days after my arrival in Greece gives additional details of my experiences in Geneva and Salonica, besides reflecting the emotions of the moment better than they can be recalled by later memory. I wrote as follows:

November 17, 1923.

My dear Children:

The day after I had talked with Venizelos I also talked separately with Mr. Michalopoulis and with Mr. Politis, and between the two they gave me a very good picture of conditions in Greece. They spoke frankly, and it was highly interesting to have them unfold to me what this small group of Venizelists were doing and plotting. There is no doubt that Venizelos is directing most of the movements of the present government in Greece from his headquarters in Paris. All concerned and interested in the future of Greece are keenly watching the developments that will occur within the next few weeks.

There are really three factions in Greece—the Royalists form one compact group, whereas Republicans are divided into two distinct factions. One of them is the Venizelists, who are still following him blindly; and the other, those who are opposed to the dynasty and want to promptly declare a republic. They do not wish to delay the declaration until

93

after the elections, but wish by immediate action to avoid the necessity of another election after the declaration of a republic. They want to abolish the present constitution, declare a republic, and then have an election that would ratify the proceedings. On the other hand, the Royalists and the Venizelists wish to comply with the demands of the larger Powers that they stop their blood feud, have the regular election on December 2d, and if they conduct it properly and the majority of the Republicans are elected, the Powers will accept this as a ratification of the revolution and will recognize the incoming government. Venizelos realizes that Greece must cater to the "Big Powers" so that she can have a successful bond issue which would enable her to solve her refugee problem.

I reached Geneva on November 7th about nine o'clock in the morning, and was met at the station by a delegation of four, consisting of Mr. Arthur Sweetser, Mr. Gilchrist, Mr. Dufour, and Mr. Berry. About half-past ten I made my formal call on Dr. Nitobe, who is the Under-Secretary General of the League of Nations. We exchanged the usual formalities and then he spoke of Japan's catastrophe and marvelously quick recovery.

At eleven o'clock I visited the Refugee Section of the League, where I discussed the matter with Mr. Gorvin, a Britisher; Mr. Lassitch, a Jugo-Slavian; and Mr. Xenakis, a Greek. They had an amazing amount of detail to tell me and I spent three quarters of an hour with them. They explained to me just how their investigations had finally led to the formation of this Commission to solve the refugee problem.

At 11:45 we visited the Administrative Commissions and Minorities Section where again I met representatives of three different countries—Messrs. Gilchrist, an American, Magalhaes, a Portuguese, and Azcarate.

At 12:15 P. M. we called on the Economic Section, which is under the control of Mr. Dufour, a Frenchman; and at 12:30 Dr. Sydenstricker of the Epidemic Section called on me and enlightened me on what they had done and what would still have to be done in Greece to prevent epidemics.

At 12:50 P. M. I granted an interview to Colonel Cunliffe-Owen, who had been the British Military Attachè in Constantinople. He is very anxious to come to Athens and join the staff of our Commission.

At 1:15 P. M. we sat down to lunch. There were fifteen besides myself and nine foreign countries were represented. Dr. Nitobe made a splendid speech and I answered as best I could.

At 3 o'clock the representative of the Greek secretariat to the League of Nations, M. Colocotronis, called. When I say "called" I mean at the office of the Secretary General, which had been placed at my disposal for the day.

At 3:30 M. de Pourtales called.

At 3:40 the representative of the Near East Relief, Mr. Berry, and Mr. Davis, of the Y. M. C. A., came to discuss their activities.

At 4:30 Mr. Sweetser and I called at the International Labor Office. Mr. Thomas was absent and so I had my talk with the Deputy Director, Mr. Butler.

At 5 o'clock I had a conference with the press consisting of Mr. Sharkey of the Associated Press, and my old friend Harry Wood of the United Press, and Mr. D'Arcis of the London *Times*, and Mr. Laya of *Le Temps*. I gave them an interview which probably you read in the papers.

At 5:45 the representatives of the Minorities Section made a second visit, as I had not been able to finish with them in the morning.

At 7 o'clock we all met at Sweetser's. There were present about ten of the men who had called during the day, and several of the wives.

At 9:30 I took the train for Lausanne. During the day I had heard that the French were anxious to participate in the loan and that M. Herriot, the Mayor of Lyons, was at the head of the group. So they telephoned to Lyons and he said that he would send a representative to Geneva if I could wait over. I could not do so as my itinerary had been arranged, so we telephoned that I would see the man at Lausanne if he was willing to come there.

At 3 o'clock in the morning M. Triboulet, former Deputy Mayor of Lyons, rapped at my door, and to my utter amazement he could not speak a word of English. I tried to have the night watchman, who spoke a little English, interpret, but I really believe his vocabulary consisted of less than one hundred words of English. We finally understood each other a little and I arranged with him to accompany me on the train for a short distance and meet my colleague, Campbell, who speaks French. This we did, and we discovered that there is a very enterprising group of business men at Lyons, and that they are very anxious to secure some of the contracts for agricultural machinery, manufactured lumber, and other things which the Commission contemplates buying. They are willing to take bonds in payment and even to buy some additional bonds if by doing so they can secure commercial advantages equal to those that they believe Great Britain will secure through her financing of the loan. This poor chap missed connections at Geneva and had to auto from there to Lausanne in the early hours of the morning. He thinks, as a great many others do, that M. Herriot will probably be the successor of Poincaré.

As we journeyed through Switzerland, taking repeated glimpses of the beautiful scenery, and through Italy, Jugo-Slavia and Greece, Campbell and I were reading the voluminous reports and documents they had handed to me at Geneva, and were discussing our plans.

I found Mr. Campbell a typical British civil servant. He has had extraordinary experiences. He has been in India many years and rose to the rank of under-secretary. It was instructive to listen to his descriptions and analysis of the Indians and of their relations toward the British. He did such good work at Geneva for Lord Hardinge, former Viceroy of India, that he secured for him the position of Financial Advisor to the University of London. I doubt if any of our colleges takes the precaution to have a special man to advise them on their investments, etc., as the British universities do. He is a Scotchman and his bump of caution is tremendously developed. He wants to have everything shown him before he believes it, and that is pretty hard in Greece. Fortunately he gracefully adjusts himself to the rule of the majority and is not inclined to ever be in the minority. He speaks a perfect English, is about six feet tall, sparely built, and possesses great self-composure, and his every move and pose and his method of expressing himself show the result of the exercise of authority for a long time.

I had telegraphed the other commissioners to meet us at Salonica. I wanted to see the refugee settlements there and also the Vardar and Struma valleys which Venizelos thought should be drained and cured of malaria, thereby redeeming hundreds of thousands of acres which are now uncultivated.

We arrived about 11:30 A. M. and were amazed at the large delegation that awaited us at the station. The representative of the Governor General with his auto, the mayor of the city, three members of the City Council, the president of the Jewish Community and the president of the B'nai B'rith Lodge, and several others. Amongst the reception committee there was also Mr. Jaquith, the representative of the Near East Relief, and Mr. Amoss of the Y. M. C. A.

The Governor General had insisted upon our stopping with him. He occupies a beautiful home facing the water. They allotted to me the room which King Constantine used when he visited Salonica, and which was subsequently used by Venizelos and also Plastiras. Though Governor General Lambros did not, his wife spoke English splendidly. He was a lawyer who had lived in Smyrna, a Revolutionist of tremendous force, and his eloquence constantly displayed itself in ordinary conversation. This charming gentleman is most alert and active-minded. They could not do enough for us.

They were rather disappointed that their preparations for my wife's reception had been futile.

We had very busy days at Salonica. We visited four of the refugee settlements. It is simply pitiful to see how those poor people are struggling for their existence. We saw several rows of people in lines waiting to have their daily ration ladled out to them. We also saw the disembarkation of several thousands out of the seven thousand that had arrived in a ship of about four-thousand-ton capacity. How they were ever jammed in the boat it is impossible to understand. The odor they gave forth as we passed them was something stifling.

The refugee settlements reminded me very much of the concentration camps for Russians we visited in Lemberg in 1919. At Salonica they have already housed a great many. They have not only refugees in the settlements, but have utilized nearly all of their schools for the past two years for the refugees, so that incidental to their other troubles they are compelled to let their children go without education, and the evil influence of that is incalculable as the youngsters are forced to street life. This same school situation prevails in Athens. They were trying to open some of the schools again.

In the evening the Governor General gave a reception to the Commission and to the Mayor and his wife, and other celebrities of the town, which lasted until about twelve o'clock.

Next day they had provided a special train for us to visit Vodena, one of the big refugee settlements, to study the lay of that land and the possibilities of redeeming it. Our party consisted of the Commission and the daughter of Mr. Delta, a fine young woman who had been educated in England, Mr. Caclamanos and another government expert, and a representative of the National Bank of Greece who is in charge of the Agricultural Department of the bank, which is practically the same as our Federal Land Banks. The car had a nice observation room in which we sat and discussed matters, studying the maps and listening to the explanations of the experts.

When we reached Vodena we were received by the Prefect of the district and the Mayor of the town and numerous other officials. It is a very old city but now very thriving as they have important factories there and the influx of the refugees has created considerable activity. They are erecting many small houses and a school. The Prefect insisted upon taking our party to his home for dinner. He had a delightful young wife whose eyes were just sparkling with joy at the privilege of entertaining such celebrities. It was the first real Greek dinner that I ever ate. Everything was cooked with olive oil.

They were building a group of sixty-one double houses, four families in each house, the entire house for the four families costing $512.

They paid the girls (who were aged from twelve years up) who carried bricks and mortar, from six to eight drachmas a day (a drachma is now about $1\frac{2}{3}$ cents); while the women who work (and many are employed) receive from eight to twelve drachmas; the young men from twelve to fifteen drachmas, while the master mechanics receive from twenty-two to thirty-seven drachmas, and they seem to be working really very hard.

On Tuesday we visited several orphan asylums. One of them is called the "Bee Hive" and is entirely supported and managed by young girls. Ten of them are the "Queen Bees" and each "Queen" has from ten to fifteen ordinary bees helping her, sewing garments and supervising the education and training of the children. We talked with some of the young girls and it was amazing what fine spirit they displayed.

One day I attended three receptions: At four o'clock the Municipality gave us a reception; at five o'clock the American Consul gave a tea in my honor, and at six o'clock all the

Jewish organizations, about eight, had combined and gave a splendid reception at the B'nai B'rith Lodge rooms, with the usual speeches. It was amusing that three of the organizations were Zionists and I could not refrain in my talk from telling them how essential it was for them to be real Greek Nationalists, which they are not.

The whole atmosphere in Salonica was surcharged with terrific excitement. Everybody talked politics and defended his point of view with an intense partisanship and a display of the intention to "fight to the finish," so that I really fear there are slight prospects of an early termination of this modern Capulet and Montagu conflict.

CHAPTER VIII

My First Days in Greece

FAITH is the first essential in solving large problems. If a man has faith, his faith gives him courage. Courage leads to success.

The problem in Greece was primarily a human problem. If I had not realized before how urgently human it was, my first day in Salonica would have impressed the fact indelibly upon my mind. I went down to the quay and saw a shipload of refugees land. A more tragic sight could hardly be imagined. I saw seven thousand people crowded in a ship that would have been taxed to normal capacity with two thousand. They were packed like sardines upon the deck, a squirming, writhing mass of human misery. They had been at sea for four days. There had not been space to permit them to lie down to sleep; there had been no food to eat; there was not access to any toilet facilities. For those four days and nights many had stood upon the open deck, drenched by an autumn rain, pierced by the cold night wind, and blistered by the noonday sun. They came ashore in rags, hungry, sick, covered with vermin, hollow-eyed, exhaling the horrible odor of human filth—bowed with despair. And yet these old men and children and women only a few weeks before had been living at peace, in happy homes, useful and industrious citizens, comfortably housed and clothed, and fed with the fruits of contented labor.

Seven thousand people in that one ship! And yet I knew that a fleet of nearly two hundred more such ship-loads would have to land before my eyes if I were to see all the human beings who were in exactly their same plight—a million and a quarter of them, a gaunt and shattered multitude of misery.

A human problem! And I at the moment, above all others, pledged to redeem this throng! What an awful responsibility! How could I dare to fail them, when my failure meant a deeper misery to these people—to thousands of them, death? No obstacle must be allowed to stand in the way of bringing succor to them. If others were indifferent, I must harrow them with the tale of this horror. If others were hopeless that they could be helped, I must fire them with my faith that they could be saved. If the money to do it could not be found in Greece, then it must be found in Europe; if not in Europe, then surely in America. My task was a task of faith—to believe, in the face of everything, that some way could—must—be found to relieve this army of woe.

Fortunately, I knew the people I was dealing with— had known the Greeks in Turkey for what they were: high-spirited, clever, energetic, capable—otherwise I might well have doubted that those animated heaps of filthy rags that debarked from that ship had in them enough of human resources to be salvaged. Imagination alone, unaided by such knowledge, might well have failed me.

Even with this knowledge it would have been easy to

approach a solution of their trouble from a mistaken angle. Moved to profound pity as I was, it would have been not unnatural to think of these people only as objects of charity—poor wretches like the poverty-stricken hordes of India, to be *governed* back toward subsistence, rather than *guided* back to their natural independence and self-sufficiency. From such an attitude of benevolent arrogance I was saved by my American upbringing. To an American's eyes these Greeks were not hapless dependents, but equals, the worthy descendants of a glorious ancestry, the capable brothers of one of the ablest and most enterprising of modern peoples. To an American, to patronize such a race would be impossible; the only thinkable attitude toward them was that "here are brethren in distress—how fine it is to be able to help them to their feet again!"

How could they best be helped? Not by condescension, surely. That would be to kill the spirit for the sake of saving the body. Not by mere charity. That would be to destroy their independence. Not by treating them as dependents, to be managed by an outsider for their own good. That would be to insult their self-respect.

Deeply as I was moved by the misery of the refugees, I was only less touched by the plight of the native Greeks. A nation only five millions strong, never blessed with an overabundance of the natural resources from which industry wrings comfort, recently impoverished by ten years of almost uninterrupted warfare, these native Greeks had suddenly had thrust upon them their destitute brethren from Asia Minor, in numbers equal to one fourth of their own population. What a staggering burden to be thrown upon their shoulders! And how nobly they had accepted it! They had greeted these brethren with open arms, had received them as full members of their national family, had given them all the citizen's rights of the native born, had spent of their treasure to relieve their distress until they had no more to spend, and now, almost in despair but with desperate courage, they still struggled to survive. They had devised a plan of relief and of positive rehabilitation worthy of their genius for business, a plan so sound in principle that it could not be improved—but they had exhausted their resources in its execution, and could not carry it on to completion without outside aid.

At this moment I appeared on the scene. My coming was not important because of myself, for I was largely unknown to the Greeks. The important thing to them was that here was the representative of the League of Nations—proof that the organized outside world had heard of their distress and was determined to help them. An equally important thing in the eyes of the Greeks was the fact that this agent of relief was an American— a citizen of that great land of democratic enterprise, where freedom of opportunity had not only made possible the creation of vast wealth but had also taught men to regard other men as equals. From an American they might expect not only help in the task of material rehabilitation, but sympathetic understanding of their spiritual distress.

And in my labors to help them I thought of myself, not as an individual, but as an American. Anything I could do for them would not come out of any personal wisdom, but would be great or little in just the degree to which I brought the American spirit to their service. If I could make the Greeks feel that I had faith in their own ability to solve their problem, and not pride in my ability to solve it for them; if I could persuade them, as I sincerely believed, that they were not mortally wounded but only a cruelly stricken patient whose recovery, none the less, was assured; if I could convince them that, as a disinterested outsider, I felt that they only needed a temporary pilot to guide them through a dangerous channel—then I was sure that they would respond with the just pride of a virile race and would soon be able again to steer their own ship.

In the days that followed my arrival at Salonica further investigation confirmed me in my belief that the refugee problem was a solvable problem. The Greeks were reeling under a terrific body blow, but they were neither down nor out. They were bewildered, naturally. The confusion engendered by so great a catastrophe was reflected in a confusion in their political life. The Royalist government, whose mismanagement had invited the calamity, had been held responsible by the people. The army had revolted and set up a provisional government, oddly enough respecting the person of the monarch, though taking a terrible vengeance on his counselors, for its first act had been to execute three ex-prime ministers, two ex-ministers and the general who had been defeated by the Turks. To King Constantine they had applied the ancient Greek penalty of ostracism; they had forced him from his throne and exiled him to Italy. His son George now occupied the throne; to say that he reigned would be to confound the fiction of royalty with the fact of ruling. The ruling was done by the provisional government, grim Colonels Plastiras and Gonatos, who, though they had not flinched at taking the lives of six of Greece's most eminent citizens, had astonished the world by the subsequent moderation and wisdom of their rule. Great patriots, they held the sovereign power in trust until a civil leadership should emerge out of the momentary chaos, capable of taking up the reins of government.

Thus, the Greeks had already demonstrated their capacity in three directions: They had mastered the monster of anarchy in a great disintegrating national calamity. They had devised a plan for rehabilitating the refugees and absorbing them into the national life that was sound in principle and practical in operation. They had proved that they had a noble national soul, by the unselfish loving-kindness with which they had received their stricken brethren.

Viewing these facts, why should an outsider despair? What could he say but this: "Great has been your faith. Mine shall not be less."

What the Greeks needed most—what I determined at the first opportunity to supply—was encouragement.

At my request my fellow members of the Refugee Settlement Commission had come up from Athens to join me at Salonica. This made it possible for us to make a brief tour of inspection in Macedonia together before we proceeded to Athens. We at once got acquainted and down to business. The Greek members, Messrs. Etienne Delta and Pericles Argyropoulos, though of very different types, are both representative examples of the brilliant group of men who are the leaders of modern Greece. Highly educated, widely traveled, speaking several languages, at home in any society in Europe by virtue of breeding and culture, abreast of the times in politics, science, literature, and business, this group would do credit to any nation in the world. And they are not, as in Turkey for example, the brilliant exceptions at the top of a stolid mass. They are rather, as in America, the best representatives of a race of intelligent, ambitious, energetic people, evolved by competition with worthy competitors into acknowledged leadership.

With my two Greek co-laborers in the Commission I was to find it an unceasing pleasure to work. Shrewd and courageous, benevolent and unselfish, they eagerly embraced every plan to help their country, tactfully advising as to what could and could not be done, and joining whole-heartedly in the execution of projects after discussion had brought agreement.

The British member of the Commission was Mr. John Campbell. He had won his spurs by many years of work in the Civil Service in India, and he had the very great merits and the inevitable minor limitations of that training. His instinct for orderly procedure was most useful in giving solidity to the administrative work of the Commission.

The situation in Greece was unprecedented. It amounted to a life-or-death crisis, and time was of the essence of its solution, for a million and a quarter human beings were running a race with starvation and death, and bold measures must be risked at once to save them. There was no time to make sure that a project was ideal; it was enough to know that it would certainly put bread in hungry mouths next season, when the crisis would reach its height. Details could be improved later; emergency understandings could be regularized or altered by negotiation when the crisis had passed.

For this reason we held our first meeting of the Commission on the train, en route from Salonica to Athens. With the broad Macedonian plain unfolding to our eyes as we rolled along, the Commission came to order and organized for the work ahead. We agreed to divide the work into three sections: financial questions and treasury were allotted to Delta; the secretarial and legal questions to Argyropoulos; technical questions and inspection to Campbell. As chairman, I would be occupied devising major plans and negotiating with the government and foreign financiers, and would retain a general supervision of all the work.

The dramatic element in large undertakings is the very first thing to be considered in the process of making them successful. Confidence and enthusiasm must be created at once. Imaginations must be stirred. Coldness, dullness, conventionality are deadly enemies of success. I had resolved to make every effort to have the Greeks and the rest of the world realize the magnitude and importance of this emergency, and the certainty and glory of mastering it.

The first thing I did toward creating this impression, after we had agreed upon our organization, was to announce that I would waive the 2,500 English pounds that had been fixed for the salary of the chairman of the Commission, and also would pay all my own traveling and other expenses. This was a small sacrifice for me to make, and the Greeks knew this perfectly; but the gesture accomplished exactly what I had hoped; it was accepted as a final proof that I had come to Greece whole-heartedly prepared to do everything in my power, and unselfishly, to help them with their problems.

My second move even more convincingly enlisted the confidence of the country. I insisted that we should at this first meeting declare our policy to be that every post to be created by the Commission should be filled, if possible, by one of the Greek refugees. I was confident that there were enough men of brains, character, and technical training among the refugees themselves to perform every service we should require. Not only would such a policy encourage the country by its assertion of confidence, but also it would make our work a truly national enterprise, enlisting the fullest coöperation of every individual in the nation. Furthermore, it would provide work and livelihood to the refugees, who were the class that needed them most. And, finally, it would build up a permanent native organization, competent to manage the administration of the problem after the need for foreign assistance should be passed.

Again, as I had hoped, this move likewise confirmed the Greeks in their confidence in the Commission. Any fears they might have had, that we were to be swayed in our decisions by any but purely Greek interests, disappeared when this policy was actually put into operation. It generated an enormous enthusiasm for our efforts, and put the country solidly behind us. When the inevitable differences of opinion between the Commission and other public agencies arose we found ourselves gratifyingly supported by public opinion. And I may pause for a moment here to add that the policy justified itself wholly in practice. We did find Greek refugees equal to every position, including those dealing with the most technical problems of construction and finance, unearthing, indeed, several men possessed of practical genius to a degree rare in any country, and of a fidelity to duty that was beyond praise. Their names and achievements will appear as my narrative unfolds.

Immediately after my arrival at Athens I found the opportunity I had been looking for to deliver a message of encouragement to the Greek people. Instead of submitting to a series of interviews by the reporters who kept coming to see me, I arranged to have the responsible editors of all the newspapers come together to meet me. They gathered in my parlor at the hotel.

It was most interesting to me to size up their mental attitude toward me. Their manner seemed to say: "Who are you, anyway; and what have you got to propose, now that you are here? We know about your friendliness toward Greece while you were in Constantinople. We have heard something of your business career in America. The League of Nations has sent you. But what can *you* do with our terrific national problem? What can you know about it that we do not know much better? We have been struggling with it for more than a year, and to us it seems nearly hopeless. You may think you have a solution, but you will have to 'show us'."

Their attitude put me on my mettle. I *did* have a solution, and I was eager to lay it before them. I said, in effect:

"You gentlemen may think it is strange that I, who am almost a stranger, should be prepared already to say that I see clearly a way out of your difficulties. I think I see it more clearly than you, precisely because I *am* a stranger. You are naturally overwhelmed with the details of a misfortune that meets you every way you turn. I am free to look at the larger aspects of your problem. If this were a military situation I might say that you have had to be entirely preoccupied with the details of the service of supply, while I am privileged to sit in the quiet map room at general headquarters and study the strategy.

"The strategy seems fairly simple, as I see it. I do not minimize the difficulties ahead in applying it. That is a complicated task, and will call for much work and much thinking. But the broad principles to be followed are clearly apparent.

"Greece's problem is primarily a business problem and one that is familiar, in its essence, to every American business man of wide experience. It is the problem of a going concern that is temporarily embarrassed. In undertaking to reorganize such a concern and put it back on its feet, the first thing to determine is whether it has enough assets to make recovery possible.

"On that point there is no question in your case. And the refugees themselves are an additional asset.

They bring you fresh manpower to develop your resources of lands and materials. For example, the Turks who are being removed from Macedonia are evacuating more than forty thousand houses and farms. The refugees will cultivate these farms more efficiently, and wholly for the benefit of Greece. Again: Greece needs more factories, new industries. The refugees will provide skilled workers for these enterprises. You will find that the refugees will stimulate your whole economic production to a point you have never dreamed of.

"But, you will say, these things will require capital, and Greece has no money, and her credit is exhausted. Yes, I reply, but credit is something that can be created. If a man has sound assets, then skilful management can so use them as to create confidence in his ability to use borrowed money profitably and with safety to the lender.

"Now, what our Commission proposes to do is to help Greece recreate her credit standing in the money markets of the world. We have a million pounds in cash at our disposal. Instead of attempting the impossible task of solving the whole refugee problem with that little money, we propose to use it in such a way that Greece can get more. If we can prove that *one* million pounds can be so handled that it definitely restores to productive independence 125,000 refugees, then it will be no trouble to convince bankers that it will require *ten* million pounds to do the same thing for a million and a quarter of refugees; and they will be glad to lend the money.

"Credit, then, is what you need. The way to get credit is to make a demonstration, on a small scale, of what you can do with a little money. Prove that, and you can get all the money you need.

"With sufficient money, you can make Greece blossom like the rose. You have the land, you have the climate, you have the geographical position, and you have the people to make a prosperous, happy nation. With a little piloting through some of the reefs that are before you, you will make port safely.

"That this is what will happen, I have not the slightest doubt. The task before our Commission is to unite your new human energy and your unused resources of land and materials. The way to unite them is through the creation of a credit. This we can do with the means at our disposal. When that has been accomplished, Greece herself can solve the problem. She will have learned how to use money to make the refugees self-supporting, and the world's bankers will have learned that it is safe to provide the money.

"You gentlemen, if you will, can be enormously useful in this enterprise. Pessimism is the worst enemy of success, and I have already observed that pessimism is in the air in Greece at present. I don't wonder that it is, but we must all coöperate to dispel it. Faith is essential to the success of any plan to create credit. You are the molders of public opinion, and you must help imbue the public with courage and with a faith that Greece is going to win out."

It was remarkable to see how these editors responded to my talk. My optimism seemed to infect them, and they eagerly fired question after question at me, to bring out additional reasons for optimism. And it was a solid satisfaction next day, on reading their reports of the interview and their editorial comment, to see how every one sounded a note of confidence that was refreshing. The effect on the whole Greek people was instantaneous. They felt that someone with courage, clear vision, and a workable program was now attacking their problem, backed by the good-will of the world as expressed in the League of Nations. Despair was replaced by hope, and lassitude by energy. Offers of coöperation by the foremost Greek officials, industrialists, and leaders poured in upon us at the Commission. We were now sure of the support of public opinion in our work in behalf of the refugees. Indeed, from that day onward we had only to ask either government or private individuals for specific aid in our labors, and it was given with eagerness.

I soon found another dramatic occasion to demonstrate to the Greeks that I was determined to take the boldest measures, where necessary, to render them prompt and effective service. This occasion arose as follows:

Dr. A. Doxiades was the Minister of Public Assistance, and as such had been in charge of the governmental part of the refugee settlement work and had distributed the dole of two drachmas a day. He had ordered a large quantity of lumber from Dalmatia and Rumania; of grain and seed from Russia, Algeria, and Rumania; and of animals from Servia—80,000 oxen, horses, and mules. They were all en route and the government had no funds to pay for them. The cost of all was about 160,000 pounds. The doctor said their predicament was frightful, as it was now November 24th, the cold winter was coming along fast, and the poor refugees would starve unless they could secure these provisions and animals. At the time we had not yet received any money from the Bank of England, which was still questioning Greece as to their spending some of their funds for repairing their navy and buying supplies for their army. We could not possibly tell how much of these provisions and animals would be used for reproductive purposes and on property to be deeded to us or already in our possession. Of course the Greek members of our committee wanted us to help if we could do so legally. My sympathies were thoroughly aroused, after listening to Doxiades' appeal and recalling the fearful condition of the refugees I had met. So I went in to see the governor of the Bank of Greece, Mr. Diomede (we were still using some of the bank's rooms as our offices), and I proposed that the bank should share the risk with us. The bank should advance the 160,000 pounds and we would agree to reimburse that part of it which could subsequently be proven to have been used for such purposes as brought it within the restrictions placed upon us by the Protocol.

Diomede surprised me by his prompt and enthusiastic reception of this suggestion. The patriot, not the financier, shone in his eyes as he agreed, without an instant's hesitation, to assume full responsibility for this use of the bank's funds, not waiting to consult with anyone about it.

On November 26th Diomede ratified our verbal arrangements by the following letter:

Office of the Governor   Athens,
                                             November 26, 1923.
MY DEAR MR. PRESIDENT:

In accordance with the conversation which we had, I have the honor to submit for your consideration the following propositions, which have been accepted by the government.

1. The National Bank will pay for the purchases made by the government, and which are in course of execution, for the establishment of the refugees, viz: wood, construction material, agricultural implements, ovens, beasts of burden (for traveling and for work), seeds, and other agricultural furnishings up to the amount of £160,000.

2. The Commission undertakes to repay this sum to the National Bank to the extent in which the wood and the furnishings are utilized by the Commission to carry out the works and establishments which the Commission will undertake. If a part of these materials cannot be used by the Commission, the material not used will be charged to the state.

3. As soon as these materials shall have been distributed or used, the appropriate minister will submit to the Commission an account of the distributions and the uses which shall have been made. The Commission will be at liberty to refuse to accept such of the dispositions which it may find not to have been justified. We make a special note that the Commission will recognize only the distribution made to the refugees established on the lands or in the houses which will have become the property of the Commission and after the transfer of the property will have been definitely made in accordance with the protocol of the 29th day of September, for it is understood that it is only then that the Commission will approve of the distributions made.

In that case, the cost of the furnishings, disposition of which will not have been found justified under the Commission's requirements, will be charged to the state.

4. The Commission will reimburse in cash these advances of the National Bank only when the Commission will have been placed in possession by the government, according to the Protocol, of the lands and the houses where the refugees who will have received the materials mentioned in this letter will have been established.

Please accept, my dear Mr. President, the expression of my high esteem.

(signed) DIOMEDE
The Governor.

MR. HENRY MORGENTHAU,
President, of the Commission to
Establish the Greek Refugees.

Although Dr. Doxiades made the request, and Diomede took most of the risk and advanced the money, and I just assented and devised the means of doing it, the Commission received all the credit from the refugees for coming to their rescue. Every possible help was expected from the Greeks whilst such sympathy and kindness from an American was generously applauded by the press and also by Colonels Plastiras and Gonatos and the other members of the Cabinet.

CHAPTER IX

Exit Monarchy—Enter Republic

THE first few meetings of the Commission made clearer than ever the nature of my task. The first essential was money; and as money was to be got only by a foreign loan, my first duty was so to use the funds in hand as to demonstrate to the British and to the financiers of other countries that the refugee problem could be solved. The first prerequisite of success was political stability. To secure political stability I could not with propriety take any initiative in the internal politics of Greece. I could, however, and I did, give sympathetic coöperation to the liberal elements in their evolution from monarchy to a republic. Greece was divided into two bitter political camps. So long as the Royalists and the Republicans waged their internecine strife, there was hourly danger of civil war. This situation must be eliminated if foreign financiers were ever to be satisfied.

The political situation in Greece, when I arrived in November, 1923, was in a state of ferment. Little wonder that Mr. Montagu Norman, speaking for the financial world, had been so insistent that political stability must be assured before large loans could be promised! The air of Athens was electrical with rumors of impending political change. Greece was nominally

118

ruled by King George II, but actually it was ruled by a revolutionary committee made up of officers of the army and navy. They had seen Constantine, the young King's father, once before lose his crown and then regain it by political intrigue. This time they would take no chances. They had therefore retained the actual power in their own hands, frankly calling themselves a provisional government and trying to organize a party of political moderates cohesive enough to take over the functions of government under an orderly constitutional régime. When I reached Athens they had not yet been able to do this, so I found myself facing the necessity of dealing with two governments, one such in name and the other in fact.

Curiously enough, I had met such a situation once before, while I was Ambassador at Constantinople. During that time I had visited Egypt, where I had been somewhat perplexed by the relative positions of the Khedive, who was nominal ruler, and Lord Kitchener, who was the real one.

In all public affairs there is some such combination of illusion and reality, of outward forms and true inner forces. Custom, however, prescribes a fairly general rule in such cases. Observe the forms first and then get down to the realities.

Consequently, in Athens I first of all sought an audience with King George II. I called at the Royal Palace, signed the register, and left my request with His Majesty's aide-de-camp. The King immediately sent word to my hotel that the audience would be granted on the following day. I was presented by the aide-de-camp. I found the King to be a pleasant, but by no means imposing, young gentleman. With his military uniform and his small mustache, he looked like an average, well-groomed, rather youthful army colonel. His pleasant smile and unaffected good manners were most attractive. He quickly showed, however, that he was not of kingly mold. The self-confidence of inward power was wholly lacking. Beneath his efforts at self-possession it was easy to perceive that he was a man of uncertain mind and possessed by fear. My audience with him was held in his office, and after the first greetings he retreated to his seat behind his desk. With his arms at rest upon it, his nervousness was less obvious. Our conversation was in English, which he spoke perfectly.

I could not help feeling sorry for the King. He knew perfectly well how insecure was his position on this throne. He was King in name, but in little else. The Revolutionary Government that exercised the real power was hostile to him. The million and a quarter refugees, freshly arrived in his kingdom, had little reason to love him and less to love his family. In this precarious situation it was little wonder that he looked at me askance, for I was another uncertainty, freshly added to the political factors in Greece. In my person the League of Nations was entering Greek affairs clothed with some of the attributes of independent sovereignty. I could see the King asking himself: What sort of person is this? How will he and his Commission affect my position?

Naturally, I talked chiefly about the refugee problem. He seemed little interested in the frightful sufferings of the refugees. His concern was chiefly about their activities in politics. He complained that they were agitating for political measures of relief instead of trying to determine how to take care of themselves. It was really pathetic to see how little he realized his inadequacy to meet such a situation. His remark, "I am no business man and must depend on logic and good common sense," sounded tragically ironical from a man so obviously mediocre and inexperienced.

Four days later I had my first meeting with the real rulers of Greece. These were Colonels Plastiras and Gonatos. Colonel Plastiras had led the revolution that deposed Constantine after the Smyrna disaster. With only the title of Chief of the Provisional Government, he (with his associates) was governing Greece until political conditions should evolve a civil government equal to the task. Colonel Gonatos was his Minister of Foreign Affairs. I was their guest at dinner and we had a long, frank talk about the political and economic situation in Greece.

These were men of a different mold. Plastiras, especially, was a man of native force and power. Instantly upon meeting him I was conscious of a strong personality unencumbered by pretense. His manner was simple, direct, and sympathetic. His actions had already proved his sincerity and patriotism, although he had seized and firmly held the supreme power. He had assumed none of the ostentation of a ruler, and had not even increased his military rank from the simple colonelcy that he had already achieved in the army. His conversation with me showed me that his entire concern was for the welfare of his country. He was warmly appreciative of the assistance given by the League of Nations, and offered to do everything in his power to facilitate my work as chairman of the Refugee Settlement Commission. He discussed at length the political situation in Greece. Personally, he was anxious to retire on account of his health, but quite aside from that consideration he was anxious for Greece to resume normal constitutional government, which would make his control of the state unnecessary. He expressed the view that no country should be permanently governed by its military leaders. He foresaw the gravest danger to the welfare of the state from the continuous exercise of civil functions by the military class. His earnest hope was that different party alignments would soon emerge under capable leaders, so that a constitutional régime could be erected strong enough to carry on the affairs of the country in an orderly manner. He was determined shortly to bring about the election of a parliament, and he declared that he would see to it that the election was fair. I may say, in passing, that Colonel Plastiras soon afterward proved his sincerity by doing all the things he said he intended to do; namely, reinstituting a civil government and retiring to private life.

Among military dictators Colonel Plastiras was most unusual in his firm faith in civil rule. Scarcely less interesting was his associate, Colonel Gonatos. A professional soldier with no previous experience in public life, his appointment as Minister of Foreign Affairs of the Provisional Government had been viewed with apprehension. To the pleasant surprise of everyone, however, he turned out to be an excellent official, administering the affairs of his office with much tact and good judgment. These qualities, indeed, were revealed by the Provisional Government in all its dealings with difficult situations. For example, one day a crowd of Royalist sympathizers in Athens suddenly decided to mob the Provisional Government. They tried to rush its headquarters. One would have expected military dictators to repel such an attack with machine guns. Instead, they ordered out the fire department and turned the hose on the crowd. Water proved as effective as bullets, and left no resentment behind.

A week later I had another and longer conversation with King George. This time Mrs. Morgenthau and I were the guests of the King and Queen at luncheon. Even more clearly than before it was evident that the King was no statesman. Colonel Plastiras had taken the broadest view of the welfare of the country. The King's thoughts were altogether of himself and his dynasty. Instead of praising the men who were trying to stabilize distracted Greece, the King could only complain and criticize. He declared that Plastiras's government was using the situation to popularize itself as against royalty —whereas the fact, of course, was that Plastiras was trying to retrieve a disaster caused by the incompetence of royalty. Queen Elizabeth, who had read my book on my experiences in Turkey, said that the younger element in Greek politics reminded her very much of the Young Turks as described in that book. The King was very critical of all the activities of the Bureau of Public Assistance, which up to this time had been in charge of the relief work among the refugees. He declared that he could have done the work better himself. His next remark proved that he could not. He declared a mistake had been made in placing the refugee settlements near the big cities. I was tempted to ask an obvious question but refrained—where in the world would the poor people in these settlements find immediate employment except in the cities?

The conversation of both the King and Queen impressed me as showing that they had not the slightest appreciation of the right of the Greek people to rule themselves. They evidently regarded themselves as divinely anointed rulers. They wished their subjects to look up to royalty for leadership without taking thought for themselves. What a strange delusion to cherish in the Twentieth Century! And how asburd in democratic Greece, of all places in the world!

I told the King that he ought to visit the settlements to show his sympathy with the refugees, citing the action of the King of Italy, who rushed to Messina after the great earthquake. The King said that the Minister of Public Assistance had never invited him to visit the settlements. To this I rejoined, "Then I, as the one responsible for the refugees, invite you now." He replied that he was afraid that the Royalist Party would criticize him if he did so. Why they should do so I could not imagine, but King George's attitude was part of his mistaken policy, according to which he acted not as the disinterested head of the state, symbolizing the whole nation in his person, but rather as the leader of one political group within the state. Exactly this attitude had cost Constantine his throne. Within a

Interior of National Opera House, Athens. Each box is
Occupied by a Refugee Family

month after this luncheon King George had paid the same price for this mistaken opinion.

Colonel Plastiras, determined to end the extra-legal régime of the Revolutionary Government, and to restore Greece to a constitutional system, ordered elections to be held on Sunday, December 30th, for seats in the National Assembly. This body, thus provided with a fresh mandate from the people, would then undertake to write a new constitution that should express the will of the people.

The chief issue in this campaign hinged upon the form of government to be set up by the new National Assembly: whether the constitutional monarchy was to be continued, or a republic substituted for it. It became clear, early in the campaign, that the general sentiment favored a republic. The issue then arose, whether the republic should be declared at once by the National Assembly, and this action then referred to a plebiscite for ratification; or whether the monarchy should be continued until the assembly could submit to the electorate the alternative issue of "monarchy or republic" and get a clear expression of the popular will upon this question, uncomplicated by the personalities or parties involved in the present election.

The three parties represented in the campaign were the Royalists, who wished to retain the monarchy; the Liberals, who wished to continue the monarchy until a plebiscite could be held upon the question of substituting a republic; and the Republicans, who wished to declare a republic at once and get the ratification of a plebiscite afterward. The leaders of these parties were

125

General Metaxas, for the Royalists; General Dangles, for the Liberals; and Mr. Papanastasiou, for the Republicans.

The position of the Moderate Liberals represented the position of Mr. Venizelos. He had no love for monarchy for its own sake, and least of all had he any reason to love the reigning Glucksburg dynasty, for King George's father, Constantine, had been Mr. Venizelos's bitterest enemy, and had interfered in every conceivable way with his plans for the advancement of his country. Indeed, the Royalist Party had become little more than the party of those who were opposed to Venizelos. Constantine had been a popular idol in his youth. He had inherited the popularity of his father, George I, who had been sincerely devoted to Greece. When Constantine was born huge crowds stood in Constitution Square waiting for the news of his birth, and it was by their acclamation that he bore the name of that Constantine who had tried to defend Constantinople as the Greek capital when the Turks besieged and captured it in 1453. But his son, George II, the present King, was a mere youth, unknown and untried. The elements that made up his party gathered around him as a common meeting ground of their opposition to Venizelos.

The position of Venizelos was the position of the Liberals: organize the new National Assembly, have it submit the issue of a republic to the country, and then, in due order, act upon the results of the plebiscite.

The Royalists felt doubts about their success, so that many of them did not take part in the election. The result was that the issue was fought out chiefly between

the Liberals and the Republicans. The Liberals won. Instantly the army and navy (still bitterly resentful of Constantine's mismanagement at Smyrna) brought pressure to bear on the government, to compel the immediate declaration of a republic. The army's leader in this movement was General Gondiles, and the navy's leader was Admiral Hadjikyriakos. The Provisional Government refused to grant their demand, but Colonel Plastiras, fearful that the continued presence of the King in Athens might provoke these elements to open disorder, asked the King to leave the country until the National Assembly had met and decided the issue. Therefore, on December 18, 1923, two days after the election, the King and Queen left Greece for a "vacation" in Roumania, from which they never returned.

The Revolutionary (or Provisional) Government at once appointed Admiral Condouriotes as Regent, and invited Mr. Venizelos to return to Greece, to act as National Adviser in this national crisis. He agreed to come on a temporary and unofficial visit. Two days before he arrived the Revolutionary Government resigned, so as to leave a free field for him and the new National Assembly to work out the problem of government.

I was present in the Chamber of the National Assembly when Colonel Plastiras made his farewell address. The session began with religious exercises—a high mass, in which six prelates participated; they carried lighted lamps, burned incense, and sprinkled holy water around the chamber whilst chanting the service. Plastiras ascended the rostrum and read with much feeling

and in a penetrating, clear voice his farewell address. He declared that the Military Party had finished its duties and was anxious to hand the reins of government gracefully to the civilians. He praised the United States for what they had done for Greece. All through the address he was frequently interrupted with applause, and at the end there was a perfect salvo of cheers.

Two days later Venizelos arrived in Athens. A week later he accepted the premiership, because he found at once that the many factions could not agree to work under anybody else, and while he had by no means unanimous support, he was the only person in Greece who could command a majority in the Assembly.

Three days before Venizelos accepted the office of Premier I had a long talk with him. He told me that he intended to delay the plebiscite for three months, as he wished to calm the country and assure a fair election. In the interval he would disband the Revolutionary army. He intended also to offer the Royalists the right to name two out of every five election inspectors, the anti-Royalists two, and the Court of Cassation (Supreme Court) the other one. He was trying to persuade all parties to agree to abide by the results of the plebiscite, no matter what they might be.

As we talked it was quite clear that Venizelos was far from well. He looked tired. It was obvious that he had not recovered from the strain upon his heart that his ceaseless labors at Paris had thrown upon it. Yet he needed all his energies if he were to face successfully the labors that lay before him.

On every hand I heard rumors of trouble ahead. The

Royalists were demanding that the King be brought back at once or they would create a disturbance. The army and navy cliques, who were the most rabid of the Republican groups, were threatening a *coup d'état.* Even Venizelos's own party was divided: there were Liberals of strong Royalist leanings in it, and Liberals of strong Republican bent. Every faction wanted something done at once, and wanted it done their way. I wrote in my diary that day (January 8, 1924), "It seems no matter what may be done there is trouble brewing."

Out of the conversation with Venizelos I got the reassurance of his cordial sympathy with the work of the Refugee Settlement Commission and of his eager desire that we should be successful. This was important, for on the day that he took over the government of Greece, January 11th, the British Government recognized Greece. A first step was thus taken in satisfying the British that progress was being made toward the political stability upon which they insisted before granting further loans to aid the refugees.

Political stability thus went to the heart of the refugee problem. I felt it to be essential that I miss no opportunity to do anything I could to help the Greeks tranquillize their internal politics. Not that I felt called upon to tell them what they must do—that was their affair, not mine. But where it was clear that the majority was surely headed in a certain direction, it was plainly my duty to facilitate their arrival at that destination if I could. And I had unusual facilities for knowing, in advance, which way events were tending. All factions realized that my presence in Greece was disinterested; that I had come to serve the nation, not a faction; and that any suggestions I offered were made impartially and in the interests of all. Consequently, the leaders of all the parties talked to me with great frankness, and I thus got a rounded picture of the whole situation day by day as it developed. On several occasions I was able to do or say something that the Greeks have been pleased to describe as being a real service in clarifying and facilitating this work of returning to constitutional government.

About ten days after my talk with Venizelos I had a long conversation with the leader of the Republicans, Mr. Alexander Papanastasiou. He proved to be a most charming gentleman, modest, unassuming, a bachelor of studious habit, and a sincere patriot, whose aspirations for his country were grounded upon a lofty idealism. If perhaps his weakness was on the practical side of political leadership, his strength lay in the firmness with which he held to his conviction that Greece must join the modern world current of democracy, and liberalize her institutions by becoming a republic.

My meeting with Papanastasiou was at his apartment where he had invited me to come for tea. His charming sister was acting as hostess to the throng of guests that filled the rooms. After a half hour of pleasant conversation Papanastasiou called me aside and led me into his private study and closed the door. Two other men were present, General Gondiles and Admiral Hadjikyriakos.

I said facetiously, "This looks like a conspiracy!"

To my astonishment Papanastasiou replied: "It *is*

a conspiracy! We can tell you, as a friend of Greece, we are contemplating a revolution."

"But why," I inquired, "can you not get what you want by peaceful means?"

"The majority will not consent to it," Papanastasiou replied. "It is essential for the welfare of Greece that the country become a republic. Our opponents are in the majority, and majorities never have to make revolutions. The only way for a minority to succeed is to revolt."

With this startling introduction of the subject, the four of us proceeded to a lengthy discussion of the situation. They did the talking, while I listened. They wished to make their position and intentions plain to me as a responsible, disinterested outsider. King George, they pointed out, had not the slightest sympathy with the refugees and no real understanding of the Greeks. Though born and bred the ruler of the country, he had never learned that the Greeks would not tolerate any but a constitutional monarchy. On the contrary, he believed that the "people were his." The Republican element in the country were determined that they would no longer submit to be ruled by a German prince. The Glucksburg family had demonstrated that they were unfit for their position and would have to go. As long as they were getting rid of the particular dynasty, they might as well get rid of monarchy altogether. The Greeks could rule themselves, and the best form of government for that purpose was a republic.

Papanastasiou was critical of the attitude of Venizelos in the present emergency. Like all the Liberals in the country, Papanastasiou had always been a follower of Venizelos. Nevertheless, like many others, he recalled that Venizelos had made a cardinal mistake in dealing with the former King Constantine under similar conditions. Venizelos had then permitted Constantine to return from exile and resume the crown. The result had been disastrous. What Papanastasiou and his associates now feared was that Venizelos would repeat this mistake in the case of King George. They were resolved that Venizelos should not be permitted to repeat this error. To prevent it, they were determined to use revolution, if necessary, as a means of forcing the declaration of a republic.

A confirmed believer in republican institutions myself, I could not fail to sympathize with the desire of these Greeks to achieve that form of government. Nevertheless, I took the liberty of pointing out to them, as a practical matter of the present situation, that the sympathy of the three great democracies—the United States, Great Britain, and France—was essential to the very life of Greece in her present refugee crisis, and that this sympathy would be sadly compromised if the Greeks failed to have an orderly plebiscite or if they should fail to abide by its results.

Mr. Papanastasiou granted the importance of this argument, but brought out other aspects of the question. It was equally important, he declared, that Mr. Venizelos should come firmly to grips with the situation at once, and, in his new rôle as leader of the government take a strong stand in favor of a republic. The country was determined to take this step and abolish the monarchy. Mr. Venizelos, he felt sure, was making a mistake in not coming out clearly as favoring what the majority wanted. He could not have the whole-hearted support of the majority Republican element as long as there was any doubt that he himself favored a republic.

The Republicans were in no mood to repeat with George II the error that had been so disastrous in dealing with Constantine. Unless Mr. Venizelos gave clear evidence of his intention of avoiding this error he would fail to have the country or the National Assembly behind him.

In this prophecy the events of the next few weeks proved that Papanastasiou was right. The fact was that now, in 1923, as in 1920, Venizelos's long absence from Greece, upon his brilliantly successful diplomatic missions in behalf of his country, had got him out of intimate touch with Greek internal opinion, and made him commit momentary mistakes in his political tactics at Athens. His general idea was perfectly sound. Great constitutional changes should be made with sufficient deliberation to impress their fundamental seriousness upon the minds of the people at home, and to give observers abroad the feeling that they represent the considered will of the nation and are not the ebullitions of caprice. But his tactics in carrying out this major strategy were not based on sufficient knowledge of the immediate battlefield. The outstanding political fact of the moment was that a large majority of the Greeks were absolutely determined to have a republic. They would probably have consented to Venizelos's plans for bringing that change to pass if he had unmistakably shown that he was equally determined to abolish the monarchy. But apparently he did not realize that the Republican sentiment was as powerful as it really was. Consequently he acted with a caution and a deliberation that the Republican leaders would not tolerate in their present mood.

The refugee problem itself had injected a new element into Greek politics with which, I believe, Venizelos did not sufficiently reckon. The arrival of the refugees in Greece had added an enormous number of voters to the electorate. These people were in the most dire distress and they not unnaturally ascribed their troubles very largely to the blunders of the headstrong Constantine. They judged royalism by its fruits, and certainly the miseries of their lot were no recommendation of monarchical government. Furthermore, as they had not lived in Greece before, they had none of the sentimental affection for royalty as a symbol of country that still held the imagination of many native Greeks. They were nearly all resentful of the monarchical system. Most of them were ardent Venizelists, but they were equally ardent Republicans and would not follow him in any temporizing with royalty.

My impression that Venizelos was not fully aware of the strength of the Republicans was confirmed a few evenings later, when he told me that the opposition of the Republicans in the Assembly was weak and not annoying. Less than three weeks later he had found their opposition unbearable, and had resigned as Premier.

Meanwhile, however, two even more dangerous enemies to Venizelos's success were working against him. These were his health and his social activities. Time and again in my diary of that period I find such entries as this: "V. looked very tired," "The party broke up at ten-thirty as V. looked tired," "The doctor who sat beside him at the session took his pulse and advised him to leave the chamber." And under date of January 25, 1924, I find this notation, written after returning from a dinner at which Venizelos was a fellow guest: "I think he is wrong in going out so much to evening entertainments and sapping his vitality. He ought to act as Wilson did—disregard social amenities and center all his energies on the state, storing up new energy each night for the coming tasks, or he'll break!"

Unfortunately these were prophetic words. Venizelos's lowered vitality at that period made him irritable and intolerant of criticism or opposition. If he had been his usual vigorous but patient self he would have listened to the warnings of his fellow Greeks and shaped his policy to meet their demands. Instead, he insisted on meeting them head-on, and he found them too determined to yield to his dictation. Even the everyday acerbities of debate were too severe a tax upon his physical resources. Thus my diary on January 29th records: "Venizelos had a passage at arms with Papanastasiou in reference to Royalist newspapers that had been suspended. The chamber voted confidence in Venizelos 210 to 50, but he got angry and had a heart attack; left the chamber and had a doctor inject camphorated oil."

That evening Venizelos was to have been a guest at a

dinner that I was giving for members of the government and of the Refugee Settlement Commission. Following this attack in the chamber, however, his doctor had ordered him to bed, so that he was unable to be present. His absence was greatly regretted, but it led to an interesting incident, of some importance in the recent history of Greece, which I shall describe in a moment. The guests that were present represented the best that Greece can offer in her public service.

The Regent, Admiral Condouriotes, was naturally the center of the scene. Strong, gentle, benign, and wise, and a patriot so transparently honest and above partisan bias as to enlist the affectionate loyalty of all Greeks, this distinguished grandson of one of the heroes of the Greek War of Independence still heads the state, as President, against his own inclinations, because of the unanimous wish of his countrymen. He illustrates a curious fact about Greek history, the fact that "Greece" has never been so much a specific territorial area or nationality as it has been an idea and an ideal—for some of the greatest patriots in the Greek war of liberation were Albanians. The Albanians are an utterly distinct race from the Greeks, but great numbers of these brave highlanders have been so fascinated by Greek civilization that they have merged their whole beings into it, never losing their racial identity, while wholly losing their racial consciousness. They occupy a position in Greek life somewhat analogous to that now occupied by the Scots in the life of Great Britain, honored for their peculiar virtues of character and their signal usefulness to the state.

Besides the Regent, most of Venizelos's Cabinet members were present, as well as his devoted secretary, Mr. Michaelopou. The absent Premier's health was toasted, and the fact that during the day his government had been recognized by Great Britain was mentioned as a happy augury of the hoped-for tranquillity of the country. After a pleasant dinner about forty other guests, mostly American residents of Athens, came in for a reception. The evening gave us all a better opportunity to get acquainted, and to cement the social ties that so greatly facilitate coöperation in the more serious labors of life.

As the last guests were leaving the Minister of Foreign Affairs, Mr. Roussos, drew me aside and asked if I would like to have him and two others stay on for a private political discussion. To this, of course, I gladly agreed. The other two were Mr. Carapanos, and Mr. Michaelopou, who was asked to be present so that he could report back to Venizelos. The former was the Greek Minister at Rome and an expert in international affairs.

Their desire for a conference with me was based on their anxiety over the acrimonious differences between the factions in the Parliament, differences which, unless they could be composed, would nullify all of Venizelos's efforts to start Greece anew upon an orderly constitutional régime. The reason I was consulted upon so delicate a question of internal politics was perfectly obvious: The welfare of the refugees was of vital concern to the very existence of Greece in the economic sense, and of course if the economic situation ended in disaster the political situation would follow into chaos. As the head of the agency set up by the League of Nations to grapple with this economic crisis, my opinion was sought regarding the effect upon that agency of whatever major political move might be in contemplation.

Several possible courses lay before the country, and our little group canvassed them all that evening. The first was to attempt to preserve the status quo. This was clearly out of the question, as the country had plainly evidenced its determination to have some kind of change. The second was to ask the electorate, through a plebiscite, whether it wished to change from a monarchy to a republic or whether it wished, while retaining the monarchical system, to change the dynasty. The third was to have the Parliament declare the republic at once, and seek the ratification of the electorate afterward.

I felt free to say to my Greek friends that, as a disinterested outsider who had been privileged to hear the views of all parties given with the greatest frankness, it was my opinion that the sentiment for the republic was so insistent that nothing short of the immediate elimination of both the monarchical principle and the Glucksburg dynasty would satisfy the country. Any other course, I felt confident, would simply prolong the controversy, embitter the factional differences, and very likely lead to public disorder. My only interest in the question was to establish a stable government, so that the economic regeneration of the country might proceed apace.

The others were inclined to agree with this diagnosis as a matter of judgment, though with varying degrees of reluctance or satisfaction. The most serious objection they could offer to its political wisdom was the possibility that foreign nations might be disagreeably affected by the abolition of the monarchy. The monarchical sentiment in Great Britain, though largely sentimental, is yet a real force in her policy. Would British sympathy be alienated by a change of dynasty in Greece so abruptly made as to seem altogether inconsiderate of the feelings of royalty generally?

We discussed this question until long past midnight. Finally I made the suggestion that I might be able to find out unofficially what Britain would think. If I cabled my friend, Montagu Norman, the governor of the Bank of England, he could sound out the British Government and give me an accurate picture of the way the proposal impressed them. Thus, in forty-eight hours I should probably be able to let my Greek friends know exactly what effect an immediate declaration of a republic would have upon British sentiment. If the effect were favorable the whole problem of the Greeks would be simplified, for that fact would permit Venizelos, if he saw fit to do so, to withdraw his opposition to immediate action, and would unite behind him the powerful Republican faction, with their support in the army and navy.

The others urged me to send such a cable at once. It would secure valuable information without involving either Greece or Britain officially. I was not disposed to acquiesce, but wanted to follow my usual habit where important decisions are involved. I insisted upon sleeping upon the question, to give myself time for subconscious reflection. We agreed to meet at breakfast in the morning for a final discussion.

Roussos and I met next morning in the hotel dining room and I handed him the cablegram to Norman that I had prepared. Roussos had it coded and sent to the Greek Minister at London for delivery to Norman. Decoded, the message read:

Confidential for Norman. To remove difference of political parties and immediately give stability to political and financial status of Greece it has been proposed to have Parliament decide now irrespective of plebiscite that Glucksburg dynasty be eliminated. It would then be left to a plebiscite to determine the now complicated question shall Greece have a monarchy or a republic. A vast majority of the members favor this settlement of their serious difference. I have been asked how I thought Great Britain and United States would view this proposition. Can you ascertain for me your government's attitude or have Arthur Henderson do so?

After luncheon that day I encountered Roussos at the Athenian Club, and he told me confidentially that Venizelos was going to resign the following day, and that he (Roussos) and Cafandaris (the Minister of Justice) had an appointment to meet for the purpose of arranging for a successor as Premier. The heart attack of the day before had convinced Venizelos that he was unequal to the physical strain of active leadership and he had decided to turn these labors over to another. What actually happened was that Venizelos did not resign until three days later, as it took his successor Cafandaris and the others that long to agree upon the distribution of portfolios in the new coalition.

That evening I dropped in at the session of Parliament. A pall seemed to have fallen upon that body. Venizelos's absence seemed to create a vacuum. The electric energy that filled the hall when he was there had disappeared. The friction between the two factions had been the life of the proceedings. The ministers present were clearly depressed by his impending retirement. Their eager interest, so manifest when they began their work, was now gone. Several were paying no attention to the proceedings of the Assembly, their time being occupied instead with the perusal of the newspaper. The Minister of Public Assistance looked most serious and absent-minded. Cafandaris seemed tired and listless.

During the following day I had occasion to see Carapanos, Roussos, and Papanastasiou, separately, and I urged them to use the fresh start they were about to make in government the occasion for uniting all factions as far as possible by confining the battle wholly to principles and disregarding all personalities. I was resolved, so far as I could by persuasion, to do everything in my power to help clear up the internal strife that so seriously endangered the work I had been sent by the League of Nations to do.

The next day I received the reply to my cable to Norman. It read:

Confidential answering your telegram received from Legation yesterday and irrespective Henderson—and assuming that in your opinion proposition would insure general domestic settlement and political stability we consider you may expect sympathy here.

NORMAN.

I took Norman's message at once to the Foreign Office and gave it to Roussos. He was naturally delighted with it, as he represented the Republican faction in the Cabinet, and shared the impatience of Papanastasiou and their followers to remove the dynasty at once.

His pleasure was shared by the Regent, on whom I called the following day (Sunday) at his home. To my surprise, Admiral Condouriotes had not heard the news, and he was equally surprised when he learned that Roussos had had the message the evening before, as Venizelos had visited the Admiral shortly before and had not mentioned it. It developed, later, however, that Roussos had not been able to take it to Venizelos the evening before, on account of a dinner engagement, and could not reach him until Sunday afternoon.

The Regent felt that Norman's message was the missing link to enable leaders to convince Venizelos that he should act decisively and at once in getting rid of the Glucksburg dynasty.

The Admiral talked most frankly about his own position as Regent. It appeared that he occupied a position very similar to that of the King of England, with almost no political powers, but with the personal influence that attached to the occupancy of an office which symbolizes the state itself. He was too modest to say so, but of course Admiral Condouriotes also wielded (and still wields) the moral influence that always attaches to high character and unselfish patriotism.

That evening Roussos told me that he had shown Venizelos the Norman message, and that Venizelos had seemed to be impressed, as he had said he would consider the question again in the light of this new information and would then decide what course to follow.

The next morning Papanastasiou called and asked to see the Norman cables, as he had just learned of their existence when calling on the Regent, whom he had just left. He gave me further light on the complex political situation. Cafandaris was slated to succeed Venizelos as Premier, and the change would occur at the session of Parliament that evening. Papanastasiou disclosed his own relations with Cafandaris. They had both been Venizelists and anti-Constantinists, though of different intensities in their republican leanings. Papanastasiou had insisted upon going full length and at once for a republic. Cafandaris had shared Venizelos's own hesitations about going too fast in the transitions from monarchy. Indeed, Papanastasiou felt that Cafandaris was still only a shadow and willing instrument of Venizelos, and that his premiership would merely serve as a cloak behind which Venizelos would continue to carry out his own policy.

Some color of justification for this theory appeared from my next conversation with Venizelos himself, which occurred on the following day. He told me that he had been called back, not by a faction, but by the nation, to clear up a great national emergency, and that therefore he had the right to expect compliance with his program from all parties. He wanted the Republic as much as anyone did, but he would insist that it be brought into existence in regular form and by orderly process. He had no doubt but that the country would vote overwhelmingly in favor of removing the Glucksburg dynasty, and he did not, for that reason, feel it was necessary to omit the formal actions that would regularize the new system of government in the eyes of history. On the contrary, he believed that the most scrupulous attention to these formalities would strengthen the Republican cause and would so increase the vote in favor of the change that no faction would ever after have the slightest ground to question the decision. Thus, he felt, one national controversy would be forever removed from Greek politics.

On the other hand, Venizelos declared, the power of a legislative chamber to change the fundamental system of a country's government is nowhere recognized as valid. To meet the impatience of the extreme Republicans he was willing to have a double plebiscite on the same day, asking the electors to express their will upon two questions simultaneously: 1. Did they wish to substitute a republic for the monarchy? 2. Did they wish to retain the monarchy but remove the Glucksburg dynasty? This procedure would to some extent placate the Royalists, even in their probable defeat, as they would have to admit that their side of the question had been fairly tested before the country. Venizelos insisted that the Royalists must be placated as far as possible, not because he personally agreed with them, for he did not, but because it was essential that all parties in

Greece should be got into the best possible frame of mind or there was no hope of a united country.

I agreed with Venizelos's general theory, but pointed out to him that it would not work out in practice in the present temper of the country. In the first place, the Royalists ought to appreciate the consideration he proposed to show them, but the simple fact was that they never would. Those who were sincere Royalists were such by deep conviction, else they would not hold to a theory so opposed to the main current of modern thought; and they could not be changed. The rest, who were Royalists only for factional purposes, had joined that party exactly because of their profound opposition to Venizelos himself, and nothing he could do would placate them.

On the other hand, I continued, the majority of his own followers were in the Republican camp. They wanted to follow him, but they insisted that he lead them on in the direction in which he himself had started them. He might feel that they were too impatient, but the practical fact was that they were determined upon immediate action, and he would only alienate them by insisting upon delay.

It was clear from our conversation that Venizelos still regarded himself as the actual power in the government, as indeed, in view of his call to come back to Greece, he was entitled to feel. But if there had been any remaining doubt in my mind it would have been resolved when Cafandaris himself called on me next day and frankly declared that he would adopt all of Venizelos's plans, including the proposition of a double plebiscite on the one election day. Cafandaris took no especial pleasure in his elevation to the premiership; he suffered a severe handicap in a chronic kidney complaint that at times completely prostrated him, and the shadowy honor (though he did not say this) of having the office without the real power doubtless was small compensation for the strenuous labors it involved.

On the following day some of the newspapers in Athens published abstracts of Norman's and my cables. This was almost certain to happen in a community where political leaders are so intimately associated as they are in Athens, and especially where politicians are frequently journalists as well. In order to prevent misunderstandings, I secured Norman's permission to publish the correct text in full. The messages created the most intense interest, and undoubtedly contributed materially to crystallizing public opinion. They removed the strongest objection to the immediate declaration of the republic by direct action of the Parliament.

That afternoon, when I made a return call upon Papanastasiou, I became aware that the military element was behind him, and not, as Venizelos had been confident, behind Venizelos, in the present political controversy. I found already there General Gondiles and Admiral Hadjikyriakos, the former the outstanding army leader since Plastiras had retired to his Thessalian home and the latter one of the foremost navy leaders in the revolt against Constantine. It was clear from their attitude that they looked to Papanastasiou for political guidance.

In a later conversation with Papanastasiou I learned that the Republicans, both the civil and the military leaders, were fearful that if the Royalists by any chance got control of the government they would wreak deadly vengeance upon all their enemies. Their fear in part explained their insistence upon an immediate declaration of the republic.

Meanwhile, both by personal observation and by conversation with many mutual friends, it became more and more evident, both that Venizelos's health was quite unequal to the present strain, and that he was insistent upon a program that he could not possibly carry out in the present political line-up of the country. The prospect that lay ahead was of prolonged controversy, quite possibly ending in public disorder. Unless this fruitless deadlock were broken, I could see no hope of the political stability upon which the refugee problem depended.

A few days later, Venizelos having expressed a wish to discuss the situation with me further, we met in the evening by arrangement at the home of our mutual friends, Mr. and Mrs. Delta. The only guests were Mr. Venizelos, Mrs. Morgenthau, and myself.

Soon after we arrived Venizelos said to me:

"I've been thinking about what you told me the other day. You said one thing that I wish you would explain more fully."

"What was that?" I inquired.

"You said that the army was not with me. What authority have you for that assertion?"

"The best in the world," I answered.

"That's a general statement. I mean, specifically, who told you?"

"As you insist on knowing, it was General Othoneos who told me so."

"I can't believe it!" exclaimed Venizelos.

"I assure you, I have this information personally from the lips of General Othoneos himself. He told me only the other day that the army would not blindly follow either yourself or Gondiles. He said the army was independent, and was determined only upon one thing, which is prompt action to secure a republic."

This information evidently made Venizelos exceedingly angry. He changed the subject, but later in the evening he got me into a corner and questioned me about the details of General Othoneos's conversation. Venizelos vigorously maintained his original opinion regarding the proper method in bringing about the change from a monarchy to a republic. He said he wanted the voting lists revised, and believed if this were done the Royalists would participate in the election and would abide cheerfully by its result.

Again, as he talked, Venizelos became more and more excited. I saw that our discussion was getting nowhere, and was only doing him physical harm. So I said:

"Come now, let's stop this heated argument and cool off with a game of bridge."

Venizelos agreed, playing as partner with Mrs. Morgenthau, while Mr. Delta was my partner. Evidently, however, the discussion still preoccupied his thoughts, for the game did not particularly soothe him, and he played as if he were angry at the cards, slapping them down on the table. At ten o'clock, in accordance with his doctor's orders, Venizelos excused himself and went home. As we were parting I said to him:

"I have arranged with Papanastasiou to meet you to-morrow, to see if you cannot come to an agreement by which he will coöperate with you."

"All right," replied Venizelos. "I will see him."

"I am glad of that," I continued, "because I am sure he wants to coöperate if he can possibly do so. All you will need to do is to treat him as the real leader of the Opposition. You told him awhile ago that you expected his group to be a true parliamentary Opposition. He has taken this remark of yours seriously. Papanastasiou does not like it when your manner implies that he is not to be treated seriously as a leader of a real Opposition. But I am sure you two can sit down quietly and settle this whole difficulty in short order."

After Venizelos had gone the Deltas remarked that there was nobody in all Greece who would have dared to speak so freely to Venizelos, and that this was exactly what he needed, because his own adherents kept from him many things he ought to hear.

Venizelos had arrived at the Deltas forty minutes late. None of us had attached any significance to this fact at the time. But the next morning, when I picked up my newspaper at the breakfast table, I became aware that those forty minutes had made a tremendous difference in the political situation in Athens. He had used them to give an interview to the newspaper correspondents. Imagine my astonishment when I read him quoted as delivering a perfectly vitriolic attack on the members of the Left of the Chamber of Deputies—the group of which Papanastasiou was the leader. With a sinking heart I realized that he had made it impossible to compose his differences with Papanastasiou.

Papanastasiou called on me shortly after breakfast. Of course he, too, had read the Venizelos interview and he was very angry over it. He regarded it as an insult to himself and his followers. Nevertheless, he proved himself a patriot, able to control his own feelings for the sake of the general good, because he expressed himself as willing, notwithstanding Venizelos's attack, to meet Venizelos as he had agreed and discuss the situation in person with him.

I was now convinced, however, that the two men were so far apart in their views, and so aroused in their feelings, that nothing could come of such a meeting. So upon my advice it did not take place. They could not agree on even the facts of the situation, let alone their interpretation. For example, Venizelos had said the night before that the Royalists would participate in the election if the voting lists were revised. Papanastasiou, on the contrary, had told me in the morning that the Royalists only an hour before declared that they would not participate.

Five days later the battle between the two parties came to a head in Parliament. Cafandaris, speaking as Premier, but representing the views of Venizelos, made a fine speech in which he declared that unless the republic were established in accordance with recognized legal formalities it would not last. General Gondiles, in reply, asserted that the establishment of the republic by parliamentary action would be legal, and declared that if he and his associates had wanted to change the government by mere force they would never have sought the council of civil leaders like Cafandaris and Papanastasiou, but would have shouldered their guns and marched to Tatoi, the country residence of King George, and settled the issue at once and conclusively there. All the members of Parliament at once realized that Gondiles was right, because they could have done so.

The fact that General Gondiles and not Papanastasiou had made the speech in reply to Cafandaris plainly showed that the military leaders of the country were not behind Venizelos but were supporting the Republicans. A more direct and grimmer evidence of this fact appeared in the person of General Othoneos, who came all the way from Salonica to Athens to tell Venizelos and the other leaders that the army wanted a coalition cabinet that would work harmoniously for a prompt plebiscite and the immediate declaration of the republic. This was the same General Othoneos who had presided over the military tribunal which tried, convicted, and caused to be shot five ex-ministers and General Hadjanestes for their share in Constantine's policy and military operations leading to the Smyrna disaster.

The appearance of General Othoneos on the scene in Athens, coinciding with the appearance of General Gondiles on the floor of Parliament as the spokesman of Republicanism, swept all the firm ground from under Venizelos's feet, and showed him the hopelessness of pursuing his policy. Indeed, as it developed afterward, before Cafandaris made his speech defending the Venizelos policy, Venizelos had told Cafandaris and his other supporters that he was "ready to surrender to the army," and had urged Cafandaris to resign, but the latter stood firm, went on to the floor of Parliament, and won a vote of confidence. Cafandaris said in his speech, "If Mr. Venizelos's position was right a week ago, it is right to-day. If he is afraid of the army, I am not." His victory, however, could be but momentary. Venizelos, finding Cafandaris obdurate in supporting the policy he himself had now abandoned, published a statement advising that a new coalition cabinet should be formed, with Roussos as Premier, and all parties coöperating for the immediate establishment of the republic.

Cafandaris, through his consistency and courage, rose greatly in the public estimation, and though his ministry fell two weeks later, he retired with the respect of the country. To succeed him as Premier was chosen, not Roussos, but Papanastasiou.

This change of ministries occurred while I was in Geneva, reporting to the League of Nations upon the progress of the Refugee Settlement Commission. The actual date of the change was March 10th, and the occasion was the re-formation of the Officers League representing the same group that had set up the Revolutionary or Provisional Government, and their specific demand upon the Premier and Regent that the republic be declared without further argument. Cafandaris had thereupon resigned, Venizelos had left Greece, and Papanastasiou had formed a new government, pledged to abolish the monarchy at once by vote of Parliament, to be followed by a plebiscite ratifying the change.

Before I left Athens for Geneva, however, I made a public speech that had some effect upon these events. The occasion was the conferring upon me of Honorary Citizenship of Athens, and the date was February 23d. Realizing that the Greeks were passing through one of their greatest crises, I had pondered upon the kind of reply I should make to the speech of the Mayor conferring this citizenship upon me—whether I should be content with merely a few words of formal appreciation, or whether I would be justified in giving my Greek friends some plain advice. I finally decided to speak quite frankly, but to soften the bluntness of direct advice by phrasing it in the form of a parable, as this would be more palatable to my hearers and would still permit me to say what was in my heart.

That afternoon a large number of the most distinguished citizens of Athens, including Venizelos, other members of the government, and the Mayor and council gathered at the City Hall. At six o'clock the president of the council made the formal motion that I be elected Honorary Citizen of Athens. It was carried and Mayor Patsis then delivered his address in Greek and his secretary read the following English version:

"Mr. Henry Morgenthau:
"It gives me great pleasure, as the Chief Magistrate of the historic city of Athens, to inform you that the City Council in its official sitting of February 2, 1924, has awarded you the title of Honorary Citizen of Athens.
"When a nation, like the United States of America, is

153

fortunate in having sons who by their genius harness the lightning to the service of man and turn the darkness of night into bright light; and when a nation like yours is blessed with citizens who conquer the world by the greatness of their humanitarian ideals—then that nation may be said to have attained such a perfection of civilization and human brotherhood that all other peoples must pray for its progress and prosperity.

"The people of Athens, mindful of the historic fact that in this ancient city the noblest ideas of the human race had their birth, has retained the immemorial custom of extending the freedom of its citizenship to those who labor in behalf of what is beautiful and useful to mankind. Following this ancient tradition, we beg to confer this citizenship upon Your Excellency, who have been laboring so long and with such devotion and self-sacrifice for the rehabilitation of our refugee brethren.

"In conferring this title upon you amid the lively acclamations of the people, the magistrates of this city wish to show such honor as lies in their power to the great American nation, of whose lofty spirit of disinterested service you are so eminent an embodiment."

In responding I first thanked them for the unusual honor conferred upon me, and told them how highly I appreciated it.

Then I gently and carefully related to them a parable: That the League of Nations had erected an Outpost in Greece to observe the country for them. That I was occupying it as a Look-Out. It stood at the Junction of three diverging roads. One day I heard a great commotion at the foot of the Tower, and I saw a large crowd of Greeks gathered there, gesticulating wildly and arguing loudly, as to which of the three roads they should choose. On seeing me descend from the Tower, their voices were stilled, and one of their leaders asked me to tell them whitherward the various roads led. I told them that the left road was the Russian Road, and was occupied by the Bolsheviks, Mexicans, and Turks, and as they could see it was in very bad shape and quite unsafe for travelers, and it seemed to end in a Morass of Disaster. The right road was the old military road used by the Monarchists and Militarists. But the Central Road was a fine, broad highway, on which the United States was serenely traveling peacefully to and fro, in pleasant competition with Great Britain— where one could see the unusual and charming sight of King George walking arm in arm with that much feared Macdonald who in reality was as peaceful and law-abiding as Lloyd George or any other former Prime Minister. Between the Center and the Right Road I had observed a most peculiar condition. One could see where the French and Belgians had left the Center Road, in order to follow the Germans who were struggling ahead in the quasi-Jungle that existed between the Roads; and that the French and Belgians, in their mad pursuit, had gone so far from the Main Road, that a new Jungle was rapidly growing up behind them, so that soon it would be difficult for them to retrace their steps, and again use the Central Road. I summed up by saying that I was not attempting to advise them: I was simply stating what I visioned to myself while I was in my imaginary Post of Observation, and that, sensible people as they were, they could now readily choose which road to take.

155

My speech was like a bombshell. The excited discussions that followed it were about as acrimonious as that of the bewildered Greeks who had stood at the parting of those roads when I came to address them in my parable.

The French correspondent immediately chided me for my severe criticism of his people, and a few days afterward I received a long letter from the French Minister, in which he explained to me that his country had relatively no more military forces than the United States or Great Britain.

Venizelos approved it greatly. Some of the Republicans objected to my stating that King George had been walking with Macdonald on the Boulevard of Democracy, as they promptly named the Central Road.

The Mayor thought it was a very courageous speech and would help their decision in favor of a republic.

CHAPTER X

Bright Promise for the Future

WHEN I returned to Athens, on March 18th, I called at once upon the new Premier, Mr. Papanastasiou. I told him of the encouragement I had received for my effort to raise an additional loan for refugee work, and pointed out that the only thing that stood in the way of getting it was the necessary assurances of stable government in Greece, and that this was his responsibility now. In reply he said the majority of the country would speedily be satisfied by the declaration of the republic, which would soon take place. The remaining minority, the Royalists, he hoped to pacify by "buying them out." He proposed to offer the royal family a handsome sum for their estates and the King a generous annuity for life in exchange for his crown.

The new Premier spoke with such moderation, tact, and good sense that I left greatly encouraged at the prospect for the future. Anything that I could do to help along this favorable tide of events was clearly my duty to do. The following morning, therefore, I wrote out a statement for the press, expressing my gratification, as chairman of the Refugee Settlement Commission, that the political situation had now reached a point where it promised to be effectually helpful to our work, and urging all the elements of the public to contribute to its stability by coöperating to make the new régime a success. In my first draft of this statement I included my approval of the plan to buy out the monarchy, but at the urgent request of my two Greek associates on the Commission I omitted this from the copy finally given to the papers. The statement as published was as follows:

Statement—March 19th

The authorities of the Bank of England desired a personal interview with me in order to discuss exhaustively the relations between the Bank of England and the Refugee Settlement Commission, not only for the temporary advances but also in reference to the larger permanent loan.

After a complete exchange of views and study of the facts, it was agreed that, as the present funds of the Commission would only last until about the middle of June, and as it would be impossible to complete before then the detailed arrangements for a permanent loan, a further temporary advance of one million pounds sterling would have to be made to enable the Commission to prolong its activities for the balance of the year. It might be unwise to prolong these activities unless there were definite prospects of floating a permanent loan. Before this could be done it would be absolutely necessary for Greece to demonstrate that it would maintain a stable government. The chief prerequisite for the success of a permanent loan was the improvement of Greece's credit in foreign countries, which would be demonstrated by the rise in the price of their existing bonds.

It was not considered impossible to accomplish this, as Greece has not since 1897 defaulted in the payments of her interest charges or amortization payments of her loans.

The financial authorities in Great Britain would deeply regret any compulsory suspension of the settlement of the refugees. Their attitude is that they earnestly wish to assist in pacifying the world, and they showed great appreciation of the fine efforts so far made by Greece to solve her terrible problem, and to maintain peace with her neighbors. At Geneva the Council of the League of Nations were equally sympathetic and responsive to the appeal made on behalf of Greece, and readily promised their moral support. Everybody consulted about the matter is unanimous that the condition precedent to securing permanent help is a stable government, on the ground that Greece's economic success depends entirely upon her ability to devote herself to the readjustment of her internal affairs and to the new conditions that this vast immigration has created.

It is safe to assert that none of them wish to interfere in the internal affairs of Greece by prescribing how and through whom this stability should be established. They want stability.

On the following morning the former Premier, Mr. Cafandaris, called to see me. He explained what his attitude would be in his new position as leader of the Opposition: objection to the removal of the dynasty prior to a plebiscite, on the ground of the unconstitutionality of this procedure, and objection to the intervention of the militarists in the civil government of the country. He expressed his surprise that my newspaper statement had made no reference to the plebiscite. I agreed with him that this was an omission that should be corrected, so on the following day I made a supplementary statement as follows:

Statement—March 20th

My attention having been called to the fact that I did not mention the plebiscite in my statement of yesterday, I wish to state that it appeared so evident to me that everyone now thoroughly understood that a plebiscite was required and would take place that it was unnecessary for me to allude to the same.

I desire to use this opportunity to add to my statement that the success of the permanent loan will undoubtedly be affected by various influences such as, the Bank of England, the representatives of the League of Nations and the members of the Refugee Settlement Commission, but in the final analysis its success is entirely dependent upon the willingness of the investing public of the world, including Greece, to put their money into Greek securities, and their decision to do so will depend upon the economic and governmental conditions of Greece.

This investing public are not influenced by eloquent appeals or a touching and sympathy-awakening account of the necessities of the refugees, but they want logical and conclusive evidence that Greece can and will pay her debts.

Financial institutions will not obligate themselves to float the loan unless, in their judgment, the investing public will readily absorb it.

During this period, furthermore, I had several talks with General Othoneos, who had come again from Salonica to Athens to advise with Gondiles, now a member of the Cabinet. I had formed the highest opinion of General Othoneos's character, but I wished to impress upon him, now that he had direct influence in the government, that Great Britain was unalterably opposed to any further military adventures upon the part of Greece, and her determination, in case any further funds were appropriated by the Greeks for the extension of their military establishment, not to lend any money for the benefit of the refugees.

There was an especial reason for conveying this fact

to General Othoneos. When I had gone to Greece, a few
months earlier, I had stopped off at Salonica for two
days, and while I was there the General had called upon
me. He had broached the subject of an enlarged army
at that time, and his hope that the British would lend
Greece five or ten million dollars for equipment.
The reasons he gave would affect the sympathies of any
disinterested listener—the isolation of Greece since her
abandonment by the British in the Corfu incident, the
danger from Serbia, which was heavily armed, and the
menace of hostile Bulgaria. Appealing as these reasons
were, however, I deemed it wrong to encourage false
hopes; and now that I had returned, and had talked with
responsible Englishmen in London as well as at Geneva,
I could with still greater positiveness assure the General that there was not the slightest chance of money
from Europe for further military preparations. Europe
was heartily sick of war. No European government,
even if it wished, could hope to persuade its people to
engage in further military enterprises, and no government would permit national funds to go abroad into
the arming of any smaller nation that might thereby
be encouraged to open hostilities again. The Great
War had started in the Balkans, and Europe was not
going to supply fresh fuel for a new conflagration there.

The General took what I said in good part. Indeed,
he seemed grateful for my counsel, and on one occasion
told me he had written down what I had said and
would govern himself by it, especially the thought that
"the army could exercise a great influence for peace and
stability." He proved himself the thorough patriot.

Both Plastiras and Gondiles had been under his command and had received their commissions from him. He had much influence, not only with the army but with the country generally, which respected his fine, upright, frank, and patriotic character.

Thus through every channel I sought to enlist the coöperation of all to bring about that stability which was the condition precedent to any large advance of foreign money for the rehabilitation of the refugees. But I must say that I often grew discouraged. With one fifth of their population in misery, and facing destruction, even the sincerest patriots among the Greeks seemed unable to agree upon a policy that would satisfy a consistent majority, and the swarm of lesser politicians seemed blind to everything but the selfish scramble for place and power.

On March 23, 1924, I wrote the following letter to Mr. Papanastasiou:

MY DEAR MR. PRESIDENT:

As you have told me that you intend to appoint a commission to act in a consulting capacity to the ministries in charge of the finances and economics of your country, I take the liberty of suggesting that you announce this intention to-morrow.

Let the world know that the republic is to be a real one, that you intend to avail yourself of all the most enlightened and experienced industrials and financiers that are ready to coöperate with you: that a divided country cannot master the great task now confronting Greece—of restoring her to her former prosperity: that a number of cabinets have tried and failed, that you desire to stop this rotation of oligarchies and establish not a government by the Left but a real republic, constituted by all the people. State that you will welcome volunteers and suggestions as to who should constitute the advisory board. There would be much more gained for the country if all unite in a determined effort to help her than if each set of men seek the satisfaction of making an unsuccessful effort to govern her for a while. I am constantly thinking of the fate of that million refugees whose future depends entirely on the stability of Greece's government and it is with them in mind that I take the liberty of writing you so freely and intimately.

Yours most sincerely,
HENRY MORGENTHAU.

In spite of so many reasons for pessimism, however, the declaration of the republic afforded a day of bright promise for the future of Greece. That historic event at last placed the destinies of the nation unreservedly in the hands of the people. Intriguing monarchs would no longer complicate the already too-complicated politics of the country.

The greatly beloved George I had wisely limited himself to his functions as impartial head of the state, and consequently he had been a constant force for healing the internecine quarrels of the politicians and preserving the essential unity of the people. But his son, Constantine, had descended from this lofty position to become the active leader of a political party (the Royalist Party), in opposition to the greatest statesman that Greece has produced in modern times—for whatever the tactical errors of which Mr. Venizelos has sometimes been guilty, his title to that eminent place in history is secure. This fatal precedent of Constantine's was inherited, whether he wished it or not, by George II, since the Royalist Party founded by his father continued to operate in the young King's name, for purely political purposes. The Greeks did well, therefore, to remove this whole subject of royalism from their national life.

The republic was declared on March 25, 1924. That day was made memorable in Athens by ceremonials and festivities. Because of my natural sympathy for republican institutions and my known help in facilitating the decision to abolish the monarchy, I was generously treated as a principal in the drama of instituting the new régime. Admiral Hadjikyriakos, the Minister of Marine in Papanastasiou's Cabinet, called for me in the morning, and I accompanied him in his automobile to the church where the religious rites were held that preceded the civil ceremonies in Parliament. Great crowds lined the streets and gathered about the church entrance, and as our automobiles made their way between the rows of people they were showered with flowers and applause. Inside the church the foreign diplomats were present, and their uniforms, added to those of the military, made the scene lively with color. The Regent here made his last appearance as such—a few hours later he was honored with the title of President of the Greek Republic, which he still holds.

The religious rites concluded, we all repaired to the National Assembly. Here the earlier scene was duplicated, with the addition of an excitement and gayety that had naturally been missing from the solemn exercises in the church. The "courtesy of the floor" had

164

been habitually granted to me by Parliament ever since my first arrival in Greece, and on this historic occasion my "regular" seat was again reserved for me beside the official stenographer, where I could hear and see and be a part of the whole proceedings. The atmosphere was joyous and informal. The Royalists had absented themselves from the Chamber, so that there was no resentful or discordant note. The vote was taken by roll-call upon the motion to declare Greece a republic. The enthusiasm of the members at times took an amusing form. When one member's name was called he was not content to vote a simple "yes," but in thunderous tones shouted, "A thousand times yes!" The next member to vote, not to be outdone, in even louder voice voted, "A *million* times yes!"

The motion was carried by a vote of 284 to 0. It provided for the deposition of the Glucksburg dynasty, for the return without compensation of royal property presented by the state, for the compulsory alienation of the dynasty's property, and for the retention of the regency until after the plebiscite, which would be held later to ratify the provision of the motion that Greece should henceforth be a parliamentary republic.

Immediately after the unanimous vote was announced by the speaker six white pigeons were set free in the chamber, as a symbol of the new freedom and soaring aspirations of the country. They made a beautiful spectacle as they fluttered overhead in the historic hall. One by one they were captured by members, to be preserved as souvenirs of the great occasion. One was handed to the Premier, Mr. Papanastasiou, and with characteristic generosity he sent it to my seat with the message that "This is for the Father of the Republic." A card was attached to the bird's neck by a cord and this I sent back to him with the request that he give me "the first autograph of the Premier of the New Republic." I treasure the inscription he put upon it: "To the Father of the Greek Republic!" Far too sweeping to be accurate, nevertheless it conveyed a thought I do have a right to treasure, that I had earned the affectionate friendship of the Greeks by a sincere effort to be useful to them.

That affection was mutual. I had learned to be immensely fond of these people, so warmly human and endowed with so many other admirable traits. And as a citizen of a great republic, and as a convinced believer in the justice and power of democratic institutions, I could not fail to be gratified to see these ideals extended to another country. I could only wish them well and hope that they might get this new engine of progress working effectively in time to help in the solution of the life-and-death problem of their country, which was the problem of the refugees.

A few days later I proceeded to Missolonghi, in company with a distinguished group of Greek and British dignitaries, to participate in the ceremonies commemorating the centennial of Lord Byron's death in that village.

Lord Byron is one of the national heroes of Greece. The Greeks are intensely grateful to all foreigners who have been especially fond of them or who have gone out of their way to be useful to them. They have never forgotten Lord Byron's magnificent gesture of sympathy. Every Greek school child knows every detail of the famous Missolonghi episode, when Byron came to Greece to espouse the cause of liberty, and of his death on Greek soil after the Missolonghi Sortie. This romantic ending of Byron's romantic life appeals as vividly to the Greek imagination as it does to ours. And it is powerfully enhanced in the Greek mind by its sentimental connection with the darkest days of their struggle for liberty.

The centenary of Byron's death fell in the sixth month after my arrival in Greece. The Greeks made a national festival of the celebration of this event. At their invitation a distinguished delegation of Britishers came from England to represent Byron's native land in this celebration. Besides Miss Lytton, a direct descendent of Byron, and a Miss Byron, this group comprised Sir Rennell Rodd, Lord Ernle, Lord Burnham, the poet John Drinkwater, and the famous journalist Harold Spender.

The celebration covered a period of five days, April 16th to 20th. Professor Andreades, of the University of Athens, who was in charge of the arrangements of the celebration, had asked whether the Refugee Settlement Commission would be willing to create a "Byron Quarter" in the Pangrati Settlement. I heartily assented, and in order to dramatize the event we had hurried the preparations of the foundation of the Infants Day Nursery, which Mrs. Morgenthau and I had agreed to erect in Pangrati to house the poor children during the daytime whilst their husbandless mothers were working in factories or doing day work in Athens to support their families. We managed to get the foundation finished in time so that, on the first day of the Byron celebration Byron's Quarter was opened with exercises of laying the cornerstone of this Infants Day Nursery. Great was our astonishment when, at the laying of the cornerstone, the acting President of the Republic, Admiral Condouriotes, decorated me with the highest order in the gift of the Greek nation, that of Commander of the Holy Savior (Megalostovros), and also decorated Mrs. Morgenthau with the gold cross of the same order.

In laying the cornerstone President Condouriotes, Premier Papanastasiou, General Gondiles, and Mr. Charilaos laid on the mortar. On behalf of the refugees, the Bishop of Ephesus expressed their gratefulness as follows:

"We are infinitely thankful to you, not only for the material assistance we have been given, but also that you, the great philanthropist, have taught us by your virtue, generosity, and love where the nation's true grandeur and glory must lie. Glory, honor, and peace be to you!"

The Minister of Agriculture, Mr. Bakalbassi, delivered the formal address. The children of the neighboring settlement of Syngros added a pleasing touch to the ceremony with their songs.

At six-thirty o'clock that evening the city authorities of Athens gave a reception at the city hall in honor of the British delegation. Mayor Patsis paid me a very graceful compliment on this occasion. Recalling to the Assembly that I was an Honorary Citizen of Athens, he insisted that before he began his address of welcome I should take my place at his right side, a distinction and honor that gave me great pleasure.

At eight-thirty Premier Papanastasiou gave an official dinner in honor of the British guests. And at ten-thirty we all made our way to the Acropolis to hold exercises in front of the Parthenon by moonlight. We found we had been preceded by not less than a hundred thousand Athenian citizens, who so crowded the summit of the Acropolis and its approaches that it seemed for a time that we would not be able to make our way through the throng to the steps of the Parthenon, where the exercises were to take place. Fortunately, we were noticed by some friends who saw our predicament and told some of the near-by officers who we were. The information acted like magic. For when it was announced that Kyrios [Honorable] Morgenthau was trying to reach the entrance the crowd obligingly made an open lane through which we were safely piloted to the scene of action.

We arrived in front of the Acropolis in time to see fifty Athenian ladies, dressed in pure white, sing Byron's "Maid of Athens." To hear their lovely voices, accompanied by a fine band of musicians, wafting over this massed throng of newly made republicans, under the splendor of the full moon, was a thrilling experience. The singing was followed by a recitation of one of Byron's poems, and a short address by Papanastasiou.

The Athenians were elated by these exercises. Every

aspect of the occasion helped to make it impressive—the beautiful Parthenon, the brilliant moonlight, the view of Athens and its lights spread all around, below the peaks of Hymettus and Pentelicus. Near by the Bay of Salamis, with its silvered waters in the distance, gave a most impressive setting to the ardor of the enthusiastic, appreciative throng, the fine music and singing and, above all, the new Spirit of Freedom.

Poor Byron never could have dreamed that the centenary of his death would have such a celebration. He, who in one of his cynical moods had declared that the world was divided into bores and the bored, certainly could not have applied the witticism to this day, for there had been neither bores nor bored.

On the following day we assembled for a convocation at the university, and we listened to speeches by Professor Andreades and Lord Burnham, and the recitation by John Drinkwater of an original ode written for the occasion. Then the honor of Doctor of Laws was conferred upon them and their associates, Sir Rennell Rodd, Lord Ernle, and Harold Spender. The faculty of the university had also voted to give me the degree but the confirmation of it was wisely deferred until a later date, when Dr. Fridtjof Nansen and Cardinal Dubois, who were likewise to be honored, could also be present. It was more appropriate that none but Britishers should be honored on that occasion.

At five-thirty in the evening exercises were held near the Choragic Monument of Lysicrates, on the site of the former Capuchin monastery where Byron resided during his visit to Athens. This ceremony was the unveiling of a *stele* (monument tablet) by the city of Athens in memory of Byron. Speeches were delivered by Mayor Patsis and Mr. Shirley Atchley, the delegate of the Byron Society.

From this point we proceeded to Zappeion Park for the purpose of crowning the statue of Lord Byron, which had long stood there. Further speeches were delivered by the Minister of Education and the second British delegate, Lord Ernle. This day of the celebration was rounded up by an unusual gala performance at the National Theater, to which everybody of importance in Athens had been invited to listen to the popular concert orchestra and a charming chorus of the Greek Ladies' Lyceum Club, all dressed in ancient Grecian costumes.

On the following day about one hundred and thirty leading Greeks and their guests, including the leaders of all the political parties, even including the Monarchists, foreign diplomatic corps, the British delegation, and my colleague, John Campbell, and myself, took a special train for Corinth on our way to Missolonghi. At Corinth we embarked on the steamer *Hiera* to cross the gulf of Corinth. As we sailed into the port of Kryoneri that evening, we were saluted by British and Greek naval squadrons. We spent the night on board and at nine o'clock landed at Kryoneri and took the train for Missolonghi. Upon our arrival there we heard an address of welcome by the Mayor and then marched through decorated and festooned streets under arches of flowers to the Heroön, where we witnessed the crowning of the Byron Monument. Miss Lytton (who as I have explained is a direct descendant of Lord Byron) stood at the side of the monument, and her resemblance to her distinguished ancestor, in face, figure, and pose, was really striking.

The most impressive event of the entire celebration occurred in the evening at six o'clock, when we all met at the spot where Byron had died at that same hour of the same day one hundred years before, on April 19, 1824. We stood with bared heads and listened to an address by the rector of the university, Dr. Papulios. It was an impressive, even sacred occasion. Priests of the Greek Orthodox Church had accompanied us, garbed in their rich costumes. After this ceremony we all returned to the church and attended a religious service that is given every year in commemoration of the Sortie of Missolonghi, including memorial services for those who fell there on that occasion with Lord Byron.

After the memorial services we all sat down to a great supper given by the authorities of Missolonghi.

In the evening we attended a splendid exhibition of Greek dancers in the town square. All the dancers wore their native garb. Later in the evening we went back by train to Kryoneri and boarded the *Hiera* again. Instead of returning directly to Corinth, we steamed to Patras, where we landed on Sunday morning. We attended Easter service at the English church, and thought to ourselves that just such services in English churches were being held all over the world. We then attended a luncheon given by the Mayor of Patras, at which two hundred and fifty guests were seated in the dining room of the Hôtel d'Angleterre. Immediately

One of the Streets in the Refugee Settlement of Pangrati, near Athens

after a special train took us away toward Corinth. We arrived there in time for tea. In that fine, old, but somewhat ruined city they had set tables outdoors at the railroad station for our entire party of one hundred and thirty, and served us an elaborate repast. We then proceeded toward Athens.

On our way the train was stopped a number of times to give our Republican political leaders, Papanastasiou, Gondiles, and Hadjikyriakos, a chance to address their constituents. At one of the stations we found waiting for us a group of Greeks, all carrying small American flags and calling my name. Papanastasiou insisted that I should make them a speech in Greek. I did so by using two of the half-dozen Greek words I knew. Waving my hand to the crowd, I shouted, "*Cito democratia.*" The brevity of my speech, and its meaning ("Long live the Republic"), evoked much applause.

We arrived back at Athens in good season, and all the guests, the British as much so as ourselves, were most enthusiastic in their praise, not only of the remarkable variety and interest of the programs we had enjoyed but also of the extraordinary perfection of the arrangements by which the whole series of events, covering five days and many cities, had been run off without the slightest mishap. I have often thought that the efficiency of this celebration was significant of the essential soundness of the Greek nation. It should be recalled that these arrangements were made during the most strenuous hours of a change in the very structure of Greek Government—the republic was proclaimed only three days before the Byron celebration.

But by the simple device of turning the responsibility for these exercises over to the educational authorities of the University of Athens, the whole program was efficiently arranged, and it would have made no difference in the execution of these plans whether Republicans or Monarchists had won. In like manner, most of the essential undertakings of life in Greece pursue the even tenor of their way, regardless of the surface agitations of politics.

CHAPTER XI
Negotiations With the Bank of England

SIMULTANEOUSLY with the political developments narrated in preceding chapters, there ran my negotiations with the Bank of England. As the chairman of the Refugee Settlement Commission, my interest in Greek politics was based primarily upon the necessity of political stability as a condition precedent to getting funds from foreign investors for our refugee work. The formula we had constantly to keep in mind was: "No political stability, no money." As we have just seen, the struggle for a republic in Greece was successful, and as its success gradually emerged out of the political chaos, our prospects brightened for obtaining the necessary funds.

The Bank of England is a very human institution. The affectionate name applied to it by the English people, of "The Old Lady of Threadneedle Street," expresses their feeling that it has a human personality. The very life of the nation throbs inside its somber portals, for here is centered the official direction of the national finances, managed for the nation's safety and progress. Finance has its purely technical and mechanical aspects, reflected in popular phrases like "cold cash"; but great financiers must have great human qualities as well. No man can succeed greatly in the

175

direction of money (which is merely the instrument
of human hopes and desires and aspirations) unless he
is very human himself, keenly sensitive in his own
nature to these same human qualities.

Montagu Norman, the governor of the Bank of
England, is just such a human person as one would
imagine from the foregoing. He has the traditional
qualities of the banker—the shrewdness, the solidity,
and the caution of the custodian of cash. But he has
also the wide vision of the statesman. He can look beyond the immediate penny profit to the eventual
pounds of permanent advantage. It was a pleasure
to match wits with him, and a profound satisfaction
to me that I was able finally to convince him that
large loans for the Greek refugees were not only a
laudably humane adventure for the relief of distress
but also a sound investment of British funds. To his
credit be it said that no effort was required to stir his
sympathies. The difficulty was to satisfy his judgment
as a banker.

My first interview with Norman on this subject
took place on October 30, 1923. I had arrived in London the day before, on my way from New York to
Athens to enter on my duties with the Refugee Settlement Commission. After paying my respects at the
American Embassy, meeting Colonel Campbell, my
British colleague on the Commission, and calling on
Mr. Caclamanos, the Greek Minister to London, I
was ready for my first meeting with the leader of
British finance. It was significant of the close relationship that exists between the Bank of England and

the British Government that my appointment to meet the governor of the bank was at the office of Sir Otto Niemeyer, at the British Treasury. There, late in the afternoon, I met Norman, who personified the bank, and Niemeyer, who, as the Comptroller of Finance of Great Britain, personified the fiscal authority of the government.

A striking contrast was presented by these two men. Norman was a typical man of action, tall, broad-shouldered, muscular. His manner was lively, alert, quick, and energetic. His pointed beard is unusual among modern Britishers, but not so the determined jaw or the shrewd, intelligent, penetrating eyes that fixed on yours as you talked to him and seemed to be boring into your inner thoughts in appraisement of your intelligence and candor. The physical energy of his gestures and movements bespoke the mental energy within. Here was a mind eager for knowledge, to be used by a spirit eager for action. Decisive but courteous, an attentive listener, positive in speech when his time came to speak, Norman was a thoroughly likeable, wholesome, fine type of British business builder. He soon showed that he had a statesmanlike outlook upon affairs, and plenty of courage, along with the proper caution of the banker.

Niemeyer was of a very different type. A short, well built man, he looked more the sedentary thinker, whose habit of weighing evidence impartially was reflected in the deliberate manner in which his carefully considered sentences were spoken. He had none of Norman's bubbling energy, but rather was quiet and unobtrusive. Nevertheless, he soon revealed the qualities that had given him his important governmental post. He had the facts and figures of international finance at his finger's ends and was evidently a master of their intricate interrelations. He had, too, what so few Americans in government have, a profound knowledge of other lands. Just as our bank presidents know the relative credit standing of all the corporations in their community, their prospects, and their management, just so did Niemeyer (and Norman too, for that matter) know the resources of every country in Europe, their products, their commerce, and their politicians, with their interrelations and prospects. It was astonishing to see with what familiarity these leaders of British finance spoke of the details of internal politics in Greece, a small nation fifteen hundred miles away on the other side of Europe.

Thus I was dealing with men who, at that moment, knew more about Greece and her problem than I did. A few months later I was to have the pleasure of turning the tables on them in this respect, in a much more dramatic interview in Norman's office; but I shall leave that episode for its proper place later in this narrative. On this present visit I found them informed and interested, sympathetic but skeptical. They wanted to help Greece, but they wanted first to have proof that Greece intended to help herself. They pointed out that a provisional, military government was all that now held that country together, and that nobody knew what might happen when this government gave up the reins of power. Would Greece fall then into anarchy? If so, she was a poor credit risk for foreign investors. Or was there enough patriotism among her politicians to enable them to sink their differences for the sake of uniting to solve the refugee problem? If so, were there brains enough in Greece to grasp and overcome the gigantic economic difficulties that confronted them?

These, naturally, were questions I could not yet answer. All I could do was to assure them that I was undertaking my part of the task in a spirit of confident hope, and that I would bend every energy to make it a success. I declined to believe that this task was beyond the power of human will to accomplish. And from what I had come to know of the Greeks, through contact with the large colony of Greek merchants and bankers who lived in Constantinople when I was Ambassador there, I had every reason to believe that the race comprised plenty of eager, intelligent, energetic men who, if they could be united upon a consistent plan for the salvation of their country, could be depended upon to carry it through. As to the political situation, I would do everything I could, as chairman of the Refugee Settlement Commission, to influence the Greeks to secure as rapidly as possible a stable government and assure its stability for the sake of the refugees. Here, too, I was hopeful of success. The Bank of England could help immensely—indeed, at the moment its help was indispensable—by a generous attitude in the matter of extending credit.

There was a profound reason why it was essential that I should give Norman and Niemeyer a favorable impression of my energy and resourcefulness at this moment. When the League of Nations had instituted the Refugee Settlement Commission, two months earlier, it did so chiefly at the instance of Sir Arthur Salter, now generally recognized as the financial wizard of the League. He had previsioned the political power for good in Greece of an independent international agency for permanently rehabilitating the refugees under the patronage of the League of Nations. To get such an agency on its feet, the Bank of England had agreed to advance three fourths of a credit of one million pounds sterling for this purpose, the other fourth to be supplied by the Bank of Greece. The security of the bank was a Protocol deposited with the League by the government of Greece.

This Protocol solemnly pledged Greece to recognize the Refugee Settlement Commission as an autonomous body, not dependent upon any Greek executive or administrative authority; and to give to it all the rights and powers of a corporation. This corporation was to receive from the Bank of Greece all proceeds of a proposed loan, from three to six million pounds, to be issued by the Greek Government for the work of refugee settlement. The Greek Government agreed to assign to this corporation 500,000 hectares (approximately 1,250,000 acres) of lands suitable for agriculture, to be its absolute property for use in settling refugees upon it, the refugees to buy the land upon long-term payments, and these payments to be applied to extinguishing the loan. The loan was to be used wholly for productive purposes, such as the building of houses, purchase of farming implements, equipment of factories, and the like. The first security for this loan was obviously mortgages upon this land and these buildings, implements, tools, etc. Additional security comprised all buildings, etc., provided by the Refugee Treasury Fund prior to the creation of the Commission. Still further security was offered by the pledge of the Greek Government to apply to the repayment of the loan all revenues derived from the duty on alcohol in the whole of Greece, besides the tobacco duty, the stamp duty, and the monopolies of salt, matches, playing cards, and cigarette paper in New Greece—that is, Macedonia and Thrace.

The "million-pound advance" promised by the Banks of England and Greece, which I mentioned in the preceding paragraph, was money that the banks agreed to let the Commission have at once, without waiting for the floating of the loan. The sale of bonds takes a long time, whereas the Commission needed cash at once, to prevent starvation in Greece. The banks, therefore, had agreed to advance one million pounds, taking some unsold existing Greek bonds as security. Later, if a market could be found for the bonds, the Greek Government would sell them and pay back the bank's advance.

There were any number of good reasons why two "statesmen of finance," like Norman and Niemeyer, should be willing to make such an advance. British prestige in the League of Nations was very high. Lord Robert Cecil was then its outstanding official, and Sir Arthur Salter, with his financial genius, had played the leading part in arranging for the fiscal rehabilitation of Hungary and Austria. Now that he had planned a similar achievement in Greece, it was good political policy that his native country should provide financial backing to make his plan a success.

Norman and Niemeyer were fully alive to this opportunity to enhance British prestige. But they were equally alive to the possibilities that lay the other way, and in their conversation showed that they had some mental reservations as to whether the advance would be made. Suppose the plan did not succeed? Suppose Greece plunged into political chaos? Not only would there be no prestige gained, but the Bank of England's money might be lost. And things certainly looked shaky in Greece. Or suppose the Refugee Settlement Commission was not handled with sufficient ability to solve the staggering economic problem presented by the million and a quarter penniless refugees? The security in the Bank of England's vaults would then be a poor substitute for the gold that had left them.

These considerations explain why I said above that there was a profound reason why I was bound to give Norman and Niemeyer a favorable impression of my energy and resourcefulness at my first interview with them. If they sized me up as unequal to the task they could very well find reasons, even yet, for refusing to deliver the money promised as an advance. Mortgages upon undeveloped real estate in Macedonia would be cold comfort to a banker in London if the developer looked too small for his job.

For these reasons I wanted to make Norman and

Niemeyer feel that I was confident of success. My career in finance and diplomacy gave them some assurance of my qualifications, but they had to feel besides that I was heart and soul in the undertaking, and that I realized its difficulties from their point of view. I must hereafter deal with them chiefly by letter and cable from distant Athens, hence they must know the kind of man they were dealing with, and form a personal estimate of his judgment. Their hearty good wishes when we parted, and the course of our subsequent negotiations, gave me satisfying evidence that I had succeeded in creating confidence in their minds.

Hardly had I set foot in Athens before these negotiations began. One of the provisions of the Protocol signed by the Greek Government reads as follows: "The Greek Government undertakes not to create any charge on its revenues by way of security for any loans not intended for productive purposes." On November 15, 1923, Norman wrote a letter to A. N. Diomede, the president of the Bank of Greece, expressing his surprise at having heard a rumor in London that the Greek Government was considering proposals to incur heavy expenditures for naval armaments, the financing of which might be provided by means of external credits. Norman reminded Diomede that such credits would be a violation of the conditions governing the advance of a million pounds, and advised him that the position of that advance would be imperiled if the rumor proved to be correct. He suggested that Diomede consult with me about it.

When Diomede received this letter he at once

showed it to me. Two days later I received a letter from Norman on the same subject, urging me to use my influence with the Greek Government to dissuade them from any increase in armaments. I knew, from my conversation with Norman in London, that the British were strongly opposed to anybody giving any encouragement to any nation to spend money on military preparations. The world had only lately come through the Great War, with its frightful destruction of economic values, and Europe generally had no desire to have any money spent anywhere on anything except enterprises looking toward economic recovery. The Balkans had set off the explosion of the World War, and the Bank of England had no intention of encouraging any Balkan nation to start preparations that might cause another explosion.

Diomede and I at once set an investigation afoot, and while we were never able to find out exactly *who* started the rumor, it soon developed *why* it started. Before the World War began Greece had contracted in France for the construction of a type-*Lorraine* dreadnaught, and had also contracted in Germany for a cruiser, to be called the *Salamis*. The outbreak of the war had prevented the delivery of either ship to Greece. The *Salamis* had been completed by the Germans during the war, used in their navy, and scrapped under the peace treaty. The dreadnaught was never completed by the French. But after the war both Germany and France demanded payment from Greece for the work they had done on these ships before the war started. The Greeks resented and had rejected the claim.

Probably agents of the shipyards had retaliated by starting the rumor that Norman had heard in London. I wrote Norman the following letter:

Refugee Settlement Commission
Athens, 27th, November, 1923.

MY DEAR MR. NORMAN:

Immediately on the receipt of your letter of the 17th. inst. we discussed the matter with Mr. Diomede, who fortunately, as a former Minister of Finance, was thoroughly familiar with the details of the arrangements for the construction of the dreadnought (type-*Lorraine*) in France, and of the cruiser *Salamis* in Germany. He made it clear at once that there was no question of undertaking new liabilities as it was solely a case of liquidating such liabilities as might have been incurred by Greece in respect of these vessels prior to the outbreak of the war of 1914. He assured us that, so far as he knew, Greece was most anxious to avoid making any payments in respect of either of these ships, which were laid down in 1912 and 1913. Her contention was that the contracts had been annulled by circumstances; the vessels partially constructed before the war broke out had since then been left untouched both in France and Germany, they were now of an obsolete type, and Greece was doing everything possible to secure the acceptance of her contention that she had no longer any liability in respect of them. Representatives of the Forges and Chantiers Company, and of the Vulcan Company, had recently been in Greece, and had attempted to force the government of Greece either to pay the sums still due in respect of work already done on the vessels, or to authorize them to complete the ships at the cost of the Greek Government. The Greek Government maintained its position that no liability of any kind attached to it, and would give no order to complete the construction. Mr. Diomede is convinced that the rumors you have heard are due to statements made by these disappointed representatives. He also assured us positively that there are no negotiations of any kind now pending for a new foreign loan.

Mr. Diomede added that the representative of the French company had suggested that the government of Greece should make over, to that company, the Greek claim against the French Government for the three hundred million drachmas arising out of the war arrangements made between France and Greece; in that event the company would then complete the construction of the dreadnought, would deliver it to the Greek Government, and would look to the transferred Greek claim against the French Government for the satisfaction of the cost. The National Bank, for its party, absolutely declined to consider this suggestion.

As we wanted a definite assurance from the government of Greece that no foreign loan was under consideration, we wrote a letter to the Minister of Finance. I enclose a translation of this, and of the reply which I have just received. In order to expedite the matter, to impress Mr. Cofinas (the Minister of Finance) and the Cabinet with the importance which the Commission attached to the question, and also with the object of explaining to him our own views, all four members of the Commission delivered this letter to him personally. During the interview I told him that, as various members of the Cabinet had assured us that they rely on our success in dealing with the refugee problem for the cure of the economic evils from which Greece was now suffering, I wished to reiterate that our success in that matter depended absolutely on the successful launching of a loan for six million pounds; and that, in its turn, depended entirely on the stability of the Greek Government, and on its financial policy and general conduct of affairs during the period whilst a test would be made with the one million pounds which the Bank of England is now providing. He positively assured us that the plan of the government was to remain at peace, and to do nothing that could in any way conflict with the success of our undertaking. In reply to a question from Mr. Campbell, he gave as a definite statement that no foreign loan was in contemplation and he explained that such charges as were essential for the reasonable upkeep of the navy materiel, were provided from the current budget. On the morning of the 26th, Messrs. Campbell, Delta and myself called on Colonel Plastiras, and the general situation was discussed. He too assured us of the government's sincere intention to preserve internal and external peace, and to prevent any untoward occurrence that might hamper the settlement of the refugee problem.

The Greek Government clearly relies on our Commission to relieve them of their urgent preoccupation, which is the pressing necessity for settling the refugees upon a productive basis. They realize the desperate condition of these people, and the effect which their presence has upon the finances and economic life of Greece.

Conversations of the frankest kind with my Greek colleagues convince me that there is a general, effective desire among the population of Greece to secure a period of rest and recuperation, to give all possible aid to the Commission in its work, and to support a government which will render it practicable to attain these ends. Messrs. Delta and Argyropoulos think that the desire for peace, and for a solution of the refugee problem, is so strong that the policy of the present government in this respect will undoubtedly be continued by any government which the December elections may place in power.

I should be glad if you would allow Lord Robert Cecil, and Mr. Niemeyer, to see this letter, or perhaps you would be good enough to send them a copy of it.

I was satisfied that the explanation as given above was correct, but to satisfy Norman, and also to impress his views on the Greek Government, all four commissioners called in a body upon the Minister of Finance,

Mr. Cofinas, and delivered Norman's letter to him. We asked for an official statement of the government's position. Mr. Cofinas positively assured us that the Greek Government had every intention of remaining at peace. He explained that no expenditures upon the navy were contemplated beyond routine repairs and upkeep, and that these were provided for by funds in the normal current budget. Mr. Cofinas telegraphed the Greek Legation to convey these facts officially to Mr. Norman. I cabled them likewise. The next day Norman cabled me that the bank was ready to advance £650,000 against bonds already delivered to it. Shortly afterward the rest of the bonds to secure the advance were delivered to the Bank of England, which in turn delivered the rest of the advance to the Bank of Greece, deposited there to the account of the Refugee Settlement Commission.

This incident had hardly been cleared up before another negotiation with the Bank of England had to be started. The Greek Government had promised to cede to the Refugee Settlement Commission absolute title to one and a quarter million acres of land upon which rural refugees could be settled. This promise was contained in the Protocol. The wording of the Protocol was intended to mean (and all parties to it understood this) that these lands would be assigned to the Commission "free of all encumbrances." Very quickly, however, it became clear that the Greek Government would be unable immediately to produce a clear title to so much land. Yet these lands were to form a large part of the security for the loan. And the

loan, in turn, was necessary to make the lands valuable, by putting settlers productively at work upon
them.

Here was a vicious circle that seemed likely to wreck
our rural program before it started. The reason the
Greeks could not deliver clear titles was interesting:
For four hundred years the fertile plains of Macedonia
and Thrace had been owned chiefly by the Turkish
conquerors. These Turks did not till the land themselves—they regarded themselves as aristocrats, above
such menial labor. Indeed, there were not enough Turks
in Macedonia to do the work. The Turks there were a
military garrison. The *beys* who held the land did so
by favor of the Sultan. To each was assigned a great
estate, as reward for distinguished military service.
Each *bey* built himself a villa on his estate, and in the
hot season he occasionally actually lived in it. But
most of the year he lived in the city—preferably Salonica or Cavalla—where he could have the pleasures of
society. In his absence a Turkish overseer ran the
estate. The actual labor of the tilling of the soil was
left to the native Greek population, who worked it on
shares. As the Turk is ever a rapacious landlord, the
Greeks produced only enough for bare subsistence,
because to produce more was merely to invite seizure
by the Turks. These absentee-landlord estates were
called *tchifliks.*

When the Greeks acquired Macedonia by conquest in
1912, they did not disturb the Turkish landlords. But
in 1923, when the treaty for the exchange of populations followed upon the Smyrna disaster, the Turks had

to leave Macedonia and surrender their lands. It was these lands, vacated by the Turks, that the Greek Government chiefly counted upon when they promised to give our Commission one and a quarter million acres. But when the Turks got out these lands were not thereby left altogether vacant. The native Greeks who had tilled them for the Turks were still on them. They naturally claimed the lands they had been working. Fortunately, for the reason given above, they had not cultivated anywhere near all these lands, so there was a great deal left, available for the refugees. But the available surplus was not "free of all encumbrances." Some of it was mortgaged, and mortgaged to Greeks at that! All the possible entanglements to which the title to property is liable were represented in one or another by these *tchifliks*, even after the Turks had left them.

Now it would eventually be possible for the Greeks to disentangle these complications, but lengthy legal processes in each case were involved before they could do so. But we needed money at once. The Protocol said we must have lands with a clear title, to offer as security for the loan of this money. And the Bank of England's agreement to lend it was based on the Protocol. What was to be done?

This was one of the first questions that I took up with Venizelos after he entered upon his brief premiership. On January 13, 1924, I wrote him a letter, enclosing a lengthy memorandum on this subject, and asking for an appointment for a personal discussion of it. The memorandum pointed out that under the Protocol "the very essence of the obligation of the Greek Government" was the cession of these lands in fee to the Commission. Even if we had the money to spend on rural refugees, we could not legally spend it until we got clear title to one and a quarter million acres. We urged that the government immediately cede us all available lands, and also put in effect at once the decree expropriating additional lands, especially those in Madeconia and Thrace. But we called especial attention to the lands now being vacated by the Turks retiring from Macedonia. These were particularly important, for several reasons: They were the largest tracts, they were already under cultivation, and they had farm buildings already on them.

As to these Turkish *tchifliks*, we recognized that special difficulties existed. They were not yet fully under the jurisdiction of the Greek Government, since the exchange of populations was proceeding under an International Mixed Commission, acting under the Treaty of Lausanne, and the exact legal status of the lands under this treaty remained to be established. But we urged that the Greek Government should at least adopt a positive policy in the matter and should instruct its representative on the Mixed Commission to work definitely for a solution in line with that policy. Everything now depended—loan and refugee rehabilitation and the economic future of Greece—upon the Greek Government's immediate compliance with the essential cession of lands to our Commission that must precede the granting of the loan.

A few days later my associate, Mr. Delta, and I had

such a conversation with Mr. Venizelos. And the next day he wrote us a letter "confirming our conversation of yesterday morning." Unfortunately, it scarcely "confirmed" it. Venizelos rather put the question back up to us, to put it back, in turn, to the Bank of England and the League. He expressed the opinion that an appeal to the bank for permission to use the million-pound advance, without waiting for final cession of the lands, might be successfully urged if we pointed out to the bank that this sum was safely secured by the bonds in its possession and also by the value of refugee settlements erected by the Greek Government before the Refugee Settlement Commission was instituted, these settlements now on the point of being transferred by the government to our Commission.

There was much justice in Venizelos's contention. The Bank of England really had ample security for its advance of a million pounds. The Turkish lands evacuated in Macedonia had been declared by the Treaty of Lausanne to rest in trust with the Mixed Commission for Exchange of Populations, to be used to indemnify Greek refugees for the lands which they, in turn, had evacuated in Asia Minor. The Treaty of Lausanne seemed to mean that a Greek, exchanged from Asia Minor and returning to Greece, had a definite option upon the same number of acres of Turkish evacuated lands in Macedonia as he had given up in Asia Minor. It was a question whether we could soon get *de jure* possession of these lands, therefore, although we could at once have *de facto* possession of them.

Accordingly, a long letter was sent to Norman, approved and signed by all four members of our Commission. In it were stated the foregoing facts, and it concluded as follows:

Therefore the Greek Government and the National Bank have requested the Refugee Settlement Commission to place the facts before you and obtain the concellation or modification of the conditions. The Commission believes that this does not involve any risk to the Bank of England and endorses the appeal.

It had by this time become clear that we should never get the big loan on the market, in time to be of any use to Greece, if we had to wait for all the details of this land problem to be cleared up. We must get the League of Nations and the Bank of England to waive the issue of "encumbrances" on these lands for the present. We held many discussions in the Commission, and negotiations with Diomede of the Bank of Greece and with Mylonas, the Secretary of Agriculture. I corresponded with Norman at the same time and at length we all appeared to agree upon a form of words that satisfied all hands. This formula was to be made effective by an amendment to the Protocol. Its substance was stated by Norman, in his letter to me dated February 5, 1924. Referring to the undertaking by which our Commission had pledged itself "to effect settlement solely on lands offered free of charge and without encumbrance by the Greek Government," Norman offered to modify this stringent restriction by adding the clause, "or on land vacated by departing Musselmen, to which latter lands the Greek Government agrees to furnish in due course free of charge and without encumbrances title in favor of the Commission."

It took us two weeks to get the unqualified acceptance of this new clause by the Greek Government. They pointed out that "it would be a very heavy burden for the state to undertake the obligation to free all properties exchanged from mortgages or encumbrances of any nature which may be on these estates, especially when the amount of the encumbrance is not known beforehand." They therefore sought to avoid this expense by proposing to add the phrase "agree to transfer free of charge to the proprietorship of the Refugee Settlement Commission in the condition, of course, in which they are when the lands are taken possession of."

Naturally, we refused to accept that proposal. The Bank of England had gone quite far enough when it agreed to accept a promise of *eventual* clear titles in lieu of actual delivery of *immediate* clear titles. The Greek Government's proposal meant anything or nothing, and we firmly declined it. They then accepted Norman's phraseology without alteration. Accordingly, on February 25, 1924, I was able to telegraph Norman:

Commission accepts your proposed addition. Greek Government has formally approved.

A day or two later I received a long letter from Norman—it takes five days for mail to travel from London to Athens—dated February 21, 1924. In it he said:

The object of the form of engagement to which exception is now taken was to place the present advance from the

Bank of England as nearly as possible on the same lines as the long-term loan which was contemplated for the purpose of carrying through the *raison d'être* of your commission. I have therefore doubted whether it is wise for the Greek Government to be absolved from the necessity at this stage of providing the necessary lands free and unencumbered for your Commission. It appears for the reasons which you give that the Greek Government cannot at once comply with that portion of its undertaking; and in that case I would assume you know on what basis and on what authority the eventual long-term loan is to be raised.

Thus, so far as the Bank of England is concerned, I am pretty well content to leave the decision as to the cancellation or modification of your Commission's engagement in your hands, only asking that this engagement and the undertaking of the Greek Government and the eventual basis of security for the long-term loan may throughout be considered as parts of one question.

I ignore for the purpose of this letter the prospect of raising a loan of £6,000,000 sterling or more. I wrote to you on this subject on January 14th. All I can say to-day is that the prospects have not improved: the illness of Mr. Venizelos, the political uncertainty in Greece, the difficulties as between Musselmen and Greek refugees, and the state of Central Europe appear since I last wrote you to have made the prospects no more hopeful. What we all need, as must be abundantly evident to you and in agreement with your views, is some permanent political settlement of the domestic affairs of Greece.

In concluding this letter Norman pointed out that the present advance would not carry the work of the Refugee Settlement Commission beyond a few months, and asked if he and I could not meet somewhere to discuss the problem.

This invitation to meet Norman again in person and to talk out our problem together fell in with my own judgment and inclinations. The ultimate goal of our labors was "the big loan." Unless we could eventually get a great sum of money—our estimate was not less than fifty million dollars—it was vain to hope that Greece could rehabilitate the refugees. Even that sum represented only about two hundred dollars for every family to be rehabilitated. Imagine undertaking to settle a family, even on free land, with less than two hundred dollars, when settling them meant building them a house to live in and providing them with seeds, farm implements, and a draft animal. Certainly it could not be done for less.

The million-pound advance had never been more than an emergency fund to enable us to "make a demonstration" of what we could do if we had the necessary larger sum. But it was daily becoming clear that even for this demonstration purpose it was not enough. As Norman pointed out in his letter just quoted, we would exhaust it in a few months—long before the few rural refugees we had been able to help could get in their first crop and so prove that our plan of help actually did make such refugees self-supporting. On the other hand, Norman's letter made clear that even if our work had already justified itself, financial conditions in Europe were unfavorable to success of the big loan if it were now offered to the public there.

Only one way out was possible. This way was to persuade the Bank of England to advance another million pounds. Such a second advance would keep the

Refugee Settlement Commission's work going through the summer and the first harvest. This period would be long enough to demonstrate that our method of financing refugees actually made them economically self-sustaining. And when this period should expire financial conditions in Europe would probably be more favorable to the flotation of the big loan.

Consequently I now turned all my thoughts toward the interview that Norman proposed, and made all my plans to fit my intention of going to London at once for that purpose. Political conditions at Athens were in a most critical state and they would doubtless be quoted against me by Norman, but I had to take that chance. Venizelos had just lately found himself physically unequal to the task of governing Greece, and Cafandaris, his successor as Premier, was struggling to carry on the Venizelos policies in the face of the rising tide of republicanism. I had become aware that some of the military group, contrary to Venizelos's belief, was on the side of the extreme Republicans led by Papanastasiou, and that it was entirely possible that a *coup d'état* might be precipitated any day and the country appear to outsiders to be again in the hands of a military oligarchy. All these things would make it hard for me to convince Norman that the Bank of England would be justified in risking another million pounds in Greece. Nevertheless, I felt I had some good arguments, and in any event there was no alternative but to try.

Accordingly, after a farewell talk with Venizelos, I left Athens by train on March 1, 1924, and arrived in

London on the afternoon of March 7th. I telephoned Norman at once, and he asked me to call the following morning.

I arrived at Norman's office at half-past eleven o'clock. I found him surrounded by all his chief counsellors. Seldom have I faced a group of abler men. The alert, aggressive Norman and the studious, profound Niemeyer I have described earlier in this chapter. Besides these two there were present Mr. Cecil Lubbock, the deputy governor of the bank; Mr. Ernest Harvey, the chief cashier; and Sir Arthur Salter, the financial secretary of the League of Nations. Probably no five men in the world carried in their heads more expert knowledge of international finance, international politics, and Greek finance in particular, than this group of five whom I faced that morning.

With Norman and Lubbock, Harvey is one of the three men "in the know" in the Bank of England. All important transactions of the bank are made with the full cognizance of all three of these men, so that there is always certain to be one responsible officer of the bank on the premises who can act promptly and with full knowledge. And as the inevitable changes in personnel gradually take place, there always remains at least one man, steeped in the traditions of the bank, who passes these traditions on to his new associates while they are familiarizing themselves with their duties.

I think it worth while to digress for one paragraph at this point. We hear a great deal of nonsense talked about "international bankers" being largely responsible for provoking wars. In my discussion with these men, the one point they constantly stressed as being of absolutely the first importance was that not one cent of the money I was asking them to lend should be used to increase armaments. They were not satisfied to be assured that the money would not be spent for military purposes: they insisted also that it should not be used to ease the burden of Greek taxes so that a clever Greek government might then be free to use the taxes, thus released, *indirectly* for military purposes. Thus these international bankers, instead of encouraging war, on the contrary were using the whole power of their money to discourage war. It may be remarked further that the late Benjamin Strong, as head of our own Federal Reserve System, made yearly calls upon the officers of the Bank of England, upon the president of the Deutsche Bank of Germany, and upon the directors of the Bank of France, and that all these leaders of the national financial systems of the four Great Powers coöperated to use their economic power for the preservation of world peace.

Sir Arthur Salter remains to be described. Not connected with the Bank of England, he was present as representative of the League of Nations. To him, more than to any other one man, was due the authorship of the League's plans to help Greece by the creation of the Refugee Settlement Commission. Below medium height, Sir Arthur yet gives an instant impression of competence and power. His keen eyes, behind the spectacles, are penetrating yet kindly. The firm jaw indicates decision and resolution. Sir Arthur's financial skill has made him famous throughout Europe. Salter would command an enormous salary but prefers the public service with nominal compensation. A general recognition of this has won him the respect of everybody.

When we started our discussion Norman asked me how long it would take me to explain the situation in Greece.

"Which part of the situation?" I asked.

"All of it," replied Norman. "We want to know both the financial and the political sides of the question as you see it, as well as the conditions and prospects of the refugees."

"To do that will take about four hours," I said.

Norman looked at his watch and turned to Harvey.

"Mr. Harvey," he said, "please arrange that we shall not be disturbed for the rest of the day."

I was frankly astonished to hear Norman give such instructions. Here were the four most important men in British finance deliberately shutting themselves off for a whole day from contact with the world, for the purpose of concentrating on one problem to the exclusion of all others. I could not help imagining what the four leading American financiers would have said if anyone proposed that they do such a thing, nor could I help admiring these Britishers in actually doing it. Naturally also it flattered me to feel that any task I should have in hand was of sufficient importance to justify them in doing it.

It was decided that I should go over the political situation first. With perfect frankness I explained the inside facts about the Greek Cabinet crisis and the seething internecine struggle in Greece over the proposal to change from a monarchy to a republic. I explained the differences over the manner of holding the proposed plebiscite, and the impatience of the military leaders who were determined at all costs to prevent the revival of any Monarchist power in the country, as their own lives would be endangered by the return of the Royalists to control. In the course of my talk I was subjected to a continuous and searching cross-examination.

I was just finishing my résumé of the political situation when luncheon was announced. We adjourned to the dining room, sumptuously paneled in dark oak, that adjoined the offices. Here we were joined by the directors of the bank, and after introductions all around, we sat down to a pleasant repast, during which all business discussion was suspended, the conversation being general and social.

After luncheon our little group returned to Norman's office. As soon as we were seated Norman turned to me and said:

"You've lost your case."

"Why so?"

"You've described the political situation, and your own account of it proves that the present Cabinet in Greece is not going to last, and that political conditions there are not stable, and give no hope they will be stable."

Norman's attack was exactly what I had anticipated, and I had a perfectly sound defense.

"Just a minute!" I exclaimed. "I have given you the

whole political situation, because you are entitled to all the facts. But there's another aspect of these facts that I had just come to when luncheon interrupted us. I have established confidential relations with the leaders of all the factions in Greece, and I know what is in their minds. And on one point they are absolutely agreed—no matter what happens in their internal politics, everybody in Athens understands that no faction will be allowed to touch the Refugee Settlement Commission or interfere with its work. All Greeks, of every political opinion, are committed to the maintenance of the Commission. They understand perfectly that its work is the only hope the country has to maintain its economic existence. Any party or leader that attempted to interfere with the Commission would get short shrift from the country, and they all know it.

"That is one aspect of the position," I continued. "But here is another that I have not even touched on yet. You gentlemen are hesitating over the advance as if I were asking you to lend additional money to an insolvent debtor whose loan was unsecured. Now the fact is that you haven't really let us have even one million pounds yet. In making the so-called million-pound advance you required the Bank of Greece to put up one fourth of the money, so that really you have only let us have £750,000. In the second place, you have security enough in your vaults to cover that advance and the new one I am asking for many times over. You have the written guarantee of the Bank of Greece. You have bonds of the Greek Government to a total face value of six million pounds, and an actual market value of at least three millions. And finally, the Greek Government has for years had a deposit in gold in the Bank of England of about two million pounds. The simple truth is that in lending Greece two million pounds you are really lending her her own money, and getting a fair rate of interest for doing it.

"Now," I went on, "I can't pledge the Greek Government to do this, but it is obvious that the Greek Government could any day withdraw its gold deposit from the Bank of England and take it to the United States or some other safe country that would be liberal about lending to anybody who brought them such a valuable account. And as an American financier I know perfectly well that any one of three or four banks in New York would be glad to get such a deposit, and would regard the Greek security that you now have as perfectly satisfactory collateral for a temporary loan. And I am also certain that, with the large and prosperous Greek population in the United States, to say nothing of the general investing public, it would be easy to go on and create a market for these bonds over there.

"Therefore," I concluded, "instead of you gentlemen feeling that I am here in somewhat the position of a suppliant, you ought to be glad that I am giving you a chance to take part, without any risk, in the biggest philanthropic enterprise in history. I am giving you an opportunity to do a big, fine thing, in helping to stabilize the Balkans."

It was interesting to watch Norman while I was making this challenge. When I began he had been leaning back at ease in his chair, the lower buttons of his waistcoat unbuttoned and his whole attitude one of relaxed unconcern, after having delivered his negative opinion. As I had warmed to my argument he had gradually straightened up in his chair, and his gaze was fixed on my face with concentrated attention. When I had declared that American banks would be glad to take over the whole proposition he had interrupted me to object, "But the Refugee Settlement Commission is committed to the League of Nations, and could not abrogate the arrangement without the League's consent." To which I had retorted that the agreement did not specify a definite time limit in which its terms might be consummated, and as a lawyer I knew that the courts would construe the agreement to mean "within a reasonable time"; and therefore, I continued, "since the Bank of England has held off from carrying the agreement into full effect, the bank itself would be held to have abrogated it."

And when I concluded my argument Norman's waistcoat buttons were again a barometer of his state of mind. Sitting up sharply in his chair, he snapped the last of them into its buttonhole and exclaimed, "You know too darned much! I suppose I will have to agree with you in principle."

And agree they all did. They insisted—properly enough—that I should get a formal statement from the Greek Government that the proposed advance of a second million pounds should not even indirectly be used to cover up any expenditures for military purposes. But they agreed—Norman and his advisers for the bank, and Salter for the Finance Committee of the League of Nations—to accept in principle the advance of a second million pounds, and to use their good offices with the League to make such alterations in the Protocol as experience had shown were necessary to make the Commission's work effective. I left the bank at four o'clock in the afternoon, after four very strenuous hours.

Our conference broke up with all hands happy in having arrived at a harmonious agreement by which we were all to coöperate to the limits of our ability in completing this monster philanthropic enterprise.

As I walked away from "The Old Lady of Threadneedle Street" it gave me a glow of satisfaction to think that this greatest bank in the world was not just a cold-blooded, impersonal, exacting money-lender, but was, instead, endowed with a heart as well as a brain and capable of acting the part of Good Samaritan by lending a helping hand to a sister nation staggering under a crushing load.

CHAPTER XII

Trips to Geneva and London

MY NEXT objective, naturally, was Geneva. Having got the agreement, in principle, of Norman and Salter to the advance of a second million pounds, the next move was to get the formal permission of the League of Nations to make such changes in the Protocol as would enable the Refugee Settlement Commission to spend the money effectively. We must have permission to settle refugees on the lands vacated by departing Musselmen before we got "clear title" to these lands. We must be allowed to assume that such title would eventually be secured by the Greek Government, and that the government, in turn, would transfer the lands to the Commission.

Accordingly, on the evening of the day following my conference at the Bank of England I left London for Geneva. Sir Arthur Salter and I traveled together. I have always counted it a privilege to have the opportunity of conversing with able men, and I improved this opportunity to the utmost. I plied Sir Arthur with questions about the work of the League of Nations, and before the journey was over I had gained also a greater respect than ever for the high-minded, able, and self-sacrificing men who do the work of the League. Sir Arthur himself, for example, is a man whose financial

206

talents would gladly be utilized by any big business concern in Great Britain or the United States, yet he has for years devoted himself unsparingly, at a merely nominal salary, to the tasks of economic rehabilitation and world peace fathered by the League of Nations. And it was astonishing to learn how successful the League has been in these tasks. A war in actual process fills the front pages of the newspapers, but a war prevented is relegated to a paragraph on an inside page. Consequently, the world in general has little idea of the many successful negotiations at Geneva that have removed serious causes of international friction that might easily have led to war.

Arrived at Geneva, I spent a day there collaborating with Sir Arthur and other League officials in preparing a resolution to make possible the change in the Protocol. I must explain that the Council had appointed a Greek Committee of the League, to which all questions regarding our work were habitually referred for preliminary study and recommendations. The Council gathers at Geneva only twice a year, in March and September. In the intervals between these meetings the Greek Committee often handled emergency problems. Our resolution was designed to empower the Greek Committee to make the necessary alterations in the Protocol as soon as further study should determine the exact nature of these changes. They could then be ratified by the Council at its September meeting.

Some member of the Council, of course, would have to introduce our resolution and be prepared to advocate it. It was agreed that Lord Parmoor should do this.

When I asked him for an appointment to talk the matter over he invited me to have luncheon with him on the following day. The luncheon was a delightful occasion. Lady Parmoor was a charming hostess, and two of the other guests were familiar with Turkish and Greek affairs, so that the conversation ran along channels especially interesting to me. These men were Major General Sir Frederick Maurice and Admiral Sir Aubrey Smith. General Maurice had been at Mudania assisting General Harrington during the peace negotiations, and Admiral Smith had been chief of the British Naval Mission that had reorganized the Greek Navy.

Our entertaining discussion ran along until twenty-five minutes past two. Then Lord Parmoor turned to me and said, "Now, Morgenthau, in five minutes you and I will have to get down to business." It was amusing to see how the guests took the hint and left at once. It was even more interesting to see the transformation that came over Parmoor when we "got down to business." From the easy, genial, deliberate host, he turned at once into the crisp, direct, energetic man of affairs. He cross-examined me intensively for half an hour, and at the end of that time, from knowing nothing about my special mission, he plainly had grasped clearly all its essentials. His legal training showed plainly in this power quickly to thread the mazes of a wholly unfamiliar set of facts.

Before his entrance into public life Lord Parmoor had for many years been what the English call a solicitor. We have no exact parallel in America, but a solicitor corresponds approximately to what is termed an "office lawyer" in this country—one who does the painstaking work of investigating a legal problem, analyzing it, and making all the preparations for trial, but who leaves the actual presentation of the case in court to other men (in England, the barristers) who are especially effective in public speaking and in dealing with the rapid give-and-take of the courtroom.

Lord Parmoor's membership in the Council of the League of Nations was doubtless a perpetual source of surprise to his friends. Before he was made a viscount he had sat, as plain Mr. C. Alfred Cripps, as a Conservative member of Parliament from 1895 to 1914. The war had given him a profound interest in the causes of peace. To the astonishment of everybody, when Ramsay MacDonald organized the first Labor Government after the War, Lord Parmoor entered his Cabinet, doubtless because he sympathized with MacDonald's intense desire to promote the return of peace.

Parmoor readily consented to offer and promote the passage of our resolution. I bade him adieu, and an hour later appeared before him and the other members of the League Council, in formal session at the League Headquarters. Others of this Council of Ten were Sir Eric Drummond, the secretary general; Edouard Benes, of Czecho-Slovakia; Branting, of Sweden; and Honataux, of France. I was accompanied by Mr. Colocotronis, the Greek chargé at Bern, as official representative of the Greek Government.

I explained to the Council the whole situation, and expressed my opinion that with about eight million pounds sterling net the whole refugee question could be settled within a few years, and that at the end of that time I considered it highly probable that the refugees would be self-supporting. As our present funds would be exhausted by June 15th, and as additional facilities for a loan would therefore have to be sought from the Bank of England before the next session of the Council, I urged that the Council delegate to the Greek Committee the necessary powers to act in the matter of the loan when the time came. Mr. Colocotronis seconded my remarks by official assurances from the Greek Government that they would coöperate fully with the Refugee Settlement Commission, and he emphasized the urgency of the need by pointing out that at least one hundred and fifty thousand more refugees were shortly to arrive in Greece from Pontus and the shores of the Black Sea.

Lord Parmoor then introduced our resolution, which had been handed to him by Sir Eric Drummond before the session convened. The resolution read as follows:

The Council has taken note of the quarterly report of the Refugee Settlement Commission dated February 28th, and has heard with great interest the statement of the president of the Commission, Mr. Morgenthau.

The Council desires to express its deep appreciation of the work of the Commission over which Mr. Morgenthau presides, and its satisfaction in the progress already accomplished in establishing the refugees in productive employment.

Recognizing that the results achieved and the work in progress through the expenditure of the funds already available demonstrate clearly that the methods contemplated in the scheme and put into operation by the Commission are such as to indicate a prospect of settling the refugees on a permanent and productive basis if the uninterrupted continuity of the work can be assured, and the necessary additional funds obtained:

Recognizing that consideration of the future work of the Commission, in view of the financial resources available, may become necessary at any early date:

Recognizing, moreover, that the provision of these resources will be impossible unless political developments in Greece in the immediate future are such as to offer a prospect of order and economic stability, and the consequent improvement in the foreign credit of the country:

Recognizing, too, the magnitude of the task which confronts Greece on the influx of some million destitute refugees, and the courageous and notable efforts which she with the help of the Commission has made in dealing with this problem, and desiring that if the conditions in Greece itself render it possible, the League of Nations shall use all its influence to help one of its member states to complete successfully a vital national undertaking and to return to a position of self-supporting prosperity:

The Council decides

To ask the Greek Committee to consider favorably any request to hold a meeting for this purpose, which may be made to it by the Refugee Settlement Commission, and hereby delegates authority to the Greek Committee to take such decisions in relation to the settlement scheme as it may consider should be taken before the next ordinary meeting of the Council.

After the resolution was introduced Mr. Colocotronis and I withdrew, while the Council discussed it privately. At six o'clock we were invited to return to the chamber, which was practically filled with interested observers, and in our presence the resolution was passed. M. Honataux then made a speech, thanking me for my interest in the League; and when, as I started to leave, all the members of the Council rose and shook hands with me in the friendliest manner, I felt repaid for the hard work I had put in on the work of the Commission.

It is display of this kind of spontaneous sympathy that made me feel that we are all working for the betterment of mankind and the establishment of brotherly love throughout the world.

Greatly cheered by this sympathetic coöperation of the League Council, following my success in securing the coöperation of the Bank of England, I started next day on my return trip to Athens, going by rail to Naples, and thence by sea to Piræus.

As I have already stated, I returned to Athens on March 18th. An entirely new political arrangement (not, however, unexpected) had been made while I was gone. Cafandaris had resigned as Premier, Venizelos had left Greece to resume his voluntary exile in Paris, and Papanastasiou was now Premier. The latter had strengthened his government by directly recognizing the republican military element in the persons of General Pangalos, Colonel Gondiles, and Admiral Hadjikyriakos, whom he included in his Cabinet. Soon Greece would be a Republic—for the first time in two thousand years, when it was a collection of city states, each a republic or a pure democracy.

Notwithstanding these political changes, and the greater ones impending, I felt no anxiety about the status of the Refugee Settlement Commission. Indeed, if anything, its position in Greece would be stronger than ever. The Royalists alone of all the Greeks had been hostile to refugee relief, and now their star was setting—probably permanently. On the other hand, fifty-five deputies in the National Assembly were refugees, representing refugee constituencies. Under a republican régime they would more than ever wield a great deal of power, especially as they had always, to a man, been ardent supporters of the republican cause. And the new Premier, Alexander Papanastasiou, was warmly sympathetic with the work of the Refugee Settlement Commission. I had come to know him intimately, and I was sure of his favorable attitude.

Nevertheless, the new personnel of government compelled us to go again over almost the whole problem with the new officials. We had to make sure that they would work definitely to secure the free title to the land of the departing Musselmen, and that they understood the close scrutiny of Greek affairs by British investors, who would be discouraged if all hands in Greece did not turn whole-heartedly to stabilize political conditions.

Just a week after my return to Athens the National Assembly declared Greece a republic, and two days later the political atmosphere had so cleared up that I was able to say in a letter to Norman:

The Prime Minister, as his first public function, gave a dinner to our Commission and the Minister of Agriculture to discuss our matters, and they positively promised us to hasten as much as possible the transfer to us of unencum-

bered land. 250,000 *stremmata* (62,500 acres) have already
been handed over.

They have now fixed April 13th as the day on which they
are to hold the plebiscite, and taking it for granted that the
vote will be largely in favor of the republic, I am arranging
with Mr. Diomede that we shall be in London between
April 27th and May 2d, and I should like to know whether
you will be there at that time; if not, when can we see you?

I am writing to Sir Arthur Salter asking him to arrange to
be there at the same time, and as Mr. Caclamanos, the Greek
Minister is a member of the Greek Committee, and I believe
that probably Lord Parmoor is, we may be able to arrange to
have the Greek Committee of the League of Nations meet in
London to act under the power given them on March
11th at Geneva.

The feeling here is one of great hopefulness as there no
longer exists the fear of a revolution by the extreme Left.
No one seems to expect any aggressive action on the part of
the Royalists. Now that the legislature has been adjourned
for forty days, the representatives are going home to prevail
upon their constituents to vote for a republic.

We have been asked by the government to build ac-
commodation for 5,000 families in western Thrace, and have
consented to do so at once, as in our budget we had provided
for 10,000 families in western Thrace, and we are to receive
from the government the tobacco taxes toward our expenditures.

The date finally agreed upon for our final conference
relative to the second advance of a million pounds was
May 5th, and the place, London. Accordingly, I returned to Geneva on April 26th, where I had long conversations with Drummond and Salter. Such radical
political changes had taken place in Greece since my
former discussions with them that I felt they were en-

titled to a full exposition of my reasons for still believing that Greece was politically sound and would now advance rapidly toward internal stability. The change from monarchy to republic had naturally produced those controversies that necessarily accompany any profound alteration of government. But the change was satisfactory to an overwhelming majority of the Greeks; the controversy had cleared the atmosphere, and the passing of time would eventually extinguish its passions. Greece was now a united country. Her new institutions would permit her to concentrate all her energies upon developing her resources.

I went on to London, where I was joined by Diomede, the governor of the Bank of Greece, and he and I had our second conference with Norman and his aides at the Bank of England. This conference and its sequel are described in the following letter, which I wrote to my fellow members of the Refugee Settlement Commission:

London, May 7th, 1924.

My dear Colleagues:

Just sent you a telegram: Procured additional million. Sailing *Lapland* Friday. This tells the result of a long story. Diomede and Caclamanos will send full report to the government and you are to receive a copy.

When I met Salter in Geneva, he was about convinced that there was no prospect of securing any further advance for the Refugee Settlement Commission as he, on behalf of the League of Nations, had become convinced from reports that he had received that the prospects for our success were slight because there was no stability in Greece and they were negotiating for war material, etc.

215

I at once took a positive stand that we did not care in the least what they would do, but that in any event the work would go on, for we would pay off the Bank of England by securing a loan on those bonds and the guarantee of the Bank of Greece—from some American banking institution. That I personally felt, and so I did, that I was doing the League a great favor in so shaping matters that they could continue their relations without risk and thereby receive some share of the credit that will follow its successful termination. I talked very independently because I felt so, and it was the only way to eradicate from him the pessimism that had penetrated him, and I succeeded before we reached London, except that he still rebels a little at our insisting on modifications of the Protocol.

On Monday we had over four hours' session with Norman, Lubbock, Harvey, and Niemeyer, and had some very acute stages in our discussion. Diomede can tell you the details. Norman felt that the stability had only lasted four weeks, and also laid great stress on their (Greece) desiring to spend money for armaments and claimed that if Greece had to spend her own money on the refugees they would not have any to spend on war measures. I told him that it was a shame to leave Greece unprotected while she is surrounded by ambitious and designing neighbors and told him they should make Greece the Belgium of the Balkans.

That it would fall to Greece's lot to stop the Turks when they attempted to invade Europe and told Norman we would sell enough bonds in the United States to pay him the £750,000 his bank had so far advanced (for £250,000 of what we have drawn was furnished by Bank of Greece) and finish our activities under the Protocol. This started him and Salter. They said Greece could not abandon the Protocol without consent of the League. I answered that the League has failed in providing us with the full loan, which it was obligated to do. Norman said no time limit had been mentioned, so I claimed that in such cases the law provides that

216

only a reasonable time is allowed and that has expired. They then switched on to another line of argument and wanted to know if they advanced the additional million we would agree to take it on the same terms as the first, and agree that the big loan be negotiated on the same lines. Diomede insisted that as to the first million, they must agree to construe the purchasing of munitions, etc., on deferred payments (such payments to be made out of current income and not out of loans) to be permitted to the Greek Government. It seems they have (and they reiterated it at our meeting) claimed that such obligations would be equal to foreign loans and could not be entered into. They finally waived this claim and agreed to Diomede's construction.

Then Diomede and I insisted that there must be modifications in the Protocol before we proceed with the big loan. I told them that it was impossible for us to use all the funds for reproductive purposes. We must have some latitude in that, and also that we cannot secure all required land absolutely free and clear. We want to be at liberty to expend some of the money on leased land and on encumbered land. I suggested that about twenty per cent. of the money should be liberated from the restrictive clauses in the Protocol. They finally agreed that, the Greek Committee having no authority to alter the Protocol, they would all consent to putting them in the resolutions, and it was so done.

Resolutions are as follows:

"The Greek Committee of the Council acting under the full powers delegated to it by the Council in March, recognizing the considerable improvement in the stability of the economic and political situation in Greece and being informed also that the Greek Government has been able to arrange a further advance of £1,000,000 under the same conditions as those of the first advance for the expenditure on the settlement of the refugees under the terms of the protocol:

"Decide to continue the work of the Refugee Settlement

Commission and indicate its intention to proceed with the schemes as described in the Protocol:

"On the understanding that the long-term loan will be negotiated as soon as conditions are opportune, the general scheme being maintained *subject* to such modifications as may be found desirable and may be agreed between the League and the Greek Government."

We agreed that I should try to meet with the representatives of the Greek Government and Campbell and the Finance Committee of the League in Geneva next September and settle the details of the permanent loan.

Last evening Lord and Lady Parmoor had Norman, Salter, and myself at their home and we had a very pleasant discussion about the affair. Lord P. was much pleased that we had secured the million and promised to facilitate the passing of the resolutions.

To-day at ten-fifteen we met the Greek Committee, consisting of Lord Parmoor, Marquis della Torretta, M. Clauzel, and Caclamanos. I made a verbal statement explaining matters and they were satisfied, but as Lord P. had to attend another meeting, hence was hurried, we adjourned to two-forty-five when the resolutions will be passed. I am writing this letter between the two meetings, so as to send it right off after the meeting has consummated the transaction.

We are now in a splendid position, the League is anxious to have us complete the work, the rise of the value of drachmas and the Greek bonds are most encouraging and will undoubtedly change the financial international standing of Greece. Norman is very glad to have the loan as he knows it is safe and he is really lending us the money which the National Bank of Greece has on deposit with him. So let us all be contented. Please accept my warmest regards and extend them to Papanastasiou, Roussos, *et al.*

The morning after everything had been settled to the satisfaction of everybody I called at the Bank of

England to tell Norman good-bye. I found Harvey, the chief cashier, with him.

"Mr. Governor," I said, smiling, "I have come here this morning, not to thank you for letting us have that million pounds, but to be thanked by you for letting you have the privilege of lending it."

Norman smiled back and replied heartily: "You are quite right, Mr. Morgenthau. I was only just saying to Harvey that you had done us a real kindness in convincing us that it is our duty to go on with our assistance to the Greeks. Now if you will only stay on the job, and help them to spend the money wisely, we'll be perfectly satisfied."

Norman's cordiality was reflected in the attitude of everyone concerned in the matter.

CHAPTER XIII

The Big Loan

LATE in July, 1924, Sir Arthur Salter arrived in New York for a visit to the United States, to speak before the Institute of Politics at Williamstown. I met him and he and I had a long private chat. I discovered that he was again depressed about the future of Greece and somewhat doubtful about securing the authorization of the big loan when the League Council should next meet in September.

Pondering afterward upon his state of mind, I came to the conclusion that Geneva was being consistently supplied with pessimistic reports by some British resident of Athens. Both in March and May, when I had visited Geneva and London, I had encountered a feeling of discouragement among the British members of the League Secretariat. On both occasions I had been able, by argument and my own enthusiasm, to restore confidence to them. Would I be able to do so again, when I returned in the fall?

Not, I reasoned to myself, if I went directly to Geneva. There I should be met with the usual prophecies of failure. On both previous occasions I had met these prophecies by producing facts to discount them. The information officially supplied to Geneva from Athens was necessarily rather colorless, as it was contained in

A Greek Family Moving from Thrace to Greece

formal reports. It was incomplete, as well, since no formal report can convey the intimate knowledge of the human elements involved in large transactions— and oftentimes the human factors are more important than the statistical facts; as, for example, in business it is sometimes more important to know that a man is honest and capable than to know that at the moment he cannot pay his bills. Unless I could go to Geneva fresh from a new study of the situation at Athens, I might not be prepared to counteract this pessimism. Consequently, I decided to proceed in the fall, not to London to see Norman again, or to Geneva to argue for authority for the big loan, but first to Athens, and then to Geneva.

I arrived in Athens on August 13th. I called at once upon Sophoulis, the new Prime Minister, and upon Mylonas, who, by the shift of Cabinets, was back in office as Minister of Agriculture. I pointed out to them that the Bank of England had repeatedly balked because it felt that the security for refugee loans was not being supplied in full under the terms of the Protocol between Greece and the League of Nations. In the Protocol Greece had agreed to give the Refugee Settlement Commission clear title to 500,000 hectares of land. Greece had never been able to make good this promise, because of the complications surrounding the title to lands of the evacuated Turks in Macedonia and elsewhere. But, I pointed out, further, Greece could relieve this difficulty, in practical effect, by giving the Commission a "blanket deed" to 500,000 hectares of land, accompanied by a binding promise of the Greek

Government to supply later deeds to specific parcels of land as fast as these titles were cleared up and the parcels surveyed so that exact boundaries could be described.

Sophoulis and Mylonas agreed to supply the blanket deed. But what, they inquired, would I accept as "a binding promise of the Greek Government" to turn over the lands in detail as available?

"By a binding promise," I replied, "I mean a decree, signed by every member of the Cabinet, and formally ratified by the vote of Parliament."

They assented to my view, and in a few days supplied both these documents, executed in due form, to the office of the Commission, whence they were formally transmitted to the League of Nations at Geneva, so that they would be of record there when I arrived for the meeting of the League Council.

I next had long talks with my Greek confrères on the Commission, and with members of the government, insisting, for one thing, that the Bank of Greece and associates must subscribe 2,500,000 pounds of the proposed loan; also talks with my friends in Greek public life; and so in every way I fortified myself with the latest and most authoritative information about conditions in Greece. Thus prepared, I proceeded to Geneva, where I arrived on August 30th. As proposals would be made to the League Council for some rather drastic changes in the Protocol, I suggested that I be accompanied by someone competent to speak with authority for the Greek Government, so the Minister of Finance, Mr. Tsouderos, was my companion. We had the benefit of the counsel of Messrs. Politis and Andreades, the former a Greek diplomat of wide European experience, and the latter a Greek historian of great reputation in England and France.

The changes that we intended to ask be made in the Protocol were, briefly:

1. To permit the Refugee Settlement Commission to settle refugees upon lands to which clear title had not yet been obtained, though not relieving the Greek Government of its obligation eventually to provide clear title lands for them. In other words, we wanted a free hand to take care at once of distressed refugees, their permanent legal status to be settled later, with safeguards to potential foreign bondholders that real values would always underlie their bonds.

2. To permit the Commission to use not more than 20 per cent. of its resources upon projects, such as schools and sanitary works, which, while not directly "productive" in the economic sense, were of social services so vitally related to the health and general welfare of the refugees that their absence definitely lowered the productive capacity of the people.

3. To permit the Greek Government to raise the amount of the big loan from the 6,000,000 pounds allowed by the Protocol to 10,000,000 pounds.

None of us anticipated any opposition to our securing the first two of these proposed changes, and none was actually offered. They had been pretty thoroughly threshed out by correspondence and previous discussion, and all hands were disposed to allow Greece any reasonable alterations in the Protocol that experience had shown would make the refugee relief work more effective.

Our difficulty was with the third question—the question of the big loan. Not merely its size, but whether the League would authorize it at all. The League had much to lose if it made an unwise decision in this matter. To authorize the loan was equivalent to recommending it to investors. The League, under the shrewd financial advice of Sir Arthur Salter, had been remarkably successful in its dealings with complicated financial problems. Austria and Hungary were monuments to its skill and judgment. If the League should sanction the Greek loan, and later events prove it to be a failure, the prestige of the League would suffer severely. It was a serious question for the Council and the Secretariat.

The prospects of the loan had been injuriously affected before we arrived by an estimate of value placed upon the lands abandoned by the Turks who had left Greece and which were to be put under the control of the Refugee Settlement Commission. Some pessimist had supplied the League with a figure of considerably less than five million pounds for these properties. As these comprised the principal security underlying the proposed bond issue, if this estimate were correct, the security clearly was insufficient. If the estimate stood, our case would practically be lost.

But I knew that the estimate grotesquely understated the real value. For example, it appraised the 500,000 hectares of land at only four pounds per hectare. I was puzzled to know how such an absurd figure had ever been offered, until I realized it was doubtless based on the value of wild land, of which some would necessarily be included in so large a total. But this was wholly to ignore the many thousands of hectares of cultivated lands, already producing cereal crops, and worth from fifteen to twenty pounds per hectare; or those other lands, producing fruits or tobacco, whose values ran as high as one hundred pounds per hectare. From my personal knowledge of these lands I was able to set a figure of nearly fifteen pounds per hectare as a highly conservative average value, or a total of 7,000,000 pounds for lands alone. Then the pessimist's estimate had ignored altogether the houses on the lands of the evacuated Musselmen, and also the urban lands and houses controlled by the Commission in the various towns and cities of Greece, upon which the Greek Government and the Treasury Fund had spent about two million pounds.

Accordingly a statement was prepared, giving a more sensible estimate of the values of the Commission's property. In this form, as an official document, it was filed with the League, and put a much more accurate, as well as more optimistic, face upon the question of security for the loan. The statement read as follows:

DECLARATION BY MR. MORGENTHAU AND MR. CAMPBELL
Refugee Settlement Commission

Geneva, September 11, 1924.

We have been asked to give an approximate valuation of the properties held by the Refugee Settlement Commission in Greece which were not purchased or constructed with its funds but were made over to it free of charge by the Hellenic Government.

Exact data are not available as to the area or quality of the lands so made over to the Commission, or as to the number of houses left by the departing Turks who have left or are leaving Greece under the terms of the Lausanne Convention.

Our estimates have been framed on a conservative basis; they are founded on the detailed knowledge we possess as to the approximate areas and qualities of the lands made over to the Refugee Settlement Commission, the approximate number of Turkish houses, and their state of repair.

Our estimates under each main head are:

1. Value of 500,000 hectares of land . . . . £ 7,000,000.
2. Value of Turkish houses . . . . 2,500,000.
3. Value of urban lands and houses in the vicinity of Athens and other towns in Greece . 900,000.

£10,400,000.

We desire to emphasize that these estimates are, in our opinion, very conservative. For example, the National Bank of Greece (which possesses a special service for the issue and control of agricultural loans to peasants, and which has unequaled opportunities for forming a sound opinion on the question) estimates the value of item 1 above at £13,000,000. In calculating item 2 the low figure of £50 a house has been adopted. Item 3 is considerably below the estimate framed by the Hellenic Government.

(signed) HENRY MORGENTHAU
J. CAMPBELL.

I found, as I had feared, other elements of pessimism at Geneva. But I was determined not to be discouraged or defeated. Consequently I began a systematic canvass of everybody who could affect the final decision regarding the big loan. No opportunity must be lost to smoke out doubt or opposition, and to meet it in advance by facts and arguments. By numerous personal interviews I felt I was making progress in creating an atmosphere congenial to a favorable decision.

Then, by a happy accident I made an ally whose help was decisive. Along the lake front at Geneva one day, on my way to the League headquarters, I observed a man walking slowly ahead of me. The cut of his rough walking clothes, the angle of the slouch hat pulled down over his eyes, even his gait, proclaimed him an Englishman. More than that, his general outline and carriage, even viewed from the back, made me think he was an Englishman whom I knew. And yet I could scarcely believe it. What would he be doing in Geneva, and how could he be there and the news of it not be common property? Nevertheless, when he turned his head slightly, to look out over the lake, and I perceived the pointed beard projecting below the rim of the slouched hat, I knew after all it really was Montagu Norman.

"Well, Governor," I called out as I stepped up alongside him, "what in the world are you doing here?"

Startled from his reverie, my friend swung about quickly and a comical look of surprise, mixed with warning, puckered up his face.

"*Sh!*" he exclaimed, in a hoarse whisper. "I'm not in Geneva. Don't give me away. This visit is incognito."

Having finished this amusing bit of dramatics, and having joined in the laughter he had provoked, Norman greeted me cordially and explained that he was taking a vacation in the Swiss Alps northeast of Geneva, visiting our mutual friend, the delightful Mrs. John Markoe of Philadelphia, and that he had come over at the request of J. Ramsay MacDonald, who had some matters he wanted to discuss.

"Incognito or not," I exclaimed, "the Lord has delivered you into my hands and you can't escape me! You're the very man I need and I want half an hour to talk things over. Will you have luncheon with me? I'll have Salter there; and let me see if I cannot convince you that the Bank of England ought to subscribe to the big loan for Greece."

Norman agreed. Besides Sir Arthur Salter, I invited also Mr. Strakosch, the governor of the Bank of South Africa, who was acting chairman of the Financial Committee of the League. After I had given them the facts I had gathered in Athens, about current political and economic prospects, Norman said:

"If the Greeks will take two and a half million pounds of the ten you propose, and America four millions, I'll pledge the British now to take three."

"That clinches the matter then!" I declared. "I know that the Greeks will agree without question. And I am positive that any part of the total that is not taken by other Europeans will be taken by the Greeks in America and by the American bankers. With your assurance about the British to complete the picture, the Council of the League can feel no hesitation in authorizing the ten millions. I told you that you were the very man I needed, and now you have proved it. You have made my visit to Geneva a perfect success."

And so, indeed, it proved to be. Norman's assurance

that British financiers would take 30 per cent. of the big loan—an assurance given in the presence of Sir Arthur Salter and Mr. Strakosch—dissipated any doubts that any of the League officials might have had about the soundness of the loan. Therefore, on September 12, 1924, the Financial Committee formally reported to the Council of the League that it approved all our proposed amendments to the Protocol, including the increase of the loan to 10,000,000 pounds. A week later the Council of the League passed the following resolution:

THE COUNCIL OF THE LEAGUE OF NATIONS:
Having noted the draft amendments to the Protocol and Statutes of the Greek Refugee Settlement Commission of September 29, 1923, proposed by the Greek Government in agreement with the Financial Committee and the Settlement Commission and annexed to the report of the Financial Committee of September 12, 1924:
Approves these amendments;
Consents to the signature by the Greek Government of an additional act amending the said Protocol and Statutes; and
Expresses the desire that the three governments which signed in 1923 a declaration regarding the duties of the International Financial Commission should give to their representatives any supplementary instructions required by the additional act.

On September 25th the Assembly of the League passed the following resolution:

THE ASSEMBLY:
Learns with great satisfaction the progress made during the last year in the difficult and important task of settling the Greek refugees in productive employment.

It notes the establishment and successful working of the Greek Refugee Settlement Commission; the arrangements made to finance the work of the past year through temporary advances amounting to three millions sterling; the allocation of suitable land by the Greek Government; the housing and establishment upon the land and, to a smaller extent, in industry of a large proportion of the refugees.

The Assembly further notes with satisfaction the improvement in the stability of Greek political conditions; the improved economic position; and the maintenance of a steady value of the Greek currency.

It is glad to learn that the Council, on the advice of the Financial Committee, considers that the time has now arrived when the whole scheme may be placed upon a definite financial basis by the issue of the long-term loan; and that, in view of the above favorable circumstances, the land and the assigned revenues proposed in the Protocol afford a sufficient security for the total sum of ten millions sterling required to complete the work of establishing all the suitable refugees.

The Assembly expresses in conclusion the earnest hope that the loan may be successfully issued and that the whole of the undertaking, so vital to the economic and political stability of Greece, may be carried through to a successful conclusion.

The favorable report of the Financial Committee, transmitted to the Council on September 12th, was all that I needed to assure myself that my work in behalf of the big loan was to be crowned with success. The favorable action of the Council and of the Assembly was a foregone conclusion. On September 13th, therefore, I tendered my resignation as chairman of the Refugee

Settlement Commission and prepared to return at once to the United States.

Two reasons decided me to terminate my official connection with the Greek refugee work. The first was that the task I had set myself at the beginning was now finished. The Commission was now established in the confidence of the Greeks themselves, of the British financiers, and of the League that had created it. The Commission's method of handling the problem was clearly defined and was a proven success. Henceforth the chairman of the Commission would be chiefly occupied with administrative details. His work, important as it would be, was not of the kind that would interest me. As a man does best those things that interest him most I felt that now another man should assume the chairmanship.

The other reason that influenced me to resign was that if I were in the United States I could help to make the American share of the big loan a success. The purpose and soundness of the loan were now thoroughly understood by the British and the Greeks, who were to take the majority part of it. They were far less well understood in the United States.

Dr. Alfred Bonzon, a distinguished Swiss economist who had acted as my substitute during my absence from Athens, was chosen temporarily to succeed me as chairman of the Commission until an American could be selected. Eventually, Mr. Charles P. Howland, a prominent New York lawyer, and now connected with Yale University, was elected as my successor. On September 17, 1924, I sailed for New York.

The detailed plan for the big loan, as finally worked out, was that a group of Greek banks, headed by the National Bank of Greece, took £2,500,000 of it; and Hambros Bank, Limited, of London, assumed responsibility for the remaining £7,500,000 with the understanding that they would find an American banking house to take over part of their share, for sale in the United States. On my arrival in New York I took up the matter with Mr. James Speyer, with the result that Speyer & Company subscribed for $11,000,000 of the bonds. The loan was offered to the public in December, 1924, in London, Athens, and New York, and was a complete success in all three places.

Before leaving Geneva I had the pleasure of receiving the following telegram of appreciation from Mr. Roussos, Minister of Foreign Affairs of Greece:

Athens, Sept. 9, 1924.

HONORABLE HENRY MORGENTHAU, GENEVA.

On the occasion of your approaching departure for America, the Greek Government has asked me to express their gratitude for your valuable and efficient assistance in settling the refugees. The Greek nation will not forget your persevering and self-sacrificing labor in this tragic hour of their history. I also wish to express again my own esteem for you and my hope that I may see you soon again.

ROUSSOS.

Likewise, after my return to America, Sir Eric Drummond wrote the following most gratifying letter on behalf of the Council of the League, in accepting my resignation:

232

Rome

League of Nations,
December 13th, 1924.

MY DEAR MR. MORGENTHAU:

I have been requested by the Council to inform you that they have learned with great regret your resignation of the chairmanship of the Greek Refugee Settlement Commission which you have filled with so much distinction and ability since the Commission started its work.

I am instructed to express to you on behalf of the Council their high appreciation of the services which you have rendered to Greece and to the League of Nations in discharging this important task and thus contributing to the settlement of one of the most serious problems with which the Council has hitherto been confronted.

I am, dear Mr. Morgenthau,

Yours very sincerely,
(signed) ERIC DRUMMOND.
*Secretary-General of the
League of Nations.*

His Excellency,
MR. HENRY MORGENTHAU,
30, West 72d Street,
New York City.

Another honor from my warm-hearted and grateful Greek friends followed later. There was called a special convocation of the University of Athens on April 17, 1925, with all the usual ceremonials and formalities of this occasion. Admiral and Mrs. Condouriotes as heads of the government, were present, and several hundred of students of both sexes. Professor A. Andreades presented me to the rector in a speech in which he reviewed in a most gracious and complimentary manner my career as business man, social reformer, and diplomatist.

233

I replied to Professor Andreades's speech as follows:
"The bestowal of so distinguished an honor as Doctor
of Laws by such an eminent institution as the University of Athens makes the recipient feel proud and indeed very happy. Also very grateful that he was so fortunate as to be selected to participate in this greatest
humanitarian work by Greece to absorb and assimilate
one and a quarter million of refugees. As the work has
now reached such a stage that its success can no longer
be doubted it is eminently proper that the accomplishment should be celebrated. But it is of course *not I
but my nation* itself that should be honored. Greece has
shown that the unredeemed Hellenes, though stripped
of all their worldly goods and deprived of most of their
gallant youths, were welcomed and treated like brothers. This is the greatest actual demonstration of what
human brotherhood really means. It is admirable that
Greece, who has given to the world so much in art,
poetry, architecture, sculpture, oratory, and statecraft, should once again lead, and this time in practical
philanthropy.

"As one journeys through your country and admires
and studies its great ruins, which so vividly recall all
that he has learned of ancient Greece, he realizes that
though the material results of that great epoch have disappeared, the *spirit* of the ancient masters still lives
and greatly influences the present-day civilization.

"It is a grave responsibility and at the same time a
magnificent opportunity for service that rests upon the
students of this university. They are to make Greece
the outstanding example of how so small a unit can,

through its own inherent strength, its inherited intelligence, and the hearty coöperation of its political leaders, be made the Sun of the Balkan Constellation. You young men who are the future bulwark of your country must first learn and then teach to your communities that in this new progressive movement which is aiming to unite all the civilized nations into one great family, it is *principles* and not *individuals* that will prevail. Principles are eternal, while men come and go. You must also appreciate that your country's reputation and standing in the community of nations depend entirely upon how fine, how progressive, and how high your principles are. Your country's credit, its economic conditions, and its exchange rise and fall according to the impression your internal and external conduct make upon the greater states who are the financial powers of the world. Greece should interweave her future with that of the family of nations. Now that the greatest effort of the ages is being made to lessen wars and improve the standard of living of the masses, present-day Greece should, like her forefathers in ancient civilization, become one of the leaders in this movement.

"Greece is to be congratulated on the disposition, already evinced and made part of her foreign policy, to settle Balkan affairs by the great principles of international arbitration and friendly negotiations with her neighbors.

"Her future economic prosperity is assured if she remains at peace and devotes all her energies to her internal development."

235

CHAPTER XIV

The Urban Refugees Absorbed

THE first thing that could be done for the great bulk of the urban refugees was to provide them with permanent homes, see to it that they were clothed and fed for a while, and then throw them on their own responsibility to find a means of livelihood. With a less industrious race the first steps of this process might easily have meant forming the habit of dependence among a large share of the population, but the Greeks almost universally were pathetically eager to earn their own way and hesitated at no extremes of labor or self-denial to accomplish that end.

The Refugee Settlement Commission was wisely limited by the Protocol to expenditures solely for permanent reproductive purposes. It was specifically forbidden to dispense charity or temporary relief. Therefore, of the three essentials of the urban refugees—shelter, food, and clothing—the Commission was limited to supplying the first. Permanent houses to be lived in by the refugees would be as useful to them when they became self-supporting as they were during their temporary dependence. Dwellings within which to recreate home life were essential to the reconstruction of the social fabric of the refugees, without which no permanent economic life could be developed.

236

The Commission therefore concentrated its chief thought, so far as urban refugees were concerned, upon a vast program of building construction to provide permanent houses. Whole new cities had to be built, housing from five to twenty-five thousand people apiece. Sites had to be chosen, lands acquired, buildings erected, community water supplies and sewage disposal systems provided, the families to occupy them sorted out and allocated, and arrangements made for eventual purchase by installment payments. It was a most complicated task, involving not only large sums of money, but problems of choice of design, materials, varying forms of contracts with builders, and so forth and so forth.

Fortunately a young genius was found among the Greeks themselves, who proved able to master their great problem under the management of the Commission. Mr. Sgouta was a brilliant young engineer whom the Commission found already employed by the Refugee Treasury Fund, the organization that had been struggling with the problem before the Settlement Commission was organized. Though barely twenty-six years old when we took him over, he speedily proved himself equal to the administrative execution of our vastly enlarged program, and when this is written is still in charge of the work. Young Sgouta was a native of Constantinople, received his engineering education in Paris, was attached to the British Army units at Salonica during the war as translator, was transferred to the staff of the late Henry P. Davison of the American Red Cross in the same capacity, and when the Smyrna

237

disaster occurred was an officer of the Greek Army in the Engineering Corps. When the Refugee Treasury Fund was organized, he was assigned to its service by the army as an engineer, and when we took over the work of the Fund, Sgouta was automatically transferred to our staff.

Sgouta proved to be not only an excellent engineer but also a born organizer and executive. A handsome little fellow, with shapely round head and black bright eyes, he has all the *savoir faire* of the very social Greek, but likewise the decision and firmness of the hard-headed business man. With an office force of only fifteen men he organized the work of construction in four departments which have successfully handled the work in all its complications: (1) Architectural design and working drawings (2) Legal matters including contracts (3) Inspection (4) Accounting. Under the leadership of this small group approximately twenty thousand dwellings have been erected in five settlements on the fringes of Athens and in three settlements in cities remote from the capital. Following the policy which I laid down at the beginning of our work, all positions in this building program which could possibly be filled by refugees were given to them, and it is interesting to record that 90 per cent. of the people who have done this great work of construction have been refugees.

The erection of these dwellings went through four stages of a very interesting evolution. When the refugees first arrived and the emergency was most acute, wholesale shelter had to be improvised out of whatever materials were at hand and could be most quickly utilized. Thus the first shelters were large crude wooden barracks into which the refugees were herded pell-mell —anything to get them in out of the inclement weather. Some of these barracks were merely frames covered with sheets of galvanized iron. None of them pretended to permanence and most of them have by now been abandoned and dismantled.

Steps soon had to be taken toward providing more permanent shelters, so designed that families could be segregated with some degree of decent privacy. Lumber in quantities was not available, as Greece long ago ceased to be timbered country to any considerable extent. The most readily available material was bricks, made of mud and straw and dried in the sun. In a semi-arid country like southern Greece, houses made of such material withstand the elements to a surprising degree, and though unlovely to look upon and far from ideal in a sanitary sense, they are yet a perfectly practical semi-permanent form of structure. Thousands of refugee families built such houses upon their own initiative and with little, if any, public assistance. A good many hundreds of such buildings were erected by the Commission in the first months of its work as being the best thing available at the moment.

As soon, however, as sound contracts could be made for the importation of lumber from abroad, the Commission began erecting a good many houses of substantial wooden construction. Properly painted, such houses will last for several generations, but of course they involve a considerable continuous upkeep charge for repairs. Therefore, as our work progressed we were constantly experimenting to find the ideal form of construction, combining permanence with low upkeep. These experiments included trials of hollow tile, concrete blocks, and various other materials.

Experience finally demonstrated that houses built of native stone, coated with stucco and roofed with native tile, could be built for little more than the cost of wooden houses, and provided a structure that for all practical purposes would last long enough and that required almost no upkeep.

Experiments were also continually carried on to determine the most economic practical arrangement of the interior of these houses. Two types finally emerged. One is a house one story high, to be occupied by two families. If a separate house were built for each family it is obvious that four walls would be required for each house, or eight walls in all. But by putting two families into one house they can still be provided with absolutely separate lodgings by a solid partition in the middle, and seven walls instead of eight enclose two separate dwellings. As light is still available from three sides of each apartment, there is no loss of health involved.

It must be understood of course that these houses were reduced to the absolute minimum possible as to size and number of rooms. All that a family gets is three rooms. One of these is usually thirteen and one-half feet square, and is used as the living room by day and as the bedroom by night. Another room, about half as large, is kitchen, laundry, and pantry combined; and a third and still smaller room (really a large closet) is provided for storage. How pathetically inadequate such a lodging is to provide real comfort may be imagined when one recalls that few of these lodgings accommodate less than five persons, who have all to sleep in one small room. Yet it is astonishing as well as most touching to see how homelike the loving care of the inmates has made nearly all these diminutive apartments. Last summer we visited dozens of them in all parts of Greece, and in every case we found them as clean and neat as willing hands could make them, adorned with a few bits of embroidery in gay colors, done at odd moments when a minute could be snatched from more necessary labors, with hand-made curtains over the windows and nearly always with at least one tiny geranium in a pot or a sprig of green growing out of a tin can to bring a touch of natural beauty into the place.

The second type of permanent dwelling, evolved by Sgouta's experiments, is merely the enlargement of this two-family house by the addition of a second story upon the same plan, so as to provide lodgings for four families. Access to each of the upper apartments is by an outside stairway, so that each family can live quite independent of contact with the others. Architecturally a pleasing effect has finally been achieved, in spite of the severe simplicity imposed by the compulsions of economy. The natural buff color of the stucco, and the natural red of the tile roofing, make a congenial and picturesque combination.

As these new villages were built upon large tracts of open land, it was possible to lay out the arrangements of streets and houses upon the most modern conception of convenience and healthful arrangements. Adequate light and air have been provided for every lodging. In these respects these new villages will doubtless have a permanent sanitary effect upon all Greek towns in the future by reason of their example.

The cost at which these lodgings have been erected is amazingly low. The cheapness of labor and materials in part accounts for this. But much credit also must be given to Sgouta and his staff for their skill in utilizing every opportunity offered by the natural advantages of mass production to make these constructions as economical as possible. Translating the figures into American money, it has been found possible to provide these permanent sanitary lodgings at an average cost of about $250 per family.

Water supply and sanitation for these settlements occupied many anxious thoughts. The rivers of Greece, except in Macedonia, are little more than those capricious streams known in our own arid West as "dry creeks." In other words, they are small channels that become roaring torrents for a few hours at every rainfall in the wet season, but which in the long summers run absolutely dry. Reservoirs to impound these waters would have entailed prohibitive expense. Springs are scarce and not conveniently located. Deep wells tapping artesian waters have been the solution in most of the settlements.

The evolution of the sanitary arrangements has followed the lines of evolution in the dwellings themselves. In the first emergency stages of the problem these sanitary arrangements can be described in a phrase

—"There were none." In the two succeeding stages (the mud-brick and wooden temporary houses) the dwellings were usually built around four sides of a city block, and communal sanitary facilities were provided in the form of latrines placed in the center of the block. Though this arrangement obviated the danger of epidemics occasioned by the absence of any facilities at all, it was at best an undesirable condition. Decency, morals, and convenience were sacrificed to an urgent necessity.

With the arrival of the permanent stone houses, however, it was found to be economically feasible to include separate toilet facilities for each family within each lodging; and as the groups of these permanent dwellings were arranged upon a better general community plan it has been possible to connect all the houses to community sewage disposal systems. The waste matter is led through mains to disposal beds. Two systems of disposal are utilized, depending upon the local lay of the land: in some places septic tanks are more practical, while in others absorption beds are better adapted to the circumstances.

Following this system of construction, the Commission had erected up to the end of July, 1929, more than ten thousand dwellings in Athens and its environs, and another seven thousand dwellings in smaller cities and villages scattered throughout Greece.

Gigantic as this accomplishment has been for a nation as small as Greece, these dwellings represent little more than a third of what is urgently required. In a recent report the Commission estimates that an additional thirty-one thousand dwellings must be erected before its urban program can be regarded as complete. To gain an idea of the crying need that still exists, one need only visit two refugee settlements on the outskirts of Salonica, where the distress is most grievous.

The first of these settlements is aptly called by its denizens by a Greek name, the exact significance of which can be translated by the term "tin town." Whatever else a Greek loses, he manages to retain a grim sense of humor. "Tin Town" was erected in the first overwhelmingly urgent days of the exodus following the Smyrna disaster, when refugees by the tens of thousands were being dumped on the beach at Salonica, and when it was impossible to do more than the most rudimentary things for their benefit. As Salonica had been a military base of allied French and English forces during the World War, it happened that there were thousands of empty five-gallon kerosene and gasoline tins piled about, gradually disintegrating. The more enterprising of the refugees seized upon these empty tins, cut them down along the edges so that they could be flattened out into sheets, and used them to make the walls over wooden frames that they improvised out of pieces of packing cases, saplings, and any other bits of wood available. By this process a whole village of tiny "tin" huts was built on the outskirts of Salonica, providing a rude shelter for four hundred families, or more than two thousand people.

These huts are characteristically about ten feet square and six feet high, and the floors are of earth.

They are indescribably picturesque, with the outlandish patterns produced by the eccentric shapes of the sheets of tin, and colored with rust. They are also indescribably uncomfortable. With such construction, it is impossible to make them wind-proof in winter, so that they are then cold and draughty. In summer the blistering sun beating down on the flat tin roofs turns these huts into small furnaces. Wretched as these quarters are, however, they form at least some protection; and as there were tens of thousands of other refugees who had no protection at all, the houses that the Commission later built had to be used to make provision for them, so that the denizens of "Tin Town" have had to stay in their present quarters and make the best of it. To an astonishing degree they have adorned even these miserable tenements. In the few square feet outside the door one characteristically finds a few castor beans growing, a melon vine or two, and a few gayly flowering plants. Indoors, the earthen floors are kept brushed scrupulously clean, and the pitifully few household belongings kept in the best possible order and repair. But at best these dwellings represent civilized life reduced almost to its lowest terms.

Life under worse conditions than these, however, is the lot of a much larger group of refugees in the Calamaria Settlement on the beach just outside of Salonica to the west. This settlement occupies the site of the wartime base hospital of the British Army. During the war the British at this point built a temporary wooden base hospital in the form of long rows of one-story frame structures divided by partitions into small wards, in which individual patients could be isolated. Several larger buildings were also erected, designed to provide large open wards for non-contagious cases. These structures were all abandoned when the war closed, and as they were all of very light construction and unpainted, they speedily began to disintegrate.

When the refugees arrived in 1922, these buildings offered a shelter much better than none, and they were promptly crowded to the bursting point. Even now, seven years later, it has been impossible to remove these people or to better their conditions. Their plight is really appalling. In the larger buildings scores of families are huddled in one huge barnlike room. Each family occupies a space about twelve feet square. The floor is the only bed available. Blankets, if the family is so fortunate as to possess such a thing, are spread directly on the bare boards. As often as not there are no blankets but only a heap of rags. Wherever possible the women have stretched pieces of burlap bags upon wires to form a sort of screen from the neighbors and to preserve some semblance of privacy. The percentage of men among these families is very small; they are mostly made up of women and children. In practically every family one or more persons are ill. The region is malarial, and hence this fever is the commonest ailment, but tuberculosis runs it a close second.

Cooking is done in little charcoal braziers improvised out of tin cans and bricks. The roofs of these buildings leak with every rain and the walls are full of gaping cracks that let in the cold damp winds of winter. In visiting this settlement, wherever one's eye turns it is greeted by signs of human misery—death, disease, and bodily suffering and semi-starvation. Two thousand families, more than ten thousand souls, live in Calamaria.

These people represent the most unfortunate bottom depths of the urban refugees problem. They are at the bottom because they include the fewest people capable of being quickly restored to economic self-sufficiency. In the terrible emergency that was thrust upon the Greek nation, with its limited resources, help had to be extended first to those offering the most hope of speedily becoming self-sustaining and thereby able in turn to contribute to the rehabilitation of those next below them. Inevitably, some of the refugees were almost hopeless from this point of view. And, while a certain amount of charitable assistance could be extended to them, they lacked the physical strength or the native abilities necessary to build on this assistance a life of self-support. Such an element exists in even the most advanced and orderly countries, even in the United States, but they are there diffused so widely among the population that their existence is seldom realized by most people.

From the miseries of Calamaria and the acute discomforts of "Tin Town" Greece eventually will rescue those who survive. The marvel is not that such pitiful settlements exist, but rather that there are not more of them.

So much for the housing of urban refugees, which, as I have already explained, was the first and most urgent

247

task of the Commission in dealing with this part of the refugee problem. This housing program occupied most of the Commission's thought and funds, but by no means all. Definitely constructive efforts were made to stimulate the revival of gainful occupations among the urban refugees, and a very considerable degree of success in this direction has been achieved.

In canvassing this situation for opportunities to help, we early came to the conclusion that one of the most promising fields of industry was the manufacture of oriental rugs. So-called "Turkish rugs" had been for centuries one of the two or three main exportable products of the Turkish Empire. I have already pointed out, however, that the Turks themselves were unable to practise any skilled craft to any great extent. Thus the beautiful carpets exported from Asia Minor, and sold as Turkish rugs in Europe and America, were largely made by Greeks and Armenians. Their fabrication was a domestic art practised in the home by the women and children at odd hours after the household tasks were finished. Each district had its own traditional patterns, handed down through the succeeding generations and representing a local adaptation of some floral design or some Mohammedan religious symbol. The almost endless variety of these rugs, which has made them inexhaustibly interesting and almost always charming to foreign eyes, has been largely due to the inevitable minor variations that occur in the practice of a household handicraft.

When the Greeks were suddenly thrust out of Asia Minor and dumped on the shores of Greece they were naturally unable to bring their looms with them. When the Commission set about reviving this industry among the refugees it was first thought that the only expense involved would be to supply this lack by the purchase of new looms. It immediately became clear, however, that an additional obstacle had to be surmounted. The houses in which the art was practised in Asia Minor had been large enough to allow space for the erection of the family loom. As the living quarters of the refugees in Greece were restricted to the lowest endurable limit, there was not a spare inch of space available. To erect the heavy timbers of a carpet loom in a refugee dwelling was out of the question.

Evidently the solution was to transform this household industry into a modern factory industry. In every refugee settlement, therefore, the Commission has financed the erection of one or more large buildings, in each of which numerous looms have been placed and the manufacture of rugs undertaken on a large scale. In some cases, these factories were run as community coöperative enterprises, the refugees themselves selecting a manager from their own number and sharing the profits of the enterprise. In other cases, a factory was leased by the Commission to some capable man, who operated it as a private business. In either event, the women and girls who performed the actual work at the looms were paid wages on a piece-work basis, so many drachmas per thousand knots tied. In many of these factories preference in employment is given to widows and orphans, and this work often constitutes their sole means of livelihood. Though the factories pay as high wages as the economics of the business permit, these wages are pitifully small. The price paid is from two and four-fifths to three drachmas per thousand knots. As the drachma is roughly equivalent to one and one-third cents, this means that the pay amounts to from three and three-quarters to four cents per thousand knots. As a fast worker can average about fifteen thousand knots a day, working ten or twelve hours, the highest wages run from fifty-five to sixty cents a day. Slow workers and apprentices of course make less. And it frequently happens that there is only one worker in a family. This means that many families in Greece are fortunate to have one-half dollar a day upon which to feed and clothe from three to five persons, and that many more families subsist on half or two thirds as much. Such wages translate themselves in practical terms into half a loaf of bread per person per day, a handful of olives, a little olive oil, and meat or fish perhaps once or twice a month. Virile as the Greek race is, there is little cause for surprise that tuberculosis is endemic throughout the land, definitely threatening the future of the race unless the scale of living can be much improved.

The rug industry did not exist in Greece five years ago. To-day there are between eighty and one hundred factories equipped with more than three thousand looms, producing nearly three hundred thousand square yards of carpets yearly, of a gross value of perhaps two and one-half million dollars. The United States is the largest purchaser of these rugs, one company in New York alone taking a considerable percentage of the entire output. The industry is continually growing. As all the Greeks who formerly practised the art in Asia Minor are now in Greece, and as the Armenians have been reduced by massacre and privations to a mere remnant of their former number, and as the Turks are unequal to its practice, it is reasonably sure that Greece will eventually dominate this field of manufacture.

This industry graphically illustrates one of the hopeful aspects of the refugee problem. Generously as the native Greeks aided their brethren from Asia Minor, it naturally seemed at first that this impoverished horde could be nothing but a liability and a burden. The development of the rug industry, however (and other industries, equally important, brought over by the refugees), indicates that on the contrary the refugees are destined to be one of the greatest assets of the country. The new arts they have introduced and the energy they have infused into the whole nation by their competition are strengthening the economic structure of the country and vitalizing its enterprises.

Another industry has been brought up to even larger proportions by the rivalry of the refugees in Greece. This is the cultivation and the processing of tobacco. I shall discuss the cultivation of tobacco in another chapter dealing with the rural refugees. The processing of tobacco, however, is a factory enterprise, and in Greece is carried on chiefly at the port of Cavalla. The degree to which the tobacco business has been stimulated by the arrival of the refugees is suggested by the increase in population of this interesting city, from

28,000 inhabitants before the Smyrna disaster to its present 58,000 inhabitants.

This tobacco industry is of special interest to Americans, as the United States takes most of the crop. It is chiefly used in American cigarette factories, where it is blended with the native American tobaccos to provide a more delicate aroma. Enormous quantities are used in such popular brands as Lucky Strikes, Camels, and Chesterfields.

The phrase "Turkish tobacco" has in the past been used roughly to describe several distinctive varieties under one generic name. An especially fine quality of small, light-leaf tobacco, for example, has always been produced in the neighborhood of Smyrna, and that port, even yet, annually sells to American merchants something like thirty-three million pounds. Other distinctive varieties have long been produced in Asia Minor, in the three districts centering, respectively, at Samsun, Brousa, and Constantinople. A fifth large tobacco-producing district of the former Turkish Empire comprised Macedonia and Thrace, which in 1912 were separated from Turkey and have since been provinces of Greece.

The tobaccos of these various regions vary in strength and quality, but they all possess the distinctive characteristic of producing a highly aromatic and pleasing flavor and odor. Greeks were the largest producers of this tobacco in all these regions. When the refugees arrived in Greece every effort was naturally made to settle those engaged in tobacco cultivation in those parts of Greece favorable to its continuance. Thus the tobacco-growing population of Macedonia and Thrace has been

Assorting and Packing Tobacco Leaves in Cavalla

heavily augmented by refugees from Asia Minor. Production has correspondingly been increased, until to-day Cavalla exports in the neighborhood of one hundred million pounds of tobacco yearly.

The processing of this tobacco for export gives employment to 12,300 men and women at Cavalla. The work to be done consists chiefly of grading the leaf. The tobacco-growing farmer gathers the ripened leaves, dries them, and then bales them for shipment with very little regard to the variations of quality in his crop. These rude bales, when received at the factories in Cavalla, are unpacked and turned over to the sorters. These sit on the floor of the warehouses, each with his little pile of leaves before him, from which he selects with expert skill those with the same size, shape, and color, arranging them into piles of about one-half dozen different grades. All the leaf of a given grade is collected together, packed into rough bales and stored about a year to undergo a natural "sweating" process, during which it undergoes a chemical change corresponding roughly to fermentation in wine, by which the desirable qualities are ripened and fixed. When this process is complete the bales are compressed and packed for shipment to America.

The processing of tobacco is light work, and a very large proportion of the sorting of the leaves is done by women. It requires considerable skill and dexterity, at which they readily become proficient.

Then there is the special living problem of the employees, due to the fact that the work is seasonal. Beginning when the crop comes in, the various processes of preparing the tobacco for export can all be finished in nine months. This leaves the workers with three months of idleness. It is too much to expect of average human nature that the workers will exercise sufficient forethought and management to save enough during the nine months to carry them through the three. An arrangement, therefore, has been worked out to take care of this problem. During the nine months an unemployment fund is steadily accumulated to relieve the other three. Employers and employees both contribute to this fund, and the national government as well. The fund is collected by the government, which utilizes a very ingenious system for this purpose. Every employee is required to carry a stamp book issued to him by the government. On every pay day he is required to purchase government stamps to the value of 4 per cent. of his wages and to stick these stamps in his book. At the same time the employer adds stamps equivalent in value to 6 per cent. of the employee's wages, and the government adds stamps to the value of 7 per cent. By this system a sum equivalent to 17 per cent. of the employee's wages is set aside every month for nine months. The fund thus accumulated is then paid out to the employee in installments fortnightly, during the three months of idleness. The government can afford to contribute to the fund, since it receives in excise taxes 19 per cent. of the price paid to the producer of the tobacco. As the export value of the tobacco shipped out of Cavalla amounts to about thirty-five million dollars a year, the government has a very considerable revenue from this source.

Though it has nothing to do with the refugee problem, I may digress here for a moment to remark upon other facts of interest about Cavalla. It is a very ancient city and was known for many centuries under the name of Neapolis. Here Paul the Apostle landed when he came over from Asia Minor to answer "the Macedonian cry." Through the city still runs—and in many places in perfect repair—the ancient Egnatian Way, the famous Roman military highway that ran from Constantinople westward through Thrace and Macedonia to the shores of the Adriatic at Durazzo. Beyond doubt, it was along this Egnatian Way and upon these very cobble stones that Paul made his way westward to Thessalonica (which, by the way, still is the lettering of the Greek postmark used in Salonica to cancel postage stamps). A few miles inland from Cavalla lie the ruins of ancient Phillipi, and the broad plain outside its walls is the site on which the battle was fought in which Brutus was killed. Towering above this plain is Pangaion Mountain, in whose veins Philip of Macedon found the gold with which he and his son, Alexander the Great, financed their conquests.

Few cities in the world have a more magnificent site than Cavalla. Ringed with mountains that rise abruptly from the water's edge to four thousand feet in height, the city is built upon the curving flanks of these mountains and upon a high and rocky promontory projecting boldly into the purple sea. Seen from above, it surpasses the view of the Riviera from the Grande Corniche in both magnificence and color. In the distance, across the waters, rise the rocky outlines of the Island of

Thasos, whose silver mines were a main dependence of the Periclean glory of Athens. Much farther away, in the purple haze of distance, but still clearly outlined at the far horizon across seventy miles of water, one may see the uniquely interesting peaks of Mount Athos, the site of those famous monasteries, dating from the earliest centuries of the Christian era, that house to-day probably the largest and most valuable collection of early manuscripts relating to the history of the Christian Church.

Until three years ago the water supply of Cavalla was received entirely by means of the ancient Roman aqueduct that still towers upon its triple tiers of arches over the lower sections of the city. And upon the highest point of the promontory which was the site of the older part of Cavalla there is still preserved the birthplace and home of the famous Mohammed Ali, the celebrated Albanian who defeated the Wahabees at Mecca and who received as his reward the revenues of Thasos in perpetuity. The present King Fuad of Egypt, who is a lineal descendant of Mohammed Ali, founded the near-by orphanage which is now used to house refugee families. The rents paid by these refugees are still paid to Fuad.

But to return to the refugees in general. A third industry that largely occupied the Greeks in Asia Minor was the growing of silkworms and the manufacture of silk fabrics. Silkworm culture has been largely developed in Greece by the refugees and will be discussed in a chapter devoted to rural rehabilitation. The manufacture of silk fabric has been revived in Greece, but only on a relatively small scale as yet. It offers promise, however, of growing eventually into an industry of considerable value.

The making of pottery was an art practised by Greeks in all parts of Turkey. The designs and qualities were of almost infinite variety. Each district perpetuated traditional patterns with local variations, and the qualities were determined largely by the materials available in the neighborhood. Potters among the refugees now ply their trade in all parts of Greece, and though the industry has not been developed in factories (with one striking exception), the trade value of the product of the individual workman makes a considerable addition to the national revenue.

Besides these industries that lend themselves to factory production, the Greeks have always practised several other valuable crafts. Particularly numerous have been the coppersmiths, silversmiths, and tanners. It has not been practicable to foster these workers by utilizing them in large-scale factory operations. They flourish best as independent artisans or as small groups employed by a master craftsman. The Refugee Settlement Commission has been able to encourage these men in many cases by providing them with replacements of tools lost in their flight, leaving to the men themselves the problem of securing their materials and finding their markets.

Much as the Refugee Settlement Commission has done in the encouraging of urban refugees to find their place in the national economic situation in Greece, all that it has been able to do amounts to only a small fraction of the total work; much more has been accomplished by the refugees themselves. The majority have solved their own problems by their own resourcefulness and energy. The native Greek industrialists also have done wonders in the employment of refugees by the expansion of their industries.

Too high praise cannot be given to the refugees for their courage and ingenuity in solving their own problems. I cannot describe what they have done better than it has been described in the nineteenth quarterly report of the Refugee Settlement Commission published by the League of Nations at Geneva on August 22, 1928. The following paragraphs written by Mr. Charles D. Eddy, the present chairman of the Refugee Settlement Commission, give an admirable description of this aspect of the urban refugee problem:

In all matters connected with the life of the masses, the factors which escape control are often those which exercise the most decisive influence on their future. During three years at least, the urban refugees, urged by some strange instinct, were continually on the move. There are very few urban families which have not flitted again and again from one large town to another in order to see with their own eyes the possibilities offered by each locality visited. Advice from distant relatives and the exchange of correspondence helped to foster these movements and maintain the population in a state of effervescence, in spite of all that the authorities could do to hinder and prohibit these changes of residence which interfered with their plans.

Gradually, families have sorted themselves out in such a way that each is now settled in the locality it considers most suitable.

The process is terminated, and what neither the State

nor any form of management could have accomplished when the refugees were arriving in Greece—namely, the selection for each category of the locality in which it would be most likely to settle down without difficulty—has been achieved by the refugees themselves.

If we seek to connect all these events by going back to a remoter cause, we shall find perhaps that the answer to the problem lies in the special characteristics of the race, which have remained unchanged throughout the ages.

In expressing an unfavorable opinion—and there seemed to be every justification for doing so—with regard to this excess of urban population which had crossed the Ægean Sea, we were inclined to take as a basis for comparison the social order as it exists in most other countries. We were apt to forget that this excess of urban population has always been an inherent characteristic of Hellenism in Turkey, that it is due to one of the most striking features of the genius of the race. For centuries, indeed, the Greeks have congregated mainly in the towns of the eastern Mediterranean seacoast, where they have displayed a very decided inclination for navigation, commerce, and industry. It might be said that this nation shows a natural tendency to gather about some great city, some powerful center of intellectual life; indeed, when no such city exists, the Greeks themselves create one. After Athens came Alexandria, and after Alexandria, Constantinople. We must delve deep to discover the causes of these phenomena; it is perhaps fairer to believe that the prosperity of the towns of Asia Minor which have now been abandoned was due as much to the industry and intelligence of their inhabitants as to the fertility of the surrounding country. If this be true, the peculiar gifts of the Greek people will again bear fruit, and Athens, Piræus, and Salonica will witness a future worthy of their past.

The various facts which we have mentioned in our endeavor to explain the altered situation of the urban refugees also show that the standard of living among these refugees is gradually improving, in spite of the obstacles that were at first held to be insuperable. We should not, however, indulge in more than moderate optimism; we should merely note that the facts entitle us to conclude that Greece can quite well absorb the Greeks from overseas whom destiny has cast into her territory. The rest is merely a matter of time and peace. We should remember one cause of weakness which the arrival of the refugees engendered; the disproportion between the number of males and females over twelve years of age. At present this disproportion only exists as between individuals over eighteen years of age. Equilibrium will be restored when the new generation grows up. It will be a generation which will have passed its youth in trials and mourning, but it will have received, in the hard school of adversity, a training that after all makes for character and rejuvenates both individuals and nations.

CHAPTER XV
The Rural Refugees Take Root

AS AGRICULTURE is the most steadily productive industry in a nation's economy, the Refugee Settlement Commission concentrated its greatest efforts upon establishing on the soil as many refugees as quickly as possible. Thousands of these newcomers had practised agriculture in one form or another in Asia Minor. The lands available for their settlement in Greece included such varieties of soils under such variations of climate as to lend themselves to the same varieties of agriculture. Thus the tobacco growers from Asia Minor could grow tobacco as well in Thrace, Macedonia, and some parts of the Peloponnesus. Silk culture can be carried on as well in Macedonia as in Asia Minor. Fruits grow well in the lower uplands in which mountainous Greece abounds. The vine, the fig, and the olive flourish in all the southern parts of Greece. Cereal crops do well in Thessaly, Macedonia, and Thrace, except in the not infrequent years of drought or late rains.

A glance at the map of Greece, accompanied by a few figures for comparison, clearly pictures the agricultural possibilities and limitations. Greece, as at present constituted, includes a multitude of inconsiderable islands in the Ægean Sea, most of them too small to be of much

261

consequence agriculturally. Some of the larger islands, such as Crete, Mytilene, and Eubœa, have fairly large agricultural areas. On the mainland, the coastal fringe of the Peloponnesus is fertile. But the greatest agricultural possibilities lie in the northern part of the country, Thessaly, Thrace, and by far most important of all, Macedonia. It must be remembered, however, that Greece is the mountainous tip of the Balkan Peninsula and that only 20 per cent. of its area is estimated to be cultivable at all.

Greece at best is a very small country. Its total area is only 49,000 square miles (this includes the islands). It is thus almost exactly the size of New York State. The 20 per cent. of arable land, therefore, means that only 10,000 square miles can be used for agricultural purposes. The present population of Greece is about six and one-half millions, and this means that about seven hundred thousand farmers and their families (or about three and one-half million people) must find subsistence upon this small area. Some of these farmers are engaged in cattle raising and consequently live on grazing lands outside the arable area. Leaving them out of the calculation, the foregoing figures work out to mean that on the average there are available in Greece only somewhere between twelve and fifteen acres of arable land for the support of each family of five. Fifteen acres is ample for the support of an average family engaged in such forms of agriculture as bee keeping or sericulture. To wheat farmers, however, it represents an irreducible minimum, so that to them a crop failure is a calamity of the first order.

The foregoing gives the reader some idea of the physical facts involved in fitting the agricultural refugees into the national economy in Greece. With their families, the agricultural refugees numbered approximately seven hundred thousand souls. Obviously there were enormous physical difficulties involved in settling such a great number of people on the land in such a small country already densely peopled. The task would have been quite impossible had not the Bulgarians and the Turks in Macedonia and Thrace been required to leave the country. Their departure (especially the departure of the more numerous Turks) left vacant for the use of the Greek refugees large tracts of land, some of which had long been under cultivation. Nevertheless, a thousand complications made it difficult to utilize even any of these lands. For example:

Many of the departing Turks had been owners of very large tracts of land over which their control was that of absentee landlords—the land for centuries had actually been cultivated by Greek tenants under a system of feudal tenure by which the tenant families were permanently attached to the soil and worked it on a cropsharing basis. When such an absentee Turkish landlord left the country his lands technically were vacant for the use of Greek refugees; but the actual fact was that the land was occupied by numerous Greek families that had been on it for centuries and they naturally regarded it as for all practical purposes their private property. Any effort to dispossess such native Greek families in favor of refugees would have been obviously both impracticable and inequitable.

Fortunately for the refugees, the Turkish landlords had been extremely inefficient. They had seldom been enterprising enough to develop more than a fraction of their land holdings. The result was large areas of virgin soil which, though it would require much heavy work to break it up for the first crop, was nevertheless available for new settlers. Complications, however, almost invariably arose when these settlers arrived. The native Greeks had used a good deal of these open lands as common pasture for their domestic animals. When they were required to confine their animals within the constricted limits of their own small cultivated plots they naturally felt themselves deprived of an immemorial right. Some of the more ignorant were disposed to resist the innovation. The best efforts of the more intelligent leaders, both of the natives and the refugees, were required to accommodate the innumerable quarrels that arose over such details of the distribution of the land.

The human element also naturally played a very large part in the rural refugee problem. The Greek character has special qualities that had to be taken into account. Like his ancestors, the modern Greek is an intense individualist. Interference with his personal independence, or his freedom to order his life in his own way, is sharply resented. Every Greek has his own ideas about everything and hesitates neither to express them nor to act upon them. He would be quite impossible to manage were not this disintegrating characteristic counterbalanced by his equally intense social instinct. He is the most gregarious of human beings, and will not live where he cannot foregather in the evening with his fellows.

The daily gatherings in the local café are as dear to the heart of the Greek as were the weekly gatherings at the meeting house to the Puritans of old—and for many of the same reasons. At them the news of the day is exchanged, local gossip discussed, political questions argued, and business disputes accommodated. Life on isolated farms, as we know it in America, is inconceivable to the Greek and would be intolerable to him. An "agricultural community" in Greece does not mean, as in America, a community made up of farms detached from one another. It means first of all a village, where all the families of that community live side by side. The farm lands lie all about this village. These lands are marked by boundaries and are the private possessions of the various families. When the fields are to be tilled the family goes out to them from the village every morning and returns home to the village when the day's work is done. In the old and normally settled districts this means only a short walk in most cases.

This "hiving" habit of Greek families naturally resulted in the perpetuation of farming villages in Asia Minor in which the same families had lived and known one another, generation after generation. Each such village group of families, in time, naturally became in reality one large family through constant intermarriage. Besides these ties of immemorial association and blood relationship, there was also the powerful bond of religious association through continuous worship at the local church. All these influences worked together to produce in each village group almost unbreakable bonds of sentiment that bound them together.

These human aspects naturally exerted a powerful influence upon the problem of settling the rural refugees in Greece. Instinctively each village group from Asia Minor tried to reconstitute itself as the same village group in Greece. This instinct simplified the work for the refugees in many cases. Such a reconstituted group, when settled in Macedonia, for example, automatically took care of itself as a political and social organism. Democratic local self-government was invented by the Greeks many centuries ago as a natural expression of their racial character, and the Greek has not changed in this respect.

An even greater advantage accrued from this village instinct in the first emergency of the refugee problem. The first major necessity of these refugees was shelters over their heads. If it had been necessary to provide every farm family with a dwelling isolated on a separate farm, the problem of erecting such dwellings would have been almost impossible of solution. Since, however, the Greek farmer insisted on living in a village, the housing problem that was actually confronted was the problem of building anywhere from ten to five hundred dwellings in one place. Obviously, this was infinitely easier to do, since the necessary building materials and machinery could be concentrated and the work carried on as one job in each large community. Under the American system of farm living it would have been impossible for the Greeks to do what they actually have done, namely: in five years to provide comfortable lodgings for about fifty thousand agricultural families in new rural dwellings.

As it has been estimated that there are approximately one hundred and fifty thousand families of rural refugees, these new constructions take care of only about one third of them. The other two thirds have been housed in the dwellings vacated by the departing Musselmen and Bulgarians, and in temporary structures. Most of the Turkish houses were old and dilapidated. For this reason, if for no other, it has been necessary to continue the erection of the new type villages, and this work is proceeding continuously under the direction of the Commission. The most casual traveler in Greece proceeding through Macedonia and Thrace can instantly identify these new villages as far as he can see them by the bright red of the new tile roofs. Nearly all the Turkish houses were built of wood, and the roofs of the older Greek houses, though made of tile, have weathered with time to a rich brown.

Practically all the rural refugees are concentrated in the Island of Crete and in the two northern provinces of the mainland, Macedonia and Thrace. These were the least densely populated districts containing adequate areas of arable land. Of the three, Macedonia is by far the most important. Not only is it the largest but it contains also the largest percentage of lands susceptible to cultivation. I shall confine myself, in discussing the rural refugee problem, chiefly to Macedonia—not only because it is the most considerable area involved, but also because what has been done there is quite characteristic of the work done in the rest of Greece.

It should be remembered that Greece had been struggling with a small refugee problem for ten years preceding the Smyrna disaster. The two Balkan wars that preceded the World War should be briefly recalled. The first, in 1912, was a war between a coalition of Greece, Serbia, and Bulgaria against Turkey. It resulted in a complete defeat of the Turks, driving them out of Macedonia, Thrace, and southern Bulgaria back upon the famous Tchataldja Line, a few miles outside Constantinople. This war was followed in 1913 by a quarrel among the victorious allies over the division of the territorial spoils. This second Balkan War involved Serbia and Greece as allies opposed to Bulgaria, whom they severely defeated. The final treaty liquidating these two wars resulted in the present boundaries.

As thousands of Greek families had been living in the border lands of Bulgaria and Turkey before these wars, they were naturally subjected to dangerous forms of reprisals from their neighbors, the two defeated countries. These persecutions often assumed violent forms, with the result that from time to time many of these Greek families pulled up stakes and fled to Greece. This process was in operation during the ten years preceding the Smyrna disaster and early assumed such proportions that a special Bureau of the Ministry of Agriculture was set up by the Greek Government to deal systematically with the repatriation of these refugees. The experience of this Bureau of Colonization was invaluable when the wholesale refugee problem came upon Greece in 1922 and 1923. The Bureau had a small but efficient staff of agricultural experts, engineers, and legal counsel, all experienced in finding homes for refugee families and settling them on the land. The Refugee Settlement Commission eventually took over this entire staff and made it the nucleus of their organization for dealing with the larger problem.

This earlier refugee problem had also forced the Greek Government to take certain measures of far-reaching effect that helped simplify the handling of the later and bigger influx of refugees. These measures were concerned with the estates of the large landed proprietors. Not only had the lands of Macedonia characteristically been held in large tracts by absentee Turkish landlords, but similar large tracts had also been held in the same way by Greek proprietors in Epirus and Thessaly. The number of Greek farm families straggling back into Greece from Bulgaria and Turkey during the years from 1913 to 1920 was sufficient to raise the question seriously as to where they should be placed. It became clear that some means must be found to give them access to the surplus land of these large proprietors. It finally became necessary (about 1920) for the Greek Government to pass a law expropriating all unused lands in Greece above a certain rather small maximum area.

This measure was, of course, revolutionary in character and provoked the bitterest opposition. The usual cries of socialism were raised, and the usual furious resistance of a conservative landed aristocracy was exerted. The national emergency, however, was so great that the measure was accepted as inevitable. Nothing could have been more fortunate in the light of succeeding events. When the great emergency came in 1922 this absolutely essential measure had already passed through the crucible of politics and had been accepted as the policy of the country. If this had not so happened in advance of the great emergency the refugee problem would have been complicated by a major constitutional controversy. Happily, that ground had been cleared before the flood of refugees arrived. The breaking up of the large estates was already in process, and the Bureau of Colonization had had several years' experience in the practical details of the process.

Out of this Bureau of Colonization arose one of the great figures of modern Greece. The name of Karamanos is not known outside Greece—though there it is a name to conjure with—but this young man has demonstrated abilities which on a larger scene would have brought him international fame. He has been characterized as "the Hoover of Greece," and in many respects it is an apt designation; though the two men are as poles apart in their personalities and methods.

Karamanos was a young agronomist in the Bureau of Colonization, in charge of its technical staff as chief agricultural expert. A native of Greece, he got his professional training in Italy. When the Refugee Settlement Commission was organized, and took over the staff of the Bureau of Colonization, young Karamanos was put in charge of the execution of the Commission's rural program in Macedonia.

Karamanos proved to be an ideal choice. His mind and spirit rose at once to the high level demanded by the great human problem of the refugees, soaring above the mere technical details that so often narrow the outlook of professionally trained men. He did not shirk the technical problems—indeed he handled them in a masterly manner—but he viewed his task as something infinitely broader as well, surveying it with the outlook of a statesman and great humanitarian. His emotions were involved as well as his intellect. He proved himself a born leader of men. Nature had endowed him with every attribute for this rôle. Physically, he combines the two outstanding Greek types. He has the dark olive complexion, black hair, and flashing black eyes of the southern Greek, but the larger frame and more vigorous physique of the northern. His profile is that made familiar by the classical Greek statues of ideal young manhood. Temperamentally, he is Greek to his finger tips. Voluble, eloquent, impassioned, both his actions and his speech are informed with a torrential energy that is resistless. Charming in conversation, truly terrifying in wrath, and aflame with a passionate sympathy for his suffering countrymen, his zeal to accomplish their immediate relief gave his manner much of the quality suggested by Robert Burns's phrase, "Isaiah's wild seraphic fire."

Karamanos threw his whole heart into the work of refugee relief and plunged headlong into the activities it required, without sparing himself physically or emotionally. He did not sit at a desk coldly directing chessboard moves of subordinates in a calculated process of distribution of refugees and supplies. He had, indeed, such a calculated plan, but in the execution of it, as each emergency arose, he jumped into his car, dashed to the center of the difficulty, and dealt with it in person on the spot. Thus he acquired an enormous acquaintance among the refugees and an intimate and hourly-renewed familiarity with the details of his problem.

Greece is a small country, where family is almost abnormally important as the center of the social structure and where "my cousin's cousin's" influence is powerful and far-reaching. Karamanos resisted this influence, and all other forms of pressure, and decided every dispute on the sole basis of justice. This inflexible fairness, combined with the effect of his personal presence at the scene of every emergency, and with the obvious fact that he was sacrificing himself unsparingly in the service of the refugees, gave him an immense moral prestige among the peasants, by whom he is fairly idolized. Whenever he appeared in a rural village, the whole population turned out to greet him, and streamed after him as he went about his work, the air resounding with a truly Greek chorus of mingled supplication and praise. His mobile personality responded like the antistrophe of the chorus. Fluctuating moods brought out his flashing smile, his caressing sympathy, or at times his towering rage. When he left, the air of the village was cleared as if by the passing of an electrical storm and the sudden after-shining of the sun. Whether the villagers had got what they wanted or not, they had received something of greater value, which was the tonic contact with a great spirit that had ennobled their labor by the magic of his ideal of its worth, and heartened them in its prosecution by the invincibility of his courage. Recently the value of his services has been recognized by his elevation to the post of Minister of Agriculture, which places him in charge of the problem in all parts of Greece.

Along with this extraordinary moral uplift, by which

Karamanos dramatized and spiritualized the refugee work in Macedonia, has gone an equally amazing progress in tangible material accomplishment. Under Karamanos's direction the program of rehabilitation of the rural refugees has been carried to 75 per cent. of completion in five years. This means that nearly ninety thousand families have been installed upon farms in Macedonia, provided with dwellings, implements, animals, and seed, and started upon a new permanent life equipped for self-support. This figure can be safely multiplied by four to give a conservative number of individuals—women and children as well as men—so that it means that practically one third of a million human beings have been rescued from destitution and hopelessness and restored to a normal social and economic life, in conformity with the traditions of their race, gathered into communities of acquaintances, friends, and relatives, with their churches and schools and institutions of local self-government.

This work has been achieved in the face of heartrending difficulties. For example: Even now, Macedonia possesses only about three miles of practicable highways in every one hundred square miles of area. This means that building materials have had to be hauled practically across open country where agricultural villages were being erected. Under the best of conditions this meant rough going. In wet weather it meant endless miring in the soft soil. In winter it meant frozen ruts. The problem of transport alone called for endless patience and unbreakable will.

The largest areas of available lands in Macedonia are

in the low, level country near the mouths of the rivers Struma, Vardar, and Aliacman. Much of this land is swampy and frequently is inundated by spring floods. The whole region is infested with malaria, much of it of a malignant type. The hardships already endured by the incoming refugees had lowered their bodily resistance to disease, and they were further weakened by the vicissitudes of the first years of settlement on the new soil, while shelter and adequate food were being gradually accumulated. The result has been practically every year a seasonal attack of malaria, so severe as completely to incapacitate the victims for labor for days or weeks at a time. The climate of Macedonia severely taxes mankind, even in the best of health. In summer the blistering heat of the sun in midday is so intense as to compel a cessation of work from noon till three o'clock. Winter, on the other hand, is a season of biting cold, penetrating dampness, and often of heavy snowfall. Most of the refugees came from regions of a more equable climate, and few had acquired immunity to malaria. The whole situation, of course, made the refugees an ideal breeding ground for tuberculosis, and its ravages have been widespread in Macedonia. Just recently a new hope has been held out in the warfare on malaria by the prospect that the long-discussed plans for controlling the flood waters of the Macedonian rivers seem likely soon to be consummated through contracts with associated American and English engineering firms. These plans include the draining of the swamps, and when this is accomplished familiar methods of mosquito control can be applied to eliminate malaria.

Tuberculosis will be brought within normal limits as more settled conditions improve the standards of living among the peasants.

Seventy-six per cent. of these peasants are engaged in growing cereals of various kinds, but chiefly wheat. Cereals provide the quickest return from the soil, and the destitution of the peasants did not permit of the delay inevitable with other crops. The peasant who planted wheat in the fall of 1923 could eat bread from his own land in the following spring. He could not wait for fruit trees to come into bearing. Land that will grow anything at all will grow wheat; whereas tobacco, the other quick crop of the country, requires very special circumstances of soil, climate, and exposure. Wherever this happy combination existed tobacco was planted, as it is not only a quick crop, immediately convertible into cash, but also because its cash yield per acre is very high. Enough lands suitable for tobacco culture were found so that about 14 per cent. of the peasants are engaged in its culture.

The remaining 10 per cent. of the peasants comprise about 3 per cent. who grow grapes and 2 per cent. growing fruits, the last 5 per cent. being engaged in miscellaneous occupations including truck farming and the mechanical crafts bound up with agriculture, such as blacksmithing, milling, and the like.

As I have already indicated, a very large proportion of the lands in Macedonia had lain fallow for centuries due to the thriftlessness and indifference of the Turkish landlords. Other great stretches of virgin land were also in a wild state because of a situation, to find an analogy for which one must go back to the Europe of the Middle Ages. The monastic orders of the Greek Orthodox Church have from the earliest centuries of the Christian Era formed a large and powerful class in Greece. Radiating from the great picturesque center on the rocky pinnacles of Mount Athos, monastic settlements were established in all parts of the country. These monasteries resembled medieval fortresses, and the abbots resembled medieval feudal lords in the extent of their holdings of land in the name of the Church. During the four centuries of Turkish rule the Turkish Government seldom interfered with these Church holdings. With the universal depression of national life during these centuries, there was a natural decadence in these monastic communities. The numbers of the inmates dwindled; the lands tilled by the monks themselves naturally tended to be the irreducible minimum necessary to provide subsistence. The Church lands tilled by Greek tenants likewise contracted to the lowest possible limits, because the rapacity of Turkish tax gatherers destroyed all incentive to excess production. When the refugees arrived in 1922 and 1923 the national necessity compelled the Greek Government to take over most of the Church lands for their use. Most of these lands had reverted to primitive wildness and the soil was matted with the accumulated grass and weed roots of centuries. The breaking up of this soil for the first season's crop was beyond the power of the peasants with their primitive implements. The Refugee Settlement Commission met this problem by introducing American tractors and gang plows, which did this work on a wholesale scale for the peasants.

I cannot do more than suggest to the reader's imagination the infinite varieties of the problems that Karamanos and his organization had to solve. Endless disputes arose between native tenants and the refugee settlers over the possession of lands that the former had used in common for generations. Practically every new family that was introduced into Macedonia implied a boundary dispute. None of this region had ever been accurately surveyed and so boundaries had always been vague, as always happens in a country not densely populated. The arrival of the refugees, however, peopled the land to its limit and made the possession of every foot of soil a matter of serious importance to the owner. One of the great works undertaken by the Commission is a cadastral survey—still in progress and impossible of completion for some years to come—by which boundaries henceforward may be determined with the precision to which we are accustomed in America. Meanwhile, the Colonization Service in Macedonia has had to accommodate these controversies by rough approximations of the physical facts and by the use of infinite tact in dealing with human nature.

Not only have Karamanos and his assistants dealt with these instant things in masterly manner, but they have looked to the future and have simultaneously developed means of directing the agricultural progress of Macedonia toward a rounded and scientific rural economy. Macedonia must not permanently rely upon cereals and tobacco alone. Crops must be rotated to preserve the fertility of the soil. Fertilizers must be made available. Agriculture must be diversified. Dairying, poultry raising, bee culture, fruit growing must all be introduced wherever practicable. At least 20 per cent. of the lands in Macedonia cannot be counted upon for stable production until they are irrigated, and thus far only 3 per cent. have been brought under irrigation.

To assure the coming of this necessary improvement in Macedonian agriculture, the Refugee Settlement Commission has organized six agricultural stations in that region. Some of these stations are nurseries specializing exclusively in the development of stocks of trees of the various varieties of fruits adapted to that region. Other stations specialize in the breeding of cattle. A system has been introduced that is familiar in the dairying regions of America, by which the Commission lends to the agricultural settlers imported registered bulls long enough to improve the quality of the local herds. Some of the experimental stations specialize in poultry. Bee culture has long been a favorite occupation of the Greeks, and these stations have encouraged it by the introduction and multiplication of hives.

I have already indicated that many of the refugees had practised silk culture in Asia Minor. Parts of Macedonia are naturally adapted to this pursuit, and last year the Colonization Service distributed more than one million mulberry trees to refugee farmers who wished to renew this most interesting art. The Service also breeds selected "seed" (worms) of a very high quality, even better than the Italian seed. As the care of silkworms is light work, most of which can be done by women and girls, and as it can be carried on along with the production of cereals on the same land, it is an ideal use of the soil where conditions favor it. It takes four years for the mulberry trees to grow to a size at which enough branches can be taken from them to feed the silkworms, but wheat can be grown between the trees in the meantime, and after the trees are matured the annual toll of leaves can be taken from them without injury, and practically indefinitely. The trees have to be watered by artificial irrigation. A farm of fifteen acres will support five hundred trees that produce in all from twelve to thirteen hundred kilograms, yearly, of cocoons worth from fifty-five to eighty cents per kilogram. Last year Macedonia produced about five hundred thousand kilograms of cocoons, and it is estimated that in 1932, when the mulberry trees have grown to maturity, the production will have grown to two million kilograms per year.

One of the outstanding things that Karamanos has done is to rescue the wheat farmers from the destructive effects of the treacherous local climate. Chalcidice—that oddly shaped peninsula southeast of Salonica that looks on the map like a hand with three fingers outstretched—is frequently swept by the Sirocco, a dry wind that withers and burns the vegetation. The farmers of Chalcidice were growing the native small-grained wheat, which proved to be extremely susceptible to injury from the Sirocco. Karamanos introduced the Australian big wheat, and this hardy variety from the hot plains of the Antipodes flourished in Chalcidice and saved the situation.

The lands occupied by the refugees have not been given to them by the government, but are sold to them on extremely easy terms. The value of each parcel is conservatively appraised and the purchaser gives a mortgage to the Refugee Settlement Commission to guarantee payment. Amortization payments are made on an easy basis and interest is charged on the unpaid balance.

The financing of the crops is done through Farmers' Coöperatives. All the farmers of the village are organized into a society which holds the pledges of the personal assets of all the members as collateral for loans for current financing of the crops. This coöperative system falls in with the national character and political practice of the Greek, with his highly developed sense of local self-government. Nearly a thousand such coöperatives have been organized in Macedonia, with a total capital of more than three million dollars. The leaders of these coöperatives are chosen by an interesting system: The farmers of a community are organized into groups of twenty-five men, who elect one of their members to be their delegate. Later these delegates from many neighboring committees meet and elect one head man, who must receive three fourths of all votes.

CHAPTER XVI

American and British Relief

ONE cannot omit the work of the Near East Relief from any account of the refugee problem. I wish here to add my tribute to the work of this great American philanthropy. Immediately following the Smyrna disaster, the Near East Relief transferred several members of its staff from their work among the Armenians, and sent them to Greece. Their services in Armenia had been chiefly in behalf of the orphans. As many thousands of Greek refugees were orphaned children, the Near East Relief provided one of the most useful services possible when it took over the work of caring for these. As a result of their previous experience, they were able quickly to organize efficient settlements at which these children were cared for. Orphanages were promptly established in Athens, Corinth, Salonica and in the beautiful Island of Syra. Thousands of orphans were cared for in these camps.

Some of the most important Greek officials, intensely preoccupied with their onerous public duties, were hardly aware of the extent and importance of this work. I shall never forget the effect I produced on them one night in Athens when I took them to the local settlements. I had been dining with Mr. Roussos, the Foreign Minister, and Mr. Carapanos, when I suggested that they go with me to Zappeion and see the orphans. When we arrived it was late in the evening and we found only a few dim lights still lit. We were escorted into the great unfurnished barracks and there beheld one of the most touching scenes—eight hundred small boys all sound asleep on blankets laid on the bare floor. Despite the lack of comfort, their faces indicated that their sleep was troubled by none but pleasant dreams. My Greek friends were greatly affected at this evidence of the sympathy and efficiency of distant America for the childhood of their nation.

On another occasion I took Mr. Venizelos and Dr. Doxiades, the Minister of Public Assistance, to an entertainment given by the children of this same settlement. Some of the children gave recitations for our benefit and other forms of entertainment. But the outstanding feature of the occasion was a concert by a band made up of small boys, every one of whom was blind. All these children were being taught means of self-help and eventual independence.

On one of my trips to Corinth I took advantage of the opportunity to inspect the Near East Relief work there. An old regimental headquarters had been turned over to the Near East Relief, and I found Miss Cushman in charge. This delightful and cultivated lady, from one of the best families in Massachusetts, struck me at once as a typical Dickens figure—stout, muscular, armed with a big cane and with a general bearing of autocratic severity. This outward show, however, was as unlike as could be the facts about Miss Cushman's real disposition. Her warm affection for her young charges and their affection for her were reflections of the self-sacrifice and devotion that had impelled her to give up a life of pleasant ease in America in order to spend her time in this remote region caring for the unfortunate children of a distant land.

Miss Cushman had shown extraordinary administrative powers. She had turned this old army camp into a fine home for 2,000 orphans, about half of whom were Armenians. She had instituted most effectively a method of self-government among them; to every child was assigned so many square feet to keep clean and in order. By this simple device she had provided a perfectly successful system of discipline and an equally effective system of sanitation of the camp.

When we visited Miss Cushman we found her most entertaining. She had spent twenty-seven years in the Near East, and with her energetic mind and her keen sense of humor she naturally had an endless stock of most interesting stories to tell about her experiences. She had, besides, made a magnificent collection of oriental rugs, which were beautiful in themselves and about many of which there were interesting stories. Nearly everywhere she had gone in her long sojourn in the Near East she had picked up additions to her collection and had carried them about with her from place to place. They did much to brighten and make homelike her quarters in the old army barracks. The part of this barracks which she occupied had been divided into various rooms by a double layer of cloth that shut out sight but not sound. Miss Cushman had no money available for plaster partitions and got along just as well without them, for her sprightly spirit made light of minor inconveniences. While we were there Dr. Hill and Dr. Blegen, the archæologists who had shown and explained to us the ruins of Old Corinth, joined us all at dinner and Miss Cushman served us a good old-fashioned American meal.

The orphanage ran a shoe shop of its own, making all the footgear for all the children; and likewise carpenter and tailor shops. All the girls in the orphanage were taught sewing on Singer machines.

An able assistant in the person of Miss Alice G. Carr, a trained nurse attached to the camp, did a very remarkable task of clearing up the malaria with which this region is infested. With the assistance of a hundred of the boys she searched out and applied crude oil to all the breeding places of mosquitoes in that neighborhood, speedily eliminating locally a pest that has plagued Greece since earliest historic times. So successful was Miss Carr in this work, and so astonished were the municipal authorities of Corinth, that they persuaded her to undertake to rid the whole district of malaria, and with her faithful band of boy helpers she speedily completed this task likewise. At first she had trouble persuading some of the peasants to permit her to put oil in their cisterns, but it was not long before the news of her success at the camp spread throughout the country-side and she found willing coöperation from all hands.

While I was visiting Miss Cushman's camp I had a most peculiar experience. I happened to encounter a very pleasant twenty-four-year-old Armenian lady in charge of the Armenian children in the camp. Speaking

Entertainment of Near East Relief Orphans—Which Venizelos, Dr. Doxiades, and Morgenthau Attended

in perfect English, she called me by my name and asked if I did not remember her. Naturally I did not, since it developed in the subsequent conversation that the time I had seen her before was ten years earlier, when she was a little girl in Brousa over in Asia Minor. There her father had been the richest silk manufacturer of that community. He had owned three factories, which I had inspected, later visiting his home, where he had called on his little daughter (then fourteen years old) to play a piece on the piano. Naturally I did not recognize the childish pianist of Brousa in the dignified woman of Corinth. She told me that all that was left of her fortune was the same piano, on which she had entertained me ten years earlier and which now stood in Miss Cushman's parlor. It seems that in 1916, when the Turkish atrocities against the Armenians were taking place all over Asia Minor, Miss Cushman had seen this little girl sitting on this piano on the pier at Constantinople—her parents gone and the child left a waif with this one reminder of past luxury. Miss Cushman had taken her in charge and had sent her to a college in Geneva from which she eventually graduated, deciding thereafter to devote her whole life to her own people, and determined to spread the benefits of her education amongst them.

I beheld a most touching sight at meal time in this orphan camp. Twelve hundred boys were fed at once. Before the distribution of their simple meal of figs and bread, all joined in unison in outspoken prayer, the Greeks praying in the Greek tongue and the Armenians in Armenian, after which all joined together in singing an American hymn. As the meal was served cold, it took

285

less than ten minutes to clean up after the boys had eaten, and to prepare the tables ready with a fresh supply of figs and bread for the one thousand girls who followed the boys.

I asked Miss Cushman what I could do for the children. She said that the greatest happiness of the boys in the orphanage was the band of music and that I could do nothing that would give them so much pleasure as to provide money for additional instruments, which of course I gladly did. For the girls, silk hair ribbons were suggested. So, on our return to Athens, Mrs. Morgenthau ordered these ribbons, in various colors, and the next time we visited Corinth all the girls appeared bedecked in them. The boys' band serenaded under Mrs. Morgenthau's windows, while the girls sang the Star-Spangled Banner and hymns.

This orphanage at Corinth, as well as the other American orphanage for Greek children at Syra managed by Mr. and Mrs. George White, would have done credit to any community. They evoked a spirit of gratitude toward Americans among the Greeks and Armenians that will not be diminished in the lifetime of any of those children, and probably will not disappear for generations.

Another great service performed by the Near East Relief was the collection in America of thousands of bales of second-hand clothing, their shipment to headquarters in Greece, and their distribution to destitute refugees. When this clothing arrived in Greece, work was provided for many of the refugees in the task of sorting, repairing, and distributing the garments.These garments thus performed a double service to the refugees —"Chop your own wood and it warms you twice."

All these beneficent activities of the Near East Relief not only performed a grateful service to the Greeks, but, equally important, they spread abroad among them a consciousness that America was willing to share the burden of the Greeks by caring for the orphans and in this way provided an almost equally important moral encouragement. One of the most striking things about this work was its demonstration of how little outside guidance was required to bring up these orphans to take care of themselves.

The Near East Relief and its able foreign manager, Mr. Harold Jaquith, and all Americans who supported their work with contributions, however small, are entitled to take a profound pride in a noble achievement.

Not to be forgotten is Dr. Esther Lovejoy, the soul of the American Women's Hospital, who ran a number of hospitals most effectively at various refugee camps and was most helpful in Smyrna at the time of the disaster.

Besides the American activities, there was that splendid British representative, Dr. Kennedy, who on behalf of the British "Save the Children Fund" was dispersing much needed food and was at one time supporting thousands of the most hopeless and despairing cases. The soup kitchens he maintained were so well organized that they saved thousands of lives. It was all done so unostentatiously that everyone admired the spirit prevailing there.

Dr. Pennell from India rendered much help and did not spare herself in doing so.

CHAPTER XVII

The Greatness of the Greeks

THE greatness of any nation lies in its people, not in its possessions. Greece is a poor country but the Greeks are a valuable people. The wealth of Greece lies in their courage, their energy, their lively minds, and their physical virility. The amazing progress that has been made in six years toward absorbing a 25 per cent increase in population speaks volumes for the character of the absorbers and the absorbed. I think it worth while, therefore, to devote a chapter to a study of the Greeks themselves. It may help the Western world to understand and better appreciate these worthy descendants of a glorious race. When the Greeks are mentioned in Europe and America it is too much the habit to dismiss them mentally as only another of "those hopeless Balkan peoples." The Greeks are, however, very different from the other peoples of the Balkans, and it is a grievous injustice to misunderstand these differences.

First of all, the Greek has a passion for excellence and progress unique in that part of the world. Whenever he is poor or ignorant or backward he is so against his will. Education is a passion universal among the Greeks, and parents there, as in America, will make every sacrifice to provide schooling for their children. I recently

288

saw a most touching illustration of this fact. Making a rapid tour of Macedonia, I arrived at Edessa, the ancient capital, late in the evening and spent the night and following morning there. Even before my early breakfast I was informed that a delegation from a distant village was on hand awaiting my convenience to pay their respects and offer a petition. When I saw the delegation I found the local priest, the schoolmaster, and three head men leading it. They had come to see me because they thought that I had the ear of the central government and could get what they wanted from headquarters in Athens. Of course, I could not do this; but the point of the story is their errand. They explained that they represented a group of refugees from the Black Sea region of Asia Minor, who had finally been got together again after their dispersion, and were now settled in the mountains of western Macedonia. They had an exceedingly hard time getting started in their new surroundings, and at times their sufferings had been severe. They were so poor that they had not been able to build even a church, but for five years had been holding their church services in a barn. The priest himself then explained what they wanted. It was not relief from taxes, nor an extension of time on their land payments, nor any of the selfish advantages one might have expected; it was not even a church they wanted. Said the priest: "We are willing to go on worshiping in a stable until better times come, but we implore you to help us build a school, so that our children shall not grow up in ignorance."

Democracy is ingrained in the Greek. From the most

ancient historic times, ever since the decline of the tiny monarchies of the heroic age described by Homer, the Greek has resented, and has refused to accept whenever possible, any political system in which he did not share on an equality with every other Greek. So far did he carry this individualistic democracy in ancient historic times that even his military organizations were built on this principle. Some historian has pointed out that the immortal Ten Thousand, whose successful retreat from the Indus River to the shores of the Black Sea is described by Xenophon in the Anabasis, was more like a debating society than an army. Surrounded as it was by enemies, harried by day and by night, in a strange and difficult country, it continued in its darkest hours the practice of taking common counsel, deciding its strategy and changing its commanders by popular vote. Nevertheless it won its way back to Greece.

Exactly this quality, and very largely these methods, characterized the refugee mass when it arrived in Greece in 1922—seven years ago. The refugees welcomed the organized help of the Greek Government and of the international Refugee Settlement Commission, but they did not wait for these outside agencies to help them. Every Greek instantly set about helping himself. Instinctively he sought his old acquaintances and tried to reorganize his old social groups. Once gathered together again, these groups at once set up their familiar processes of local self-government.

Like the American, nearly every Greek is intensely ambitious to succeed in business. When he succeeds he gains honor (again as in America) by the lavishness of his gifts of money to the public welfare. From immemorial times preëminence in Greek communities has been given chiefly to the poet, the artist, the teacher, and the public benefactor. This is as true to-day in Greece as it was in the days of Sapho. The arts have declined in modern Greece (probably due to the centuries of foreign oppression) but the instinct for learning and for commerce is as strong as ever. In both fields the modern Greek excels.

The disruption of normal political life among the Greeks during the many centuries of foreign rule was followed by the century (just past) of self-government in Greece proper; but self-government based upon a fallacious theory. The monarchical form of government, imposed a century ago upon the Greeks by the European powers after they achieved their independence, was not adapted to their political genius. The Greek instinct is for local self-government. The monarchical idea implies the centralization of government. Under the monarchy an inevitable bureaucracy grew up at Athens, undertaking to direct from the capital the local developments of education, agriculture, and even local political and judicial administration. This system has worked after a fashion, because it had to work. But it runs counter to the nature of the Greeks, and has never been better than a poor makeshift.

For example: In most Greek cities there is an intense and healthy rivalry among the best citizens to secure the honor of election to office. So greatly is the honor prized, of being preferred above one's fellows for public office, that the ablest citizens have used every effort to secure election. The man chosen has been driven, by the same aspiration for honor, to try to excel his predecessor's record. Not only could he do this by a wiser administration, but also by a more lavish giving of his personal means. Thus it has been by no means uncommon for a man of wealth to give practically his whole fortune for the erection of a new school building. Similarly, the holders of other local offices have been known to bankrupt themselves to build a new water system for their town, or to create some other tangible and enduring evidence of their local patriotism.

The centralization of government at Athens obviously dampens or destroys this generous competition. Thus, when a new school is needed, the village, however remote, must now look to Athens for a subsidy, instead of to the munificence of its own citizens. Log-rolling at the distant capital is more effective than appeals to local pride. This situation is not merely demoralizing. More serious than that, it dries up the very fountainhead of the Greek political nature. Greece will not demonstrate its full capacity for self-government until its constitutional system is rearranged to recognize and capitalize the distinctive political qualities of the people.

Such a reorganization has hitherto been impossible. At the instance of the European powers, a foreign dynasty has sat on the Greek throne. The Greek parliamentary system has been an imitation of the French parliamentary system, which itself in turn is a none too successful imitative adaptation of the British Parliament. Ill adapted as it is to Greek conditions, the Greeks have had to put up with it because they have been under the tutelage of France and Great Britain. Now, however, since they have expelled the dynasty and have become a republic, it may well be that a natural evolution will bring about a political organization more securely based on the Greek character.

The Greek has suffered in Western eyes also by his enforced association with inferior peoples. His destiny has been wrapt up for centuries, against his will, with those of the backward Turks, and with the relatively backward Serbs and Bulgarians. To a marvelous degree the sturdy Greek has resisted the superstitions and vices of the Orientals and barbarians about him. With anything like a fair chance in the world, he will again demonstrate the possibilities of his virtues.

Endless stories could be told of the courage of the Greeks, as illustrated in the lives of the refugees. One of the pleasantest comes from a little fishing village, built by the Refugee Settlement Commission near Volo, at the foot of Mount Pelion. The inhabitants of Epivato are like all the other refugees, in that they arrived in Greece destitute and suffering the loss of most of the breadwinners. In many of their little homes beside the water only a mother and her three or four young children form the whole family. They live in two rooms and eke out a bare living by endless industry and vigilant thrift. Poor as the village is, however, it supports the best educated woman in the settlement as a teacher. Freed from other gainful labors, she gives her time to educating the children—of course, she still has her domestic duties and the care of her own children to manage. She is a widow, and life is hard; nevertheless, in her characteristically neat living room there hangs on the wall an embroidered motto which, translated into English, reads:

Wherever there is Faith there is Love,
Wherever there is Love there is Peace,
Wherever there is Peace there is Benediction,
Wherever there is Benediction there is God,
Where God is there is no want.

A faith equally genuine and sublime has been characteristic of tens of thousands of the refugees. I have visited hundreds of them in their little homes, and never has courage been found lacking in the inmates. One family in the Kaisariana Settlement just outside of Athens comprises an aged widow mother, a son incapacitated by tuberculosis, and a widowed daughter with three small children, besides an unmarried daughter. The two younger women manage to find a certain amount of casual employment but no steady work. The average total income of the family is barely enough to provide food so meager that one wonders how they can survive. Tragic memories of the violent death of husbands and sons are still fresh. These bring their moments of impassioned sorrow. But these people do not yield to despair or lassitude. They face life with resolution and with many a touch of grim humor. Questioned as to how they could possibly carry on in the face of their difficulties, the young widow flashed back a brilliant smile and shrugged her shoulders, in the characteristic Greek fashion: "God gives us strength to go about" was her laconic reply. No oriental fatalism here!

Moodiness and melancholy, as well as despair, are alien to the Greek temperament. The air is too clear, the sunlight too intense, the colors of the landscape too vivid to breed that grayness of the mind which broods in duller climates. Everything in his natural surroundings tends to stimulate the Greek rather than depress him. Only two things run counter to this general statement. In summer the dry intensity of scorching sunlight, by its overstimulation, finally tends to depress the heart action, and makes one feel dispirited. The brilliancy of the scene, however, largely counteracts this emotional effect, and constant resort to small doses of coffee helps further.

Such a climate, in another setting, would tend strongly to produce a frivolous people. The Greek is saved from this result by the effect of the scenery in which he lives and which powerfully affects his psychology. A famous historian has said that when he was writing about Greece his readers must assume that any place he mentioned was mountainous unless a plain were specifically expressed. Mountains surround the Greek on every hand. They are bold and massive, impressing the beholder with a sense of the majesty and power of nature. A highly intelligent Greek has recently said: "The Greek is not morbid, but neither is he gay or light-hearted. He loves life but reflects emotionally the climate and the scenery. The latter is rugged, difficult, and unsmiling, its every harsh outline made clear and naked by the pitiless sunlight. It is not a joyous scene nor a joyous people. We accept life as it comes, and relieve its grimness with merrymaking."

The simplicity of Greek life impresses every stranger, and deceives many. It is not the simplicity of shiftlessness but the simplicity of an inevitable poverty. The humble homes characteristic of the country are nevertheless clean and neat and orderly within. Industrious as he is, the Greek values some things above the material returns of industry. Above all else he is a social being, and he will pay almost any necessary price to gain the few hours in the evening when he foregathers with his fellows for social purposes and the exercise of his mental powers by matching them against those of his neighbors. Politics is the favorite theme of conversation, and there is in Greece no day laborer too humble to be well informed upon the facts of the current "situation," and to have his own independent opinion upon it. The democracy of the Greeks, to which I have constantly alluded, is no mere phrase that is bandied about to conceal something quite different. If the word "democracy" did not exist in Greece it would have to be coined to express the universal fact.

Out of this political equality and this perfect freedom of expression comes afresh every day a consensus of opinion probably more complete than is arrived at in any other country in the world. It explains, too, the sudden and violent fluctuations in government that so perplex and irritate many foreign observers. As the Greek is an individualist, and as almost every individual Greek is a person of thought and ideas, the political results are bound to be very different from those arrived at in America. For example: in America, team-play is as instinctive as breathing, and politics occupies a very small part of anybody's time or thought. The American gives his loyalty to organizations and institutions. He tends strongly to think of himself as a member of a party, and to follow his party right or wrong. The Greek's loyalty, on the other hand, is to his ideas. He follows the leader who, at the moment, most nearly embodies those ideas. The moment the Greek's idea changes, he shifts to another leader. The practical result is an endless variety of leaders, factions, and coalitions. The political line-up shifts from day to day, almost from hour to hour. The American views with impatience what seems to him the resultant chaos. Nevertheless, it is not chaos. Kaleidoscopic as are the changes in the political instruments of government, the eventual aims of Greek policy are as clearly defined and as steadfastly pursued as are, for example, our Monroe Doctrine and our protective tariff. It is idle to criticize their system simply because it is different. Also it is a mistake to confuse the frequent "revolutions" in Greece with the frequent revolutions in Central America. In the first place, practically all Greek revolutions are bloodless. In the second, they are usually simply short cuts to constitutional changes in a nation highly intelligent and exceedingly conscious of what it is about, politically. It may be granted that some of these revolutions are comic affairs, but even these are harmless and transitory.

The position of woman among the Greeks is in striking contrast with that of most of their neighbors. Except among the remote mountain peasantry of Epirus, woman occupies a very high position. She has a full share in life, and by no means infrequently dominates the family, her husband included, by force of superior intelligence and character. It is very common in Greece for a widow to inherit the entire estate of her husband and to manage it with conspicuous success. In most parts of Greece women live in that kine of modest retirement which we in America would call old-fashioned. But there, as formerly here, no one is deceived by the outward conventions. Inside her home the Greek woman shares equally in the family councils. Her position is one of dignity and respect. In Athens she is as fully emancipated as she is in New York or Paris. I know, for example, one highly educated Greek lady, who keeps up to date in the current literature of four languages, who, after the World War, undertook to restore the family estate, which is situated near the Bulgarian boundary and consequently had been devastated by border raids. She went alone to the remote ranch home, traveling by horseback and taking a plentiful supply of arms and ammunition along with the food and blankets. She lived alone on the ranch for many months, bought the lumber to reconstruct the buildings, hired the mechanics and directed their labors, and supervised the restoration of the soil to cultivation. Neither the loneliness of the place nor the frequent proximity of brigands daunted her in the least, nor was her independence regarded as an unwarranted unconventionality.

Marriages are "arranged" in Greece, after the French system, by the parents of the contracting parties. Romance plays little or no part in them; nevertheless, conjugal affection is the rule rather than the exception, and family ties are perhaps the strongest single influence in the life of a Greek. Moral standards are exceedingly high and are enforced by the rigors of a peculiar code regarding the family honor. Custom provides that when a woman deviates from the path of virtue she shall be killed by a member of her family. The executioner in the case of a married woman is not her husband but her brother. The theory is that her delinquency is a stain on the honor of the blood relatives and must be expiated with blood. The husband's attitude is merely that he was cheated in the bargain when his parents arranged the marriage contract. Not *he* is dishonored, but the wife's family. So rigorous is this custom, and so universally accepted, that in the rare cases where this situation arises it usually follows that the brother that has killed the woman is tried for murder, is convicted of second-degree manslaughter, is sentenced to two years in prison, and is released after serving a few weeks of the sentence. In other words, the community conscience approves the drastic action of the family to clear its name. The result, naturally, is that the practical certainty of the family penalty operates powerfully to prevent the occasion for its use.

Hospitality is a universal virtue among the Greeks. No home is so poor but that the welcome stranger is offered, at the least, a cup of Turkish coffee and cigarettes, or the sweetmeat accompanied by a glass of water, which are the characteristic between-meals refreshment. In the isolated settlements in Epirus the stranger is a welcomed contact with the outer world, and his entertainment has been worked out by custom into an elaborate and time-consuming ritual that is sometimes embarrassing to a hurried traveler. The guest must go through with the whole program of his reception, however, or his host will be so offended that he will set the wolflike dogs upon him as he leaves.

The Greek is warlike; he has to be. He has lived for five thousand years and longer in the presence of hostile tribes. Of his nearest neighbors, the one that requires the closest watching is the Turk, while the Serbs and Bulgarians are always potential, and frequently active, enemies. If the Greek's attitude toward war is different from an American's, it is only natural. To him, war is as inevitable as sunrise, and he looks forward to the next war with perfect calmness, with neither elation over its fictitious glory nor any morbid forebodings over its inevitable tragedies. To him, war is simply another of the facts of life.

Nothing has revealed the essential soundness of Greek character more vividly than his conduct in the last seven years, during the greatest emergency of his recent history. The tremendous migration of a million and a quarter people to new surroundings under the most trying conditions has been accomplished with amazingly little disorder. The sufferings of his race have not unnerved him. Tragedy has been another familiar fact of life down through all the ages of his history. He has always been acutely conscious of it but has never yielded to despair.

It would be hard to overstate the emotional strain upon the refugees. What the Psalmist meant when he said "I cannot sing the Lord's song in a strange land" has afflicted every one of them. This almost unbearable homesickness is revealed in many touching forms. Natives of Macedonia were astonished to see refugees, newly arrived from Pontus, wandering through the oak forests, almost distraught, wildly searching for walnuts, as they had done every year for centuries in their native land, and to see them smitten with a heartbreaking sense of loss when they discovered that walnuts do not grow in Greece. Some of the refugees from Asia Minor had lived for centuries in pleasant dry caves along the seashore. Their neighbors in Attica were dumbfounded to see them abandon the houses to which they had been assigned on their arrival in Greece, and, finding no caves available, proceed to dig them.

Such incidents reveal the strength and tenacity of these people's rootage in the old soil, and suggest the violence of the emotional break with the continuity of life involved in their dispersion. Examples could be multiplied. Imagine having to get your olive oil out of a single bottle when you had been used, all your life, to having it out of a barrel; or having to buy olives and wine at a store, when the idea had simply never occurred to you or your neighbors that these things should not come off your own lands, by your own hands, and endeared by the annual practice of an immemorial art. Even the everyday utensils were strange. The clothes were different. The local dialect was hard to understand. The church one attended was some new, raw structure, not the mellowed and hallowed little edifice, eight hundred years old, to which one and one's ancestors had beaten a timeless path.

CHAPTER XVIII
Looking Ahead

THE refugees are proving to be a blessing to Greece. The past six years have been time enough to demonstrate this fact. It is true that the blessing has been bought at a frightful price in human blood and suffering and in material treasure. No gains for the future could justify such a price if the purchase were voluntary. The price having been paid, however, it is proper to weigh the gains it has brought. I cannot cover this point better than by citing Mr. A. A. Pallis, one of the Refugee Settlement commissioners, who has written as follows:

By the establishment of the refugees, Greece has obtained a net accretion of population of about 1,000,000 inhabitants (the total number of refugees is estimated at about 1,400,000 against which must be set the emigration of about 400,000 Turks and Bulgarians). The refugees represent about 22 per cent. of the total population of Greece. They are proving a valuable asset in increasing production, both agricultural and industrial. Those settled on the land have been responsible for a notable increase in the production of cereals, tobacco, raisins, and silk. The following figures, comparing the situation in 1922-24, *i.e.* before the settlement of the refugees, and in 1926, when the settlement had already been partly completed, are particularly eloquent in this respect.

		1924	1926
Import of cereals	Tons	545,000	462,000

		1922	1926
Tobacco production	Kilos	25,800,000	56,500,000

	1922	1926
Silk cocoons (Macedonia and Thrace)	2,230,000	2,646,000

The cultivation of high-class Sultana raisins—introduced by refugees from Smyrna—in Crete, and the planting of vines on a large scale by refugees from Bulgaria in Macedonia are the other most striking agricultural improvements due to the refugees.

In the towns, a large number of miscellaneous industries have been started by refugees, or by local capitalists with refugee labor; by far the most important is the carpet industry, which, before 1922, was practically non-existent. Thus in 1922 there were only 130 looms employing 230 workmen. To-day there are about 5,500 looms employing 12,000 workmen with an annual production of 219,900 kilos as compared with 16,000 kilos in 1923.

There can, therefore, be no doubt of the beneficent effects of the refugee loan which has, very wisely, been devoted, in the main, to resettling the lands left vacant by the Turkish and Bulgarian emigrants. In return for the very heavy financial sacrifices imposed on her as the result of the Smyrna disaster, Greece has, at least, the compensation of seeing her soil more intensively tilled, her agricultural production increasing, the quality of her products improved, and her industry in course of steady development.

The first of Greece's gains from the refugee influx is a new national unity. The price here has been very heavy. Unity has been bought at the cost of the shattering

303

of a racial ambition, tenaciously sustained through five hundred years of disaster and foreign oppression. I have remarked elsewhere that, up to the time of the Smyrna disaster, every Greek had cherished the ambition that the ancient Byzantine Empire should some day be restored, with its capital at Constantinople. This fond illusion has been destroyed. Greece knows now that probably for centuries to come this vision is utterly impracticable. Deeply as it has shaken the national soul to relinquish it, the Greeks of to-day have accepted it as a fact, and have turned their thoughts in other directions.

The compensating gain lies in the new geographical unity of the race. Practically all the Greeks now live in one unified area on the mainland of the Balkan Peninsula and upon those Ægean Islands peopled by them from the earliest historical times. Not only have the Greeks been concentrated in this area naturally theirs, but practically all the alien intruders have been removed from it. The Turks and Bulgarians, whose presence in Macedonia and Thrace has for the last century kept alive the intolerable "Macedonian Question," have all removed to their several countries and have left Macedonia purely Greek. The Turks of the Ægean Islands (especially the great numbers of them in Crete, Chios, Samos, and Mytilene) have disappeared like the sudden passing of a swarm of locusts, and the memory of their long and hateful presence is now little more than the recollection of an unpleasant dream.

Thus united and thus limited, Greece as a nation turns to the future with an outlook much simplified and much more practicable than that of the past. Dreams of territorial expansion have been replaced by solid prospects of internal improvement. Poor as Greece is in many of the essential national resources, the land is nevertheless capable of a much more intensive development than it has ever received. The restless energy of the Greeks, and their gift for practicable achievements, will revolutionize the economic aspect of the country. The credit of the nation has naturally been strained to its limits by the gigantic program of refugee rehabilitation. Nevertheless, vast public works of the greatest utility are being pushed forward. Such works as the drainage of the fertile swamps in the plain of Salonica, with the accompanying works of flood control, will more than pay for themselves by their additions to the arable lands in Macedonia, and by the increased efficiency of the people due to the eradication of malaria.

The settlement of the agricultural refugees has been wisely accompanied by the development of great agricultural stations, that are rapidly improving the methods of the Greek farmers, so that eventually the soil of Greece will yield its theoretical limits of produce.

The industrial rise of Greece has been enormously stimulated by the influx of refugees. Indirectly, they have spurred existing industries to greater production by supplying plenty of capable labor at a low price. More directly, they have enlarged the industrial output by the creation of new industries. Rug making, silk weaving, ship building, and the manufacture of Portland cement are industries either entirely due to the presence of the refugees or multiplied in production by them.

Greece still confronts many serious problems. The hope for their solution lies in the new energy infused into the race by its exertions to meet the refugee situation, and in the experience of the nation in dealing wholesale with great emergencies under the direction of technically trained men. Probably the most serious of these difficulties ahead of the Greek people lies in the health of the nation. The hardships incident to mass movements of populations, and the lowered physical resistance of the race due to several years of undernourishment, have made tuberculosis a national menace. The figures are alarming. In the United States, the death rate from tuberculosis is 77 in every 100,000 of the population. In Athens and the Piræus, the death rate is 350 in every 100,000, and in Cavalla it is 500. In other words, in the cities where the refugees are most crowded the death rate from this one disease is from five to eight times normal. Practically no hospital facilities exist to meet this situation. A patient in these cities, whose ailment is diagnosed as tuberculosis, usually has to wait at least six months for the opportunity to enter a sanitarium. Meanwhile, he lives in a small room with four or five other people. As often as not, at the end of the six months the patient is dead and one or more members of the family have been infected. As one fifth of the population is now made up of refugees, and as half the population of Greece lives in towns and cities, the menace of tuberculosis is most serious. Unless it can be checked, it threatens the economic efficiency of the entire urban population.

On the side of health the toll of the Smyrna disaster

has by no means all been taken. The simple fact is that many thousands of these people are still lingering but doomed to eventual extinction, as a result of ailments acquired during the exodus from Asia Minor. The hope for Greece is that, as these disappear, their successors will not fall heir to their disabilities. Fortunately, the Greeks are a hardy race as well as highly prolific. The storks, that lend a picturesque touch to every rural habitation in Macedonia with their great, crude nests atop the chimneys, might fittingly be the national emblem of Greece. The birth rate has remained high through all the vicissitudes of the last seven years. It will doubtless continue to counteract the high death rate. Eventually, when the standard of living rises, when more houses have been provided, and when public health control has had time to produce results, the virile Greeks will be found to be again in their ancient health and vigor.

Greece still needs money to accomplish these results. They can be secured only by the expenditure of large sums. Fortunately, these expenditures will ultimately be more than repaid by the increased efficiency of the race.

The most advanced Greeks are planning ahead for another source of national income, as yet undeveloped. The flood of tourists, chiefly Americans, who cruise the Mediterranean shores every winter, does not yield much revenue to Greece. A day or two in Athens is about all the attention they now pay to a country which is one of the most fascinating in the world, and abounding in memorials of a glorious history. Easy access to the archæological wonders of such places as Mycenæ, Old Corinth, Delphi, Olympia, Salonica, Olynthus, and scores of other famous places has been hampered by the lack of good roads and good hotels. As these are provided Greece will become a tourist's paradise. In the season the climate is ideal, the scenery magnificent, and the historical remains endlessly fascinating.

The first step has been taken to remedy this situation. Last year the Greek Government decided to award contracts for the construction of about three thousand kilometers of new roads. A nine-year building program and a twenty-year maintenance program, costing approximately thirty million dollars, are anticipated.

The great reclamation projects for Macedonia and Thrace have been worked out in their engineering details and remain only to be financed and executed. Both health and prosperity are involved in these works. They are bound up in a sanitary sense with the practical success of the plans to eliminate the malaria-carrying mosquito that is the cause of endemic malaria in those regions. Not only reclamation but flood control is involved. Vast new areas of fertile land will be made available to settlement. These will provide great additions to the yearly food supply of Greece, besides providing a gainful occupation for many thousand families.

The rural problem in Greece is clearly on the way to solution. Steady progress is being made along lines carefully mapped out in conformity with the best technical methods, patterned, by the way, very largely upon the work of our own American Department of Agriculture.

Time, and the industry of the Greek peasants, will bring these plans to happy fruition.

Much more serious is the urban problem. The growth of modern industries, which is proceeding rapidly, will absorb the laboring class among the urban refugees. The greater difficulty lies with the so-called white-collar men. These comprise too large a percentage of the population not only for the present conditions of Greek life, but also for any foreseeable demand. Desk jobs in government, industry, and commerce tend to increase everywhere in the world under the modern conditions of civilization. Nevertheless, the number of such jobs that will probably ever be available in a nation of six or seven million people is definitely limited. Also, it is clear that there are even now more people in Greece equipped for such desk jobs than can be used now or in the near future. Not only their training but their inclination and social pride as well make it peculiarly difficult to divert these people into less attractive occupations. The force of circumstances will ultimately drive the less efficient members of this class into the ranks of labor. The process will cause many heartaches but it cannot be avoided.

Emigration to foreign lands has been a habit of the more adventurous Greeks from prehistoric times. This outlet for surplus population is now practically closed. Since 1900 the major part of these emigrants went to the United States. Our stringent immigration barriers have closed this avenue. Likewise, nearly every European country now has raised similar barriers, even more strictly controlled. Certainly, for some years to come, it seems likely that most of the Greeks will have to stay in Greece. In the present state of affairs this is probably on the whole an advantage to the country. The exceptional energy and enterprise of this class will be exercised within the boundaries of the country, and will serve to stimulate industry and to intensify an improved agriculture.

The international situation of Greece still gives her statesmen grave concern. Certain dangers have been removed. The endless border feuds and misunderstandings arising out of the mixed populations that formerly occupied Macedonia and Thrace have disappeared with the exchange of populations. The removal of all the Greeks in Asia Minor back to Greece proper has destroyed the dream of a new Byzantine Empire and to that extent has simplified Greece's foreign relations and removed a source of perpetual discord with the Turks.

On the other hand, the international relations of Greece are not even yet, by any means, ideal. Her near neighbor, Bulgaria, still smarts under her defeat in the second Balkan War. She still resents the possession by Greece of Thrace and eastern Macedonia. Most especially does Bulgaria resent the control of the ports of Cavalla and Dedeagatch. The latter port in particular Bulgaria regards as her natural outlet to the sea. Greece lives in perpetual dread that the Bulgarians will sweep down from the summits of the mountains that mark the northern border line of Thrace, intent upon revenge and determined to gain possession of valuable tobacco and fruit lands of Thrace. A glance at the map will indicate to even the most unmilitary reader the difficulty Greece would confront in defending such a long and exposed frontier.

Serbia likewise is a neighbor never long out of the apprehensive thoughts of Greek statesmen. With Italy in possession of Fiume and in practical control of the whole Adriatic Sea, the instinctive pressure toward a maritime outlet for Serbia naturally turns southward down the Vardar River to Salonica. The Greeks have attempted to satisfy the Serbians by developing at Salonica a free zone and port facilities for Serbian commerce through which it is allowed to pass without customs inspection. Such an arrangement, however, inevitably breeds dispute. Serbia claims that the facilities permitted by Greece are not adequate and Greece claims, on the other hand, that Serbia's demand for extraterritorial rights on the waterfront at Salonica amounts to an intolerable infringement upon her sovereignty. The Greeks likewise suspect Serbia of casting a covetous eye upon the fertile soil of the Macedonian plain. The Greek is not now reassured regarding the future when he compares his own national population of six and a half millions with the thirteen million Serbs.

Italy is the third thorn in the side of Greece when international affairs are in mind. The various peace treaties of the last twenty years have brought under Greek sovereignty all the islands of the Ægean Sea except Imbros and Tenedos, which dominate the two sides of the entrance to the Dardanelles and which therefore were given to Turkey. The other Ægean Islands not given to Greece are the so-called Dodecanese, which lie off the southwest corner of the Asia Minor peninsula. These were assigned to Italy under an agreement which if carried out would have assured their return, eventually, to Greece. Italy, however, has shown not the slightest evidence of any intention of keeping this bargain. On the contrary, she is consolidating her military control of them and there is plenty of reason to believe that she anticipates ultimately seizing the mainland of Asia Minor near by, from the Gulf of Adalia to the neighborhood of Smyrna. This latter ambition is not particularly repugnant to the Greeks, now that they themselves have abandoned all hope of possessing Asia Minor. They rather welcome the prospect of some other power dispossessing the Turk. They recognize that Italy must find an outlet for her large surplus population and they foresee certain advantages in having Italy rather than some other nation in control of Asia Minor.

Thus, of Greece's three major international problems, one is not regarded very seriously at the moment, but the other two are sources of continual apprehension. So long as Greece cannot be sure what Serbia or Bulgaria may do, she can never be sure that all her industry and pains expended in Macedonia and Thrace may not prove to be in vain.

Only two solutions of this problem seem possible. Of these, the ideal would be that through the League of Nations the Great Powers of Europe would definitely declare that the present northern boundary of Greece will be maintained by the unanimous power of Europe. If such an agreement could be made and given force, Greece would cheerfully abandon all thought of armament beyond a nominal force sufficient to police its frontiers and waters. This would leave Greece free to devote all its financial resources and all its manpower to the intensive development of Greek agriculture and industry.

Failing this ideal solution, some hope is still maintained for the success of a Balkan confederation. The plan is to unite Greece, Serbia, Roumania, and even Bulgaria into a confederation pledged to respect mutual interests and to defend themselves and Europe against the Turk. Notwithstanding the obvious difficulties of reconciling mutual interests and of pacifying ancient hatreds, this scheme offers such great advantages to all the four countries that even yet it is not inconceivable of accomplishment.

If such a confederation cannot be achieved nor a League of Nations guarantee provided, the only security for the future that the Greeks can foresee will reside in their own military power. They do not relish such a prospect but they do not flinch from it.

But now that the destiny of Greece is in the competent hands of that practical idealist and wise international statesman, Eleutherios Venizelos, Greece is to be congratulated on her prospects of peaceful prosperity.

INDEX

INDEX

Agriculture, rural refugee work in, 261, 305.

Alexander, King, succeeds father in 1917, 6; death, 7.

Alexander the Great, conquests, 9.

Ali, Mohammed, birthplace of, 256.

Allen, General H. T., 38.

Allenby, Lord, 37.

Amass, Mr., of the Y. M. C. A., 97.

Ambassador Morgenthau's Story, quoted, 18.

Andreades, Professor A., in charge of arrangements for the Byron centennial, 167; speaks at centennial, 170; counsel to Messrs. Morgenthau and Tsouderas, 223; presents Mr. Morgenthau for degree of Doctor of Laws, 233.

Angora, Treaty of, 37.

Argyropoulos, Pericles, estimate of, 89–90, 107; joins members of the Refugee Settlement Commission in Salonica, 106; work on the Commission, 108; believes desire of Greeks is for peace, 187.

Armoza, Ourania, case study, 63.

Aslanoglou, Ekaterian, case study, 59.

Atchley, Shirley, speaker at the Byron centennial, 171.

Azcarate, Mr., 94.

Bailey, 88.

Bakalbassi, Minister of Agriculture, 168.

Balaban, Phili, case study, 70.

Balkan Wars, results of, 13.

Benes, Edouard, at the Versailles conference, 85; member of the Council of Ten, 209.

Berry, Mr., 94, 95.

"Big Four," members of, 85.

Birth rate, 307.

Blegen, Dr., 284.

Bonzon, Dr. Alfred, temporarily succeeds Mr. Morgenthau as chairman of the Commission, 231.

Branting, Swedish member of the Council of Ten, 209.

Burnham, Lord, at the Byron centennial, 167, 170.

Butler, Mr., 95.

Byron, Lord, ceremony at Missolonghi commemorating the centennial of his death, 166 ff.

Byron, Miss, at the Byron centennial, 167.

Caclamanos, Greek minister to London, 98; meets Mr. Morgenthau in London, 176; member of the Greek Committee of the League, 218.

Cafandaris, Minister of Justice, to arrange for a successor to Venizelos as Premier, 140; to succeed Venizelos, 143; his political ties, 143; declaration of policy, 145; Parliamentary speech as Premier, 150; ministry falls, 152; succeeded by Papanastasiou, 152,

317

212; calls upon Mr. Morgenthau, 159.

Campbell, Colonel John, British member of the Commission, joins Mr. Morgenthau, 96; joins fellow members in Salonica, 107; assignment of work on the Commission, 108; accompanies Mr. Morgenthau to Missolonghi, 171; meets Mr. Morgenthau in London, 176; in conference with Colonel Plastiras, 187; statement to League evaluating Commission property, 225.

Carapanos, Mr., present at political discussion at Mr. Morgenthau's home, 137; accompanies Mr. Morgenthau on visit to orphans at Zappeion, 281.

Carr, Miss Alice G., with the Near East Relief, 284.

Cavalla, described, 255.

Cecil, Lord Robert, conference with Mr. Morgenthau regarding Greek finances, 81–82; his standing in the League of Nations, 181.

Charilaos, Epaminondas, 1; organizes Refugee Treasury Fund, 71; report on the Refugee Treasury Fund, 72 ff.; Venizelos's estimate of, 89; exercises for laying the cornerstone of the Infants Day Nursery, 168;

Churchill, Winston, on the Greek occupation of regions in Asia Minor, 23; host to Mr. Morgenthau at luncheon, 39; dinner with Mr. Morgenthau, 45.

Clauzel, M., member of the Greek Committee of the League, 218.

Clemenceau, Georges, 24; member of the "Big Four," 85.

Cofinas, assures commissioners of

the government's desire for peace, 188.

Colocatronis, M., 95; Greek representative in the Council of Ten, 209.

Committee of Union and Progress, Turkish government in control of, 13.

Condouriates, Admiral, appointed Regent of Provisional Government, 127; a guest of Mr. Morgenthau's at dinner, 136; his estimate of his position as Regent, 142; confers decorations on Mr. and Mrs. Morgenthau, 168; with Mrs. Condouriates at a special convocation of the University of Athens, 233.

Constantine, King, dismisses Venizelos as Prime Minister in 1915, 6; abdicates, 6; returns to Athens as King, 7; personally directs offensive against Nationalists, 7; forced by army to abdicate, 7; reinstated, 28; Emperor-Designate of Constantinople, 29; orders general offensive against the Turkish Nationalist position, 29; commands army in Asia Minor, 29; exiled to Italy, 105; enmity between Mr. Venizelos and, 126; popularity, 126; mistake of Mr. Venizelos in dealing with, 132; active leader of Royalists, 163.

Cripps, C. Alfred, see Lord Parmoor.

Cunliffe-Owen, Colonel, 95.

Cushman, Miss, in charge of Near East Relief work at Corinth, 282.

Daily Telegraph, London, interview with Mr. Morgenthau for the, 33 ff.

INDEX

Refugee Treasury Fund, the organization and achievements of, 71 ff., disbanded, 72.

Refugees, Smyrna disaster, 47 ff.; urban, 236 ff.; report of Charles D. Eddy on, 258; rural, 261 ff.; work of the Near East Relief, 281; report of A. A. Pallis, 302; their value to Greece, 302.

Rodd, Sir Rennell, at the Byron centennial, 167, 170.

Roussos, Geo., present at political discussion at Mr. Morgenthau's home, 137; informs Mr. Morgenthau of Venizelos's contemplated resignation, 140; is recommended as Premier by Venizelos, 152; telegram of appreciation to Mr. Morgenthau, 232; accompanies Mr. Morgenthau on visit to orphans at Zappeion, 281.

Rugs, manufacture of, 248.

Salamis, Greece's contract with Germany for the, 184.

Salter, Sir Arthur, Mr. Morgenthau's interview with, 83; the Refugee Settlement Commission instituted upon the recommendation of, 180; interest in fiscal rehabilitation of Hungary and Austria, 182; in conference with Mr. Morgenthau and Bank of England officials, 198; described, 199; accompanies Mr. Morgenthau to Geneva, 206; conference in Geneva with Messrs. Morgenthau and Drummond, 214; expresses uncertainty of Greece's stability, 215; guest of Lord and Lady Parmoor, 218; talks with Mr. Morgenthau in New York, 220; financial expert of League,

224; luncheon guest of Mr. Morgenthau's, 228.

Sartinsky, Rose, her reports on refugee settlements, 55 ff.

Secrets of the Bosphorus, 39.

Sèvres Conference, 25; terms of the treaty, 27.

Sèvres, Treaty of, provision regarding Turkish territory, 7; reconsidered at London Conference, 7, 28; terms, 27.

Sgouta, Mr., engineer for the Refugee Settlement Commission, 237 ff.

Sharkey, Mr., of the Associated Press, 95.

Silkworm, culture of, 256, 278.

Singer Manufacturing Company, 26.

Smith, Admiral Sir Aubrey, 208.

Smyrna disaster of 1922, facts itemized, 47 ff.

Sophoulis, Prime Minister of Greece, confers with Mr. Morgenthau on the transfer of land to the Commission, 221.

Spender, Harold, at the Byron centennial, 167, 170.

Speyer, James, 232.

Strakosch, governor of the Bank of South Africa, 228.

Strong, Benjamin, 199.

Strother, French, accompanies Henry Morgenthau to Greece, 4.

Sunday Times, London, interview with Mr. Morgenthau quoted, 35.

Supreme Allied Council, provides for patrol of western Asia Minor, 7.

Sweetser, Arthur, 94, 95.

Sydenstricker, Dr., 94.

INDEX

DATE DUE
